Bilingual and Multilingual Learners from the Inside-Out:

Elevating Expertise in Classrooms and Beyond

Alison Schofield & Francesca McGeary

Bilingual and Multilingual Learners from the Inside-Out: Elevating Expertise in Classrooms and Beyond by Alison Schofield and Francesca McGeary —1st Ed.

ISBN 978-1539647522

CONTENTS

Preface

Alison and I share a passion for learning and teaching. When we first met in Abu Dhabi, UAE as newly-arrived expat teachers, we were excited to see where our adventure would take us. Fast-forward almost 12 years later and we never could have imagined that our journey would lead us to opening our own educational company in Dubai, creating a literacy intervention program for struggling children and finally, researching and writing a book about bilingual and multilingual learners.

Over the years, our work with students, parents and teachers has helped us gain an intimate perspective surrounding the challenges that bilingual and multilingual learners face in English school systems. Having moved from Scotland to Belgium as an adolescent and educated in French, I understand their experiences firsthand. Now as an educationalist, I can also appreciate the challenges that teachers face when working with bilingual and multilingual learners. With limited training and support but a growing student population, the need to empower educators with expertise that reflects our globalized world has never been more critical. Since teachers will always be one of the best resources a student can have, it makes sense for us to focus our attention on them.

What is found here in this book and Professional Development Program is a new approach to working with bilingual and multilingual learners in mainstream, English classrooms. It has taken us 3 years to synthesize all of the fascinating research, most of which has been done at the university level by eminent professors over many decades. Combined with our own experiences as international educators and entrepreneurs, this book and Program offers schools and teachers a new way of delivering services to impact student success immediately. Our approach recognizes the vast diversity that exists within the bilingual and multilingual population across a variety of school settings around the world. Our aim is to help educators meet students' needs in the context of their unique surroundings. There is no one-size-fits-all approach that can be applied to each and every school or student. Instead, we encourage educators to critically reflect on how they can create impact in their own classrooms and schools, armed with this new expertise.

Francesca McGeary

Acknowledgements

We would like to thank all of the teachers, parents and students who helped contribute to this book and Program by sharing their personal experiences. We would also like to thank all of the teachers who trialed our Professional Development Program in its early stages.

Many thanks to the people who assisted us with the "Language Helpers" by giving their time, language and cultural expertise: *Ziad Khabbaz, Eman Yousef, Mubeena Mohammad, Nienke Salomanns, Geert Simons, Elizabeth Leckie Schuussel, Frances Bekhechi, Juliet Nobel, Saira Abbas, Naoko Kishida* and *Americo Sampaio*. Also, we would like to thank Gee Jacome for the design of our cover image.

Special thanks to teachers of the *Universal American School* in Dubai-*Eimear O'Connell, Rianne Fox* and *Julie Krall*-who went on to develop wonderful mother-tongue initiatives for their BMLs and also allowed us to use many of their photographs within this book. Thank you also to Amanda Ennis, Rebecca McCarthy and the other teachers who have allowed us to use their personal reflections.

Our sincere appreciation goes to Dr. Paul Nation who graciously took the time to share his expertise and answer our questions about vocabulary development.

Author's Notes

Within this manual, and within our practices, you will find us using the term "Bilingual/Multilingual Learner" or "BML/BMLs" to refer to students who are learning through English and are working towards the goal of bilingualism or multilingualism within the mainstream, English-medium school context.

From country-to-country, school-to-school, and within the literature, there is still a range of reference terms for BMLs, many of which inappropriately describe students' linguistic profiles, or inadvertently stigmatize them.

We strongly believe in using language which *amplifies* and *projects a positive image* of students; therefore, we have decided to adopt this terminology to:

1. *More accurately depict students* as being bilingual or multilingual (skills which are typically held in positive regard within our society).

2. *Have the term adopted by mainstream teachers* within different schools and countries, in order to develop a common language when communicating about these students.

We hope that you will also choose to adopt this terminology within your schools so that we can begin to raise the positive profiles of our BMLs.

[1]

Language as a Vehicle for Culture

IN THIS CHAPTER YOU WILL...
- Learn different ways of thinking about culture
- Understand how language is interconnected with culture and identity
- Recognize "surface" and "underlying aspects" of culture
- Learn about "Third Culture Kids" or "TCKs"

GROUNDING QUESTION:
How do you identify and relate to different aspects of your own culture?

Several years ago, Francesca and I decided to venture out on a road trip just outside of Dubai to visit an organic farm. It was apparently run by a local man from the UAE, and we were curious to see what we could buy.

We set out on that sunny day and headed onto the back road, ready for the 40 km journey. As soon as we reached about 10 km, the landscape began to change from city to desert. Sand started blowing across the highway, and while a less-adventurous person might have turned around, we were determined to plough ahead.

When we finally came to the area where we predicted the farm to be, there were no signs of it anywhere. There were also no visible plants, crops or clues as to where we should go next.

We decided to take a risk and turned down one of the long driveways that led to a villa. We hoped to find a local person who could give us some indication as to where we were and where the organic farm was.

Looking back now, it was a little foolish of us not to recognize the conspicuous lump of sand that had built up near the foot of the driveway. Since the rest of the driveway appeared clear, we thought it was fine to push ahead through the sand bar.

As soon as we heard that fateful *grrr* of the engine and felt the unexpected jolt of the car into a sudden stop, we knew we were stuck. We tried moving the car forward, reversing, turning our tires, but nothing seemed to work. There was no way we were going to get out on our own.

We now had to try and get some help. If no one was home in any of the nearby houses, we were going to have to call a tow-truck. As we got out of the car, a white Range Rover drove up alongside us. Inside were 4 teen boys wearing *kandouras* and *keffiyeh* (cultural dress). Reacting quickly, they jumped out of the car and came to directly survey the damage. Both of us looked inside the vehicle for an adult, but none appeared. At this point, we certainly were in no position to turn the teens away.

In UAE culture, it is not customary for a male to speak casually to a female unless it is their relative or authority figure, or there is a direct context for the conversation to take place. We were comfortable knowing that our situation clearly qualified the interaction. The boys, however, found no real need to speak to us since the damage had spoken for itself!

They walked around the car, observing the tires, depth of the sand, etc., and conversed rapidly to one-another, seemingly knowing exactly what to do. At that time, we did not have very good Arabic language skills, so we had to deduce what was going on by context. We sat back, suddenly becoming passive observers while the drama unfolded in the 40 degree, July heat.

One of the boys jumped into the car, trying to release it. Another ran to the back of his vehicle to get some shovels. The third took on the role of supervisor, shouting orders to each of them while the last one helped his friend shovel the sand around the tires.

Within 5 minutes they had concluded that more intervention was needed. They again went back to their *Range Rover* and returned with a tow-rope. Just at that moment, another 4x4 spun over to us. Inside was an adult-I assumed it was one of the boys' fathers. He opened the window and shouted something to the boys in Arabic. The boys confidently waved him off, clearly communicating to him that everything was under control. The man then sped off, assured that the boys could handle the situation.

After they had tied on the towing rope and secured it to their own vehicle, one jumped in behind the wheel. Another got into our car and the other 2 stood by directing and shouting orders. With little effort, our car was released from its rut. We were both relieved and overjoyed. We thanked the boys in Arabic and sheepishly made our way back onto the highway, heading back to Dubai.

The rescue mission had taken no more than 10 minutes, and the boys didn't seem at all bothered by our error in judgment. They jumped into rescue mode as if it were second-nature to them. Growing up in the desert with its risks and protocols for safety and survival had clearly given them an advantage that we were without.

In the UAE, the local boys have a school dropout rate of around 20% and are under-represented in higher-education (Ridge, Farah, & Sami, 2013). Although they attend Western-style government schools, making the school experience relevant for them can be a challenge at best. It is one that we have experienced first-hand, after having worked directly with many of them as classroom teachers and later, educational consultants.

While many of these children could be considered "at-risk learners" in the school setting, we could actually see how their analytical and problem-solving skills had come alive while trying to free our car. The natural desert environment had shaped their ability to survive and cope with a variety of challenging conditions and our situation provided them an opportunity to show-case their real-world skills. They were well-equipped with all the tools, supplies and water that could be potentially life-saving in the harsh desert climate. Most importantly, they knew exactly how to use them.

This is an experience which we might not have been so blessed to have had, had we not gotten stuck in the sand that day. We have made reference to this story on many occasions because it so nicely illustrates the value of culture, communication and learning within the natural environment.

The UAE people and Arabs in general, are known to value hospitality to the highest degree. They treat guests and visitors with a great deal of respect and generosity. This hospitality was often lavished upon other travelers within traditional Bedouin (nomad) societies. Those voyaging through the desert were welcomed by different tribes and offered an abundance of food, water and lodging until they moved on.

We certainly felt their hospitality that particular day in the desert. The fact that the boys extended themselves to help us out of our predicament was not only kind, but also demonstrated a reflection of their cultural values and beliefs.

We must remember that culture is an *extremely* relevant factor for each and every individual. Our Westernized education models which have now spread around the world, do not always provide many authentic opportunities to showcase the different sets of skills, talents or values that our BMLs possess. This can create a major disconnect between the students' real lives and their experience of learning and education.

On the other hand, if we created more opportunities for our BMLs to connect and engage with their learning in a way that was relevant to them, we would be more likely to see higher levels of student achievement and motivation.

Providing students with a meaningful context for learning which *they* can relate to is often the key element to engagement. Giving them opportunities to demonstrate their learning through cultural and personal links offers unique perspectives to topics and projects. Classrooms with children from different cultures and who speak a range of languages have much to offer in terms of alternative ways of looking at the world. As a result of our highly-globalized world, the value of diversity has now become well-recognized. As educators, we need to realize this and maximize the opportunities that this creates.

When we allow our students to *own* and *contribute* to the world-view rather than simply offering a dominant perspective, we are creating conditions for engagement and diverse contributions.

> *We have no hope of solving our problems without harnessing the diversity, the energy and the creativity of all our people.* ~ Roger Wilkins

Who are we without our language and cultures? Both are so inextricably linked that it is difficult to imagine one separate from the other. In many cases, bilingual and multilingual people even report that they take on specific personality characteristics, or even use different body language when speaking one of their languages as compared to the other. This is because language serves as a conduit for culture: it enables the individual to gain access to social rules and conventions which then allows them to participate with members of their cultural group.

It makes sense then that people behave differently when speaking different languages, since there are very different ways of operating and participating within each culture.

PERSONAL STORY: PAUL

English is my second language and I use it a lot. I feel I'm really good at it and most people at work comment that I have excellent English. The problem is though, that I often feel I'm not the same person that I am when I speak French. I feel like I don't have any sense of humour in English, and in French I notice that I am always making jokes and I just have a real sense of freedom and fun. In English, I find myself to be a bit boring as a person and it really used to bother me to be honest. Now I wonder if it's the differences between the languages themselves, or maybe I can just be myself much more when speaking French.

When we begin to understand that language does not operate as a separate unit on its own, but that it is interwoven with threads of behaviour, social conventions and values, we can then recognize the richness and magnitude of it.

Students who come to us with another language in their repertoire will likely have a whole other side to their "self" that might not be visible when they speak in English. They may have a range of different experiences that are available to them when they speak their own language. Some may also begin to feel that they are losing a part of themselves the more they take on English as their dominant language.

A disadvantage of learning English in school and using it more often than your own mother-tongue (MT) is that you will become more enculturated in the English-speaking culture while your other culture or "self" becomes less dominant. It receives less time and focus—slowly taking a back seat to English if it is not nurtured.

Sometimes immigrant parents feel it is important for their children to assimilate as much as possible into their new culture, and so many stop speaking their MT. They may choose to speak mainly in English and reserve their MT for use with extended family members over holidays, for example. However, by the time the child gets older, they will likely have lost a good deal of their ability to have an age-appropriate conversation in their MT language. Imagine the impact this would have on relationships and families.

It is very important that we think of language not only as "language" but as *"language + culture"*. Then we can begin to give our students' languages the respect they deserve. Language also relates to *relationships* and can be the connection to *the past* and *memories*; it can also mean *tradition* and *connection* and ultimately: *identity*.

We cannot ignore the languages of our students because we will essentially be ignoring their cultures which are at the very core of their personal identities.

A Cultural Identity Horror Story: The Worse-Case Scenario

In the late 1800s and up until the 1960s, aboriginal children in Canada were required by law, to attend residential schools away from their homes and families. The goal of the government and church at that time was to "civilize" the aboriginal people who were often referred to as savages. Ultimately, the goal was to spread Christianity and help the aboriginals to become enculturated into the European way of life.

As a result of this, thousands of children were ripped apart from their families. They were beaten if they spoke their own languages. They were forced to adopt the English or French language and as a result, any communication with their families became extremely difficult; especially because parents and elders were unable to communicate in those languages.

Besides being exposed to terrible conditions and often regular abuse by staff members, one of the most detrimental and lasting consequences of the residential schooling movement has been that the government and Church were able to effectively wipe out many distinct cultures in only one generation.

Typically, North American aboriginals (or First Nations People, as most prefer to be called) belonged to tribes with their own unique cultures and languages. Each tribe held strong values regarding spiritual practices. Their traditions taught children important hunting and survival skills, celebrated rites of passage and passed on cultural values.

The fascinating thing about the First Nations peoples' language was that it was primarily oral, and was used to communicate their traditions and way of life to the young through storytelling. Because oral cultures sustain their traditions by passing stories down from generation-to-generation, this makes them very vulnerable to outside forces.

In that one generation, many of those First Nations children essentially lost their families, cultural identity and language. This meant that the language of many tribes also died out, forcing subsequent generations to adopt English or French as a mother-tongue without access to the knowledge, traditions and values of their ancestors.

The consequences of this have led to what many people believe is the cultural genocide of the First Nations people, and this is still having a huge impact on them today. Poverty and social issues are the result of a disconnected sense of culture, belonging and identity.

As a result, many new initiatives have sprung up, with First Nations people trying to rebuild and reclaim their lost cultures and identities. Special emphasis on youth is given through bilingual education initiatives (or additional English "dialect" classes to honour the First Nations English Dialect), early childhood programs and the incorporation of culturally-relevant child-rearing and social practices into schools and classrooms.

While there is now recognition of what has been lost for these cultures and what can be learned moving forward; countless tribal languages have already disappeared with no chance of reviving them or the delicate cultures that have so quickly vanished alongside them. This story is not unique to North America; countries such as Australia and New Zealand have also experienced this black mark on their histories—the scars of colonization which have ultimately had tremendous impact on the language and identities of aboriginal peoples.

Remember that when we talk about language, we are not only talking about its words or vocabulary, but about all the rich connections that language holds for us—the deep connections to family, friends, elders and our larger community. Essentially, we can say: Language= Language + Culture.

COMPLEXITY OF CULTURE AND IDENTITY

Having lived as expatriates in the United Arab Emirates for the last 12 years, both of us have been able to learn a great deal about the culture of the UAE people, their religion and Arabic language.

When we first began taking Arabic lessons, we wondered why the Arabic language was not adapted to modernize it in regards to the complicated written system which differs greatly from the oral language. We eventually learned that Arabic was the original language of the Koran or holy book for Muslim people.

Only then did we begin to understand that this was part of the reason why written Arabic has kept its classical text and language—because the language is so deeply interconnected with religious and cultural values.

Even Muslims around the world who are not Arabic-speakers attempt to learn and read classical Arabic so that they can recite prayers from the Koran in its original form. Now that we have gained a better understanding of the roots of the language and how it has been maintained by religion and culture of both Arabs and Muslims all over the world, we can appreciate more aspects of the culture and language in our country of residence.

From these examples, we can see that language essentially forms our internal "operating system" which allows us to connect with the outside world. It enables us to form relationships with our families and interact within our broader society. Language is not simply a tool for communication but helps us to encode social norms and values which get communicated through our families, friends and extended networks of teachers, elders and institutions. Words reflect the richness of our societies and the vocabularies that we use are central to our values and experiences. We cannot speak about language-learning or language acquisition without considering the impact that these words have on our culture and ultimately our "way" of behaving and interacting with one another.

In the Korean language, the pronouns for "my" and "you" are not often used; rather Koreans have a system of addressing others that reflects their social status (i.e. title) and relationships. They will say "our" instead of saying "my" because Koreans place higher value on the goals of the group rather than the individual. This can also be seen and felt through various aspects of their cultural exchanges. Their language corresponds to the norms and values of their people.

Imagine being a classroom teacher working with a student from Korea. Can you see how it might be very difficult for them to use these words even with extra support, time and explicit instruction? Deep down they may feel awkward, simply because of the deeply-entrenched cultural significance that these words activate.

Now it might be very difficult as a classroom teacher to find out about each of your students' cultural and linguistic differences, but you can see how just a few pieces of information can lead you to a much deeper, significant understanding of both. In the Appendix, we have included *Language Helpers*, which offer basic information about many different languages, their characteristics and cultural features. This will help you be better equipped to understand and work with students from these backgrounds. Always keep in mind though, that your students and their families will be your best teachers because descriptions or categories do not always reflect everyone's precise experiences or background.

Working with BMLs does not only mean that we have to teach them the English language; it also means that we are essentially enculturating these students into our broader Western societies and value systems. From this perspective, we must be sensitive to the reality that many of our students have to face: how to operate in 2 different cultures that may, at times, seem to have competing value systems. As a result, some students may find that it takes several years to come to grips with fitting in and finding a sense of belonging within each of their cultures, especially if these cultures are extremely different to one-another.

In some situations, individuals can retain a very strong connection to their family's original culture, yet they may still adopt aspects of the other culture which enable them to function well and participate within that society. In doing so, they may be more selective in adopting cultural aspects that are not at odds with their family culture and traditions.

In other cases, individuals may seem to totally assimilate into the new culture, seeming to forgo many of their own cultural traditions and even their MT. This does not always happen intentionally, but can be something that comes about gradually as individuals try to fit into their new culture, naturally picking-up and trying out novel experiences and adopting them into their cultural repertoires.

Of course as educators, we cannot tell our students which aspects of culture they should or should not adopt; instead we must provide plenty of room for them to try out a variety of experiences within their new cultures, until they feel comfortable. At the same time, we must allow them as many opportunities as possible to relate to, share and practice their original culture's traditions, customs and language. Our role should also be to support families by educating them about cultural assimilation and significance of their home language(s) as well as providing links to external community resources and networks. Whether families are economic immigrants, expatriates or refugees, it is essential that they have access to this valuable information so that they can make the best, informed decisions for their children as possible.

Within our schools and classrooms, our aim should be to provide as much recognition as possible between the individual's different cultures so that they themselves can reflect on how they connect to each one. How an individual relates and lives out their culture and traditions might change often while they go about experimenting with what feels right for them at different phases of their lives.

While some elements of an individual's cultures might seem to be at odds with one-another especially when it comes to values, it is important to support them as they try to navigate the complex road, figuring out how they relate to each one. This process can lead them to greater awareness of "self" and their socio-cultural identities.

This process is not always destined to be easy. Some individuals may go through a searching stage while trying to define their personal identities. They may find it challenging to figure out how to allow each culture to peacefully co-exist within themselves. This can be especially true for adolescents who, at this time in their lives, are already trying to define themselves within the context of their peer groups and families.

If you find students struggling to come to terms with their cultural identity, allow them to have opportunities to observe and reflect on their own values and experiences. Remember that learning to accommodate and develop one's own cultural identity can sometimes take a lifetime.

When students feel accepted and valued for themselves, they will likely be more open to sharing their gifts and talents in a way that enriches the learning environment. Whether it is a different perspective, a new way of solving a problem or interacting with others, the best place to start is always from the unique point-of-view of the individual student.

A TEACHER'S EXPERIENCE: REBECCA

Thinking back on my years teaching in Korea, it was often very difficult to get students "out of their shell." Having students speak up in class, share their ideas and participate in presentations often took a lot of work. When I first started, I couldn't understand why they seemed so shy. I know I transmitted some of my culture to my kindergarteners because when their parents would see them interact with me, they were quite surprised at how outgoing they behaved. Parents often reminded their children to show me more respect by bowing to me and so on. I also had issues with eye contact. I remember on one occasion in particular, telling a student who had been causing me a lot of problems to "look me in the eye" when I was talking to him. At the time, I didn't realize how difficult that must have been for him—he *was* actually showing me respect by not looking me in the eye.

THIRD CULTURE KIDS (TCKs)

The concept of *Third Culture Kids* (or TCKs), originally coined by Ruth Hill Useem in the 1950's, refers to children who live abroad and who incorporate aspects of their parent's culture and culture of their host country to create a "third" or other distinct culture.

This concept is becoming more widespread as globalization dictates movement for business and educational opportunities. When children spend an extended period of their development in a country which is not their parents', they are said to be "third culture kids." TCKs may be children of military personnel, diplomats, expatriates or even missionaries.

TCKs do not always have a strong connection to their family's home country or culture(s) due to the fact that their primary residence is in a foreign country. Some TCKs might even move around the world to different countries every few years. Naturally, these children have very unique childhood experiences compared to most. This can include extensive travel, diverse cultural interactions and international education. In many cases, TCKs are bilingual or multilingual or at least exposed to people who speak other languages. This kind of alternative education enables them to greatly expand their world-view.

Along with the benefits also comes challenge. TCKs may find it difficult to relate to one particular culture, even when it is the culture of their parents. The knowledge they possess about their own background culture(s) may not always come from direct exposure or interaction, but through parent stories and information that they have encountered through second-hand sources. Many TCKs identify with others living outside their country-of-origin, often because they share similar kinds of experiences and lifestyles.

TCKs are often said to be authentic "citizens of the world" because they tend to be extremely open to internationalism, travel, different cultures, languages and diverse situations. However, some TCKs experience a sort of culture shock when they are taken back into their "home" country. This can happen when their parents return after their foreign contracts or diplomatic missions have completed, or when they have finished secondary school and are moving on to university, for example.

Working with TCKs can be very interesting and enlightening; however, understanding their unique outlook is essential to supporting them through their learning, alongside the complex aspects of social and cultural identity.

Providing an open and accepting approach, free of assumptions will allow you to best learn about the TCK and their unique perspective. Meeting with parents and getting important background information about the countries they have lived in, the kinds of schooling systems they have been educated in, as well as the cultures and peers they have been connected to, will provide you with pivotal information.

Unpacking "Culture"

Most of us speak of "culture" in terms of its general aspects: traditions, customs, religion or language, for example. However, culture itself has several layers, some of which are easy to observe while others are much more subtle.

Culture has been described as an iceberg by Gary Weaver (1986), where there are "surface" aspects above the water and then deeper traits which are hidden below the surface. Surface aspects can be more easily observed by others. Cultural dress, art, festivals and foods are very common surface connections that we make with other cultures, especially when traveling or getting to know someone from a culture different to our own.

If we mistakenly believed that a culture is only represented by these kinds of surface characteristics, we are limiting our understanding. Cultural norms, rules and values that are concealed below the surface can be so expansive that it can take years of living within a particular culture to truly feel that you recognize and understand them. It is essential to look beyond the surface aspects of a culture to learn the more subtle social etiquette or meanings of particular behaviours, gestures and "unsaid rules".

Cultural elements are deeply ingrained and not always easily visible

In 2014, we went on a trip to India to visit one of our former colleagues who lived there. During our time sight-seeing around temples and markets, one of the immediate things we noticed was the different perceptions of acceptable personal space. It was very common to see Indians traveling comfortably through crowded public spaces or queuing up very close to one-another; however, because of our own cultural need for more personal space, these kinds of crowded areas became quite stressful for us. This was a good conversation point later on in our trip because our Indian friend did not seem to be aware of this until after we pointed it out. It was something that was so engrained in her that it had become an unconscious way of operating.

Pinpointing your own culture's unconscious rules can also be difficult. Until you begin to see your culture through someone else's eyes, you can then start to identify its aspects more clearly. When I first became an expat in the UAE, I would find myself in situations that sharply contrasted my cultural norms with what I was experiencing at that time. For instance, I had a bank that was run by people from a variety of different nationalities. In that bank, I found the systems for queuing (or lining up), were stressful. Each of the 3 tellers at the counter would have separate queues, with people having to arrive and select a particular line to queue up in, (which often meant that you would have to wait longer than someone who had just arrived, simply because their queue moved faster). I would often find myself getting very annoyed and impatient because I could not understand why the bank did not use one queue for everyone! It was highly likely that someone at the bank had decided that this system had worked in his/her home country, so they simply applied the same system to this particular bank. Perhaps no one else had complained so management assumed that the system was working well.

As I thought about the situation further, I realized that I was actually annoyed at the fact that the system itself was unfair. At the time, I had even voiced my concern to the manager. What did this situation tell me about my culture? I concluded that somehow being Canadian meant that we value fairness and efficiency. We also believe that we as individuals have the right to voice our opinions in order to create change. Had I been back in Canada, would I have been able to view my culture in this way? Probably not. The situation would have taken a different turn because all the individuals were Canadians who would be operating with the same values. They would understand why I was complaining and they would react in a very "Canadian kind of way": by listening to my concern, trying to make me feel like they would do their best to rectify the situation and then I would leave feeling satisfied that at least my voice and viewpoint was heard.

Now, after having lived in a foreign country for the past 12 years, I notice that I no longer respond to situations in a purely "Canadian" kind of way. I have changed a great deal and have even adopted some cultural aspects of my multicultural home. I notice I have now become much more flexible in my approach to situations that might have caused me significant stress compared to when I first arrived years ago. I have taken on much more of a laid back attitude rather than responding with my Canadian directness. Living in the UAE where the dominant culture is Arabic or Middle-Eastern, individuals are not very direct or confrontational as compared to my culture. Whereas we Canadians tend to deal with issues or conflicts head-on because we believe in getting to the bottom and resolving them quickly, Arabs are much less confrontational in response to issues. If there is a challenge or problem, it is often deflected or discussed in a positive way (e.g. "don't worry, it will get done") rather than confronted head-on causing conflict or a negative reaction in public. Also, Arabs do not like to tell you "no" directly. It is very uncomfortable for them as they feel they are being impolite or may "lose face." After all these years, I too have come to adopt many of these qualities myself, which can make me feel like my Canadian culture has become somewhat diluted.

Many of the expatriates living here start using Arabic expressions and words within their regular English conversation in a way that has become second-nature. For example, when someone gives me an invitation to dinner or an event, I find I no longer respond with a direct "yes" or "no," as a typical Canadian would, but I now find it very comfortable to say, "Inshallah" which in Arabic means, "God-willing" (and then translates loosely in this situation to mean "maybe"). I have found *Inshallah* to be quite freeing actually, especially when you receive an invitation from a less-than desirable acquaintance. You do not get uncomfortable from declining politely or making an excuse which can lead to awkwardness; instead you simply defer to *Inshallah* and then the individual is meant to understand maybe you will or maybe you won't. Then if you follow up with them later, they know you have accepted. If not, then usually nothing more is said about it. This is quite different to how we would handle an invitation in Canada.

Culture is not a hard and fast thing. It provides some moral and social conditioning for us but it is susceptible to external influences as well. Children born in one country who move to a new country with very different cultural norms are likely to be influenced. They will often assimilate aspects of that new or dominant culture somehow. This is normal. Individuals want to belong and be accepted within their dominant societies; however, there is a major problem if they do not feel like they can actively engage and share in their own cultural practices within that society and its establishments. This creates isolation and an "us vs. them" mentality. Individuals should adopt new cultural practices and norms which allow them to participate and thrive within the dominant culture and society, but it does not always have to be at the expense of losing their own cultural roots, language or values. Societies, organizations and schools themselves need to build acceptance and practices which promote the benefits of cultural diversity into their philosophies and core values. This will create more cohesion, participation and collaboration.

When an individual moves to a new country or different cultural environment, it is essential to understand that they are going to experience a journey of self-discovery and self-awareness. At times this will be a rocky road with stressful situations, and they may be confronted with scenarios that challenge their core values and beliefs; however, at other times it can also be exciting to discover the new experiences their new environment has to offer. Individuals need time to adapt and learn about their new culture. These students require teachers who can understand their unique perspectives and support them in this process.

Helping students to stay connected to their roots while building classroom communities that celebrate and show appreciation of different cultures is a key role of all teachers. As we encourage students to share their cultures, we are empowering them to truly be themselves while giving them per-permission to fully explore all aspects of themselves and who they can become.

A.T.C.O.D.E. – TIPS FOR BUILDING CULTURAL CONSCIOUSNESS

AWARENESS:

Build up an awareness of the common "surface" and "deep" aspects of your students' cultures. Do research and/or speak to parents or other colleagues who can educate you (e.g. especially around taboos, religious beliefs, etc.). Allow students to educate you when appropriate. Learn about their linguistic background.

TIME:

Allow newcomer students time to settle in and adjust to their new classroom environments. Provide support as needed to scaffold class participation and social interactions.

COMMUNITY:

Create an open school and classroom community which celebrates the diversity of students. Openly engage in discussions that demonstrate the values of different cultures and languages. Celebrate the traditions and festivals of your students.

OBSERVE:

Be aware of how students respond across different situations (social contexts, challenging learning situations, in conflicts) and support them when required. Teach them the cultural norms and values of the culture they are currently living in.

DO NOT ASSUME:

Never assume that a child identifies or even connects with his/her heritage culture. They may have moved early on, lived abroad or might even show disdain for the particular country they come from (e.g. in cases where students come from war-torn countries or countries where they may have been persecuted). Get to know what cultural perspective(s) your students have.

ENGAGE:

Allow students to engage in the learning through their own and others' cultural lens. For example, look at issues from different cultural perspectives and allow students to share their viewpoints and cultural interpretations whenever possible. Create opportunities for students to learn about each other's cultures and languages.

DIG DEEP:

1. How has learning (or speaking) a language other than your mother-tongue allowed you to access different cultural experiences?

2. As a teacher, what aspects of your own culture do you transmit to your students, either knowingly or unknowingly?

3. Identify issues that enculturate students into the "dominant culture." What are the consequences for your classroom and even broader society? What are the benefits?

4. If you have worked with "Third Culture Kids (TCKs)" previously, what aspects of their first, second and third cultures have they seemed to take on?

5. With a partner(s), discuss the "surface aspects" and "deep aspects" of your own cultural background. Are these aspects easy or difficult to pinpoint?

BREAKOUT:

6. What values does your school culture convey?

7. Do you feel these values are responsive and flexible to (linguistically, culturally) diverse groups of students?

8. How do you enable different groups of students to express and engage with their culture within the school environment? Do you feel that these approaches are sufficient?

EXPLORE:

Think of a common stereotype related to a particular cultural group. Research and explore alternative perspectives on the issue providing greater insight into the culture along with the origin of the stereotype. Discuss and share your insights.

[2]

Bilingual and Multilingual Learners: An Exploding Population

IN THIS CHAPTER YOU WILL...

- Understand the dramatic increase of BMLs in primary and secondary education around the world and what it means for teachers
- Understand the shift in economies and the implications for education and employees of the future
- Learn about the common experience of anxiety within the BML population
- Understand the need for all educators to learn more about BML issues and teaching approaches that support them in mainstream classrooms

GROUNDING QUESTION:

Why do teachers need to learn more about the population of bilingual and multilingual students? Shouldn't we treat them like any other students?

The number of bilingual and multilingual students in English-medium classrooms is increasing rapidly around the world. Social and economic upheavals along with a desire to gain a better quality of life are contributors to this dramatic rise in globalization.

Most teachers in urban cities (and now increasingly in smaller communities) will be working directly with BMLs in their classrooms. This requires some adaptations to their teaching skill-sets in order to better meet the unique needs of these learners.

While there have always been waves of migration, the expectations for teaching BMLs are quite different now than they were when our grandparents or great-grandparents would have attended school. Classroom learning back then was much more homogenous, with the teacher focusing on lessons that were delivered to the whole class and usually pitched to the average-ability student. BMLs who struggled to acquire the language of instruction often had very limited, if any, additional help or resources available to them. There were no such things as specialist teachers or teaching assistants to give them additional lessons or break down their learning. In most cases, students had to fend for themselves in a sink-or-swim situation.

Of course good teachers have always made an effort to support their struggling students; however, the *expectation* that they should accommodate individual student needs along with the broader awareness of why they should, began to take shape around the 1970s with changing attitudes. Later, Carol Tomlinson's book, *Differentiated Instruction* (1999), also began to raise the bar by promoting the value of teacher responsiveness to individual student differences in the classroom.

This approach, differentiated instruction, shed light on the notion that each student has particular strengths and preferences for learning experiences. The idea of differentiating instruction encouraged teachers to adopt practices to customize instruction based on the content (information) they teach, the processes (activities) for teaching and the products (work student carries out to demonstrate learning).

Differentiating instructional approaches makes learning much more personalized and encourages a range of different abilities and talents including cultural and linguistic diversity. The idea that teachers should help every student access the curriculum in a way that is relevant and meaningful for them has now become a core educational philosophy.

While there is now a broad acceptance of students with a variety of differences within classrooms today, there is still an enormous gap in the understanding of issues that surround bilingual and multilingual students. The abundant amount of research in second (additional) language acquisition has not yet filtered down to classroom teachers in a widespread, practical way.

With globalization and the increasing numbers of BMLs coming into mainstream classes, it has never been more important for every teacher to become an "expert" in understanding more about BMLs and how to support them with the right instruction. The days of BMLs "sinking or swimming" are hopefully long-gone as educators become more interested in and willing to embrace specific instructional practices that will mean the difference to the success of all kinds of students, as well as BMLs.

Since "ESL" specialist teachers and consultants are often weighed down with heavy caseloads and increasing cuts to funding, they are already a scarce phenomenon. While bilingual education models have been shown to be the most successful model for helping BMLs achieve success over the long term (Thomas & Collier, 1997), the practical and economic feasibility of implementing bilingual models in ultra-diverse urban centers, or even in international school settings is greatly reduced.

Working with BMLs does not have to translate into extra work for teachers. Instead, "working smarter" is the best approach to take in regards to using instructional strategies that have high-impact. Also, being creative with the resources and staffing that are available within each and every school is essential. With the huge numbers and the diversity of BMLs entering English-speaking classrooms these days, there really can be no other way.

CASE IN POINT

Janelle is a second-year classroom teacher in London, UK. This year she is teaching 28 Year 4 students who come from 12 different cultures and language backgrounds. Some of these students are new immigrants, while others are UK-born and speak another language at home with their parents.

While Janelle has a strong handle on her curriculum and classroom management skills, she admits that her challenge is how to work with her students' differing abilities as well as raising their level of the English language. Janelle's students are all at different stages of their English acquisition. Some are "beginners" while others are more "advanced". She only has 4 students who are native speakers.

Janelle is currently coping by differentiating her lessons, but feels out of her depth since she does not have a solid understanding of their language needs and how best to address their developing English language. Sometimes she feels overwhelmed because she has limited access to the school EAL specialist, who supports several different schools and students at one time.

In a classroom as linguistically and culturally diverse as Janelle's, what do you perceive are the opportunities and challenges?

INTERNET, THE NEW ECONOMY AND GLOBAL MOVEMENT

Internet usage has now exploded across the world and global sales of smartphones have tripled in the past few years. Advanced technologies have made communication between people from across the globe as easy as pressing a button.

The human population is in the midst of globalization, with immigration and international travel becoming increasingly popular. English-medium international schools are a growing phenomenon around the world, serving expatriate families as well as local children. As a result, the English language has become the lingua franca for most global communications. Since we are now in a knowledge-based economy, workers must have a greater level of proficiency with information handling, data, research skills and technologies. An increasing number of companies now have a global reach and are successful in creating multinational teams of employees who must communicate effectively with one another, thus again making English the preferred dominant language of international business.

The world is vastly different today compared to 20 or even 10 years ago. Our competitive, knowledge-based economy relies heavily on the skill of individuals to innovate, but to also communicate their ideas and work in dynamic new ways.

Looking in on classrooms today, we can see that they are a mélange of abilities, cultures and languages. Diversity takes many different forms, and one of the fastest growing student populations is the bilingual/multilingual learner (Harper & De Jong, 2004; McKeon, 2005; Tereshchenko, A., 2014). These are children who are not only learning English but are learning academic concepts through English. If you are a teacher, especially in a major city today, it is very likely that you are teaching children who are still acquiring proficiency with the English language.

The UK *National Association for Language Development in the Curriculum* (NALDIC) has found there to be 650,000 students in 2003 whose mother-tongue was not English (2014). In 2013, that number then jumped up to slightly more than 1,000,000 students. Similarly in the USA, the number of non-native English students in California classrooms already makes up 60-70% of the student population and it is estimated that by 2030, 40% of the school-aged population in the USA will be speakers of "English as an additional language" (Thomas & Collier, 1997).

This is clearly a growing phenomenon which is showing no signs of slowing down. It signals a greater need for specific expertise amongst teachers and other education professionals. In most pre-service teacher education programs, you will find some block of study dedicated to BMLs, but despite this, there is still a large gap in practical knowledge that appropriately prepares teachers to work with these students.

Even experienced classroom teachers lack the basic and necessary understanding of language acquisition and its normal (or typical) progression. This can have an extremely detrimental effect on students, especially because of the powerful impact and lasting effects that teacher judgment and assessment can have on students.

Teachers have a very sensitive role to play, not only informing or giving feedback to parents and children about their progress, but also in alerting them to potential problems that might be occurring within their development.

Teachers who are not aware of, or misunderstand the development of a BML's language acquisition, may unknowingly provide incorrect information to parents. This can lead to undue stress and even financial expense, especially if unnecessary tests and professionals are sought out by the family.

Similarly, teachers may not understand how to separate language issues from cognitive or developmental problems. They may erroneously assume a child's development or learning difficulty is attributed to their level of English, when in fact there may be a more complex learning, or information-processing problem.

Given the fact that teacher opinions and judgments are often held in high regard by parents, it is even more critical that teachers become skilled in understanding additional language acquisition and be able to report on their BMLs' academic progress accurately.

> *English Language learners (E.L.L.s) are the fastest growing group of K-12 students in the United States. Most ELLs spend their entire school day in mainstream classrooms where instruction is in English. It is therefore important for all teachers to have the knowledge and skills needed to facilitate these students' academic language development and content area achievement.*
>
> *(Harper & de Jong, 2004)*

How Well-Prepared are Teachers for Working with BMLs?

In looking at the international research on this topic, the sentiments are echoed loud and clear: mainstream teachers feel they do not have the required skills to be effective in meeting the needs of BMLs. In most cases, there is a wide gap in professional development opportunities despite the huge (and growing) numbers of BMLs in classrooms today.

United Kingdom

NALDIC reports that the 2012 "Teaching Standards", require all teachers to have the necessary knowledge and understanding of EAL students' needs while using "distinctive teaching approaches to engage and support them" (2014).

Although this is a basic requirement by the *Department for Education,* and despite the fact that BMLs have increased by 50% since 1997, the availability of "specialist teacher expertise in schools has become increasingly rare (NALDIC, 2014)".

United States

In the US, a 2005 study of Californian teachers found that teachers who taught a majority of BMLs, had reported receiving "no more than one in-service training session in the past five years" which focused on instructional practices for BMLs (Shreve, 2005).

Only 50% of new teachers who are mandated to receive special training around the needs of BMLs were actually reported as having received it. Up to nineteen states had an increase in BMLs by 200% between the years 1995 to 2005, and were under-prepared to meet the needs of these learners within their schools. While many of these states had not traditionally had a large number of BMLs within their school populations, they were required to adapt to the changes in their student body.

Research from an *NEA Policy Brief* (2014) into teacher preparedness for working with BMLs has reported a number of important findings:

- Only 29.5 percent of teachers had received opportunities for professional development around working with BMLs
- There were 20 states which had mandated that new teachers receive special training related to the teaching of BMLs
- 27 percent of teachers reported that they felt they were well-prepared for working with and meeting the needs of BMLs
- 12 percent of teachers felt that they were not prepared at all to meet the learning needs of BMLs

Australia

In Victoria's government schools, 145,369 students were identified as coming from language backgrounds other than English. This accounts for approximately 26% of the total students (Victoria State Government, 2014).

Similarly in New South Wales, the number of students coming from language backgrounds other than English accounts for 30.9% of the total student population (NSW Government of Education, 2013). Even with the large number of BMLs, 88% of Australian mainstream primary teachers felt that they needed more professional development in order to become adept at meeting their learning needs (Grogan, Reid & Sandal, 2010).

In one Melbourne school with an increased population of students from Sudan, it was reported that teachers found it difficult to adapt their resources, meet the emotional and social needs as well as collaborate with specialist support teachers. There was also a recognized lack of professional development opportunities for teachers (Premier& Miller, 2005).

Canada

In the province of Ontario, 60% of students in elementary school are classified as BMLs, as well as 54% in high school. Within the Greater Toronto Area (GTA), this increases to up to 85% of BMLs in the elementary schools. There are some schools who have even reported a student population of up to 94% (People for Education 2012). According to one elementary school principal from the *Peel District School Board* who was quoted in the report, he stated that "the needs of ELL students are significant and the staff allocation does not even scrape the surface."

COPING VS. THRIVING

While many BMLs can appear to cope with learning English as an additional language without any extra support, they are not always capable of thriving. This is because their English ability does not allow them to show their true potential through the traditional, age-appropriate reading and writing tasks.

When students are simply trying to cope in the classroom, they are at a clear disadvantage. They may struggle to keep up with the pace of lessons, decipher the material being taught, meet the expectations of learning tasks while attempting to find relevance or context for their learning. Since many BMLs are struggling with tasks that are far beyond their independent ability levels, they can become frustrated and experience an increased amount of stress and anxiety.

We already know a great deal about the effects of stress on learners. Years of research within the field of educational psychology has shown that when high-anxiety is present, students' performance in a number of areas drops: IQ, aptitude for learning, subject-area achievement, grades and even memory (Humphrey & Revels, 1984; Blankstein, Toner & Flett, 1990; Cassady & Johnson, 2002; Hembree, 1988). Understanding the negative impact that stress can have on learners and their learning helps to better frame our BMLs' experience. Most of them will have come to know stress and anxiety as a regular fact-of-life.

The issue of chronic stress and anxiety for BMLs is not a widely-discussed issue. While there has been a great deal of research done in this area, the phenomenon tends to be more commonly discussed within the TESOL community. Insight into this problem has not yet trickled down to teachers and education professionals in K-12 or primary/secondary education.

A typical BML must make an average of nine years progress in six years in order to "catch up" with their monolinguistic peers' academic attainment (Roseberry-McKibbin & Brice, 2005). This means that theoretically, BMLs should advance by 1.5 academic years for one year of schooling in order to make the same gains as native-speaking students. Considering this fact, the burden of pressure and stress to simply meet the expectations (not exceed them), is enormous for many BMLs who are recognized to constantly be "chasing a moving target" (Collier, 1989). As a result, the educational experience can be a rocky road for many BMLs.

WHAT IS THE IMPACT OF STRESS AND ANXIETY ON BMLS?

- Anxiety can negatively affect the short and long-term memory of foreign-language students (McIntyre & Gardner, 1991a)

- Performance in a wide range of tasks are negatively impacted by language anxiety, such as: listening, reading, comprehension and learning tasks (McIntyre & Gardener, 1994)

- Students in a mainstream-classroom setting experience anxiety related to their levels of participation and their self-esteem (Young, 1990)

- When students are asked to speak aloud in front of others, they experienced the most anxiety, reporting feelings of apprehension, forgetfulness, sweating, difficulties with concentration and a rapid heartbeat (Young, 1990)

- When students were asked to speak in front of others, Horowitz et. al. (1986) found that students had fears about speaking aloud. They were especially self-conscious, worried they might misunderstand what is being said and also nervous that they might make mistakes and be seen as less-proficient than others

- Different contexts cause differing levels of anxiety in ELL students. These tend to relate to students being perceived negatively by others, having test anxiety and feeling hesitant to communicate (Pappamihiel, 2002)

- Pappamihiel believes that language anxiety is more common within the ELL segregated classroom (2002), yet while students are amongst their regular peers and teachers in the mainstream classroom, they have more performance-related anxiety

- Girls tended to be more anxious than males (Pappamihiel, 2002)

Dr. Jim Cummins, a professor from the *University of Toronto*, has studied BMLs extensively. He has highlighted a common problem of teacher misconception about BMLs' ability levels. Because many teachers do not understand the processes of second (additional) language acquisition, they can mistakenly assume that students are able to perform higher levels of academic work than they are actually ready for (Cummins, 2007).

Once students are able to communicate and converse with relative ease, teachers erroneously believe students have much higher proficiency with the language than they actually have. They then begin to expect students to handle much more complex tasks in reading and writing. These are usually challenging intellectual tasks which require a great deal more than a basic proficiency with the oral language. In most cases, BMLs do not have enough direct experience with the required vocabulary, nor do they have the strategies needed to perform advanced tasks independently. Yet on a daily basis, many BMLs are left to cope with assignments using text books that are far beyond their reading levels, they are given worksheets they cannot understand and are even assessed on information they have not been able to fully grasp. When the bar is set too high, students cannot make the huge leap to reach it—they need time to climb gradually, moving ahead one step at-a-time.

For many BMLs, issues around stress, anxiety and frustration are a common part of their everyday, academic experience. The constant pressure to comprehend, perform difficult tasks and communicate in a language they are not yet fluent in can be overwhelming. Isolation and issues around marginalization can also impact their social interactions with other students yet teachers can play a very powerful role in mediating this stress by understanding and engaging in their students' unique experiences. They can learn more about second (additional) language acquisition, successful instructional strategies and by creating an open classroom climate where all learners feel like they are valued and have a voice. Expecting high-quality teaching like this is only possible if teachers are provided with opportunities for a solid education in BML issues. Educating teachers to better understand the needs of this particular student group will go a long way in helping them support their students with the right approaches. Not only is this kind of teacher education important, it is critical.

PERSONAL STORY: ALEJO

When I come to this school, I feel very bad. In my country I get good marks in everything because I speak my language. I am smart. But then I come here to this country and I can't do anything because I don't understand. The teachers give me easy work and also I don't get good marks with the easy work because I don't remember everything on the tests. Everything is very difficult for me. When I come home, my Mom helps me do the homework but it takes very long time— sometimes 2 or 3 hours. I get so tired and I don't have any time now to play sports or do anything. Only work, work, work. Then when the teacher gives the marks from the tests I see that I don't do good. I get so mad and also it makes me feel stupid. Even the teacher don't know how to help me.

WHAT ABOUT OUR GRANDPARENTS? DIDN'T THEY TURN OUT OKAY?

Many of us are the products of second or third-generation immigration. As we look back on our grandparents' or great-grandparents' educational experiences, why does it seem that they came from foreign countries speaking other languages but somehow managed to do fine in English-medium schools?

In those days, the economy and workforce was much different to how it is now. New immigrants were able to acquire a very basic education, with countless students leaving school before reaching graduation or even secondary school. These students would often leave school to become blue collar workers, taking up jobs as miners, dock workers, factory workers or secretaries, for example. For them, higher-levels of education were often viewed as an obstacle to money-making. Joining the workforce earlier meant that they were immediately able to start earning a stable living. At that time, work was more abundant and people often had jobs for life. This meant increased security for individuals and their families. From the period of the Industrial Revolution until the 1950s, the economy required a less-educated, more manually-skilled workforce.

These days, things are radically different. We live in a technology-driven, knowledge-based economy. The demands of employers are much more diverse compared to the days of our grandparents. Work requires higher levels of thinking and problem-solving, along with advanced levels of oral and written communication. The nature of work is shifting continuously, with new innovations in technology coming up every few years. This requires workers to be flexible in adapting to changes. The concept of having one job "for life" is no longer realistic, and workers are required to diversify their skill-sets in order to remain marketable. Lifelong learning is valued and considered an ongoing part of one's career in order to keep up with advancing business and technological trends. Our current workforce simply demands highly-educated employees.

Immigrants today are very aware of the need for their children to get a higher-level of education leading to some form of post-secondary studies (Roessingh & Douglas, 2012). Whether they themselves have arrived with a university education or not, most have high expectations for their children. These expectations typically include a university education that can pave the way to more professional career options.

Considering the requirements of our economy along with the expectations of parents and students themselves, we can safely assume that post-secondary education is the goal of most students, BMLs included. This means that educators will have to possess greater levels of expertise in order to be able to support their students in reaching this long-term goal.

More than ever, it is imperative that all teachers become proficient in the specific knowledge and strategies that will allow BMLs to thrive, not just cope. The consequences of not understanding these issues can, and do result in BMLs being disproportionately represented in special education services or even dropping out of school, despite underlying talent and academic potential.

DIG DEEP:

1. What kind of factors would lead to BMLs feeling overwhelmed?

2. How might you identify stress in your BMLs? What does it look like? What can you do to help alleviate it?

3. What are your personal perceptions about teaching BMLs?

BREAKOUT:

4. How do you feel about teaching BMLs and learning more about their specific needs?

5. How much previous preparation and experience have you already had in working with BMLs? What do you already know in relation to additional language acquisition?

6. What are the levels of achievement of your BMLs as a whole, within your school?

7. How confident are you in making particular judgements about your BMLs' learning and discussing it with their parents?

EXPLORE:

Research statistics on school dropout rates of BMLs. What kind of impact do you feel this has on the community and society as-a-whole? If the English language is an entry point into membership in the dominant culture, who are the gate-keepers? How do they manage to maintain their membership and status? Will this change over time?

[3]

Understanding Bilingualism, Multilingualism and Labeling

IN THIS CHAPTER YOU WILL...
- Learn more about the nature of bilingualism, multilingualism and their benefits
- Identify risks of subtractive bilingualism and assimilation into the dominant culture
- Examine definitions of BMLs across countries and regions
- Understand the need for an upgraded definition for BMLs

GROUNDING QUESTION:
Why are the labels we use for our students important? How do labels help us do our job?

MY EXPERIENCE AS A BML: FRANCESCA'S STORY

I grew up in Scotland but later moved to Brussels, Belgium because of my father's job. I was in secondary school when I arrived in Brussels and I joined one of the European Schools, which delivered the *European Baccalaureate* at graduation level (similar to the more familiar *International Baccalaureate*). This meant I had to take some of my core subjects in the French language (L2) as well as in English (L1). Later on, I had additional classes in German while continuing to speak English at home with my family.

In Scotland, I had already had some foreign language classes in French but once I came to Brussels, most of my peers had been learning the language since elementary school. I felt I was at a clear disadvantage in comparison.

I was expected to learn French within one year and was graded according to the same standards as my native French-speaking peers. It was extremely hard work and while I did not come close to being able to function as well as the French students, I eventually did much better than I thought I would.

I remember that it was often difficult to feel successful because I did not have the vocabulary or confidence in the first two years. The pressure to catch up and keep up so that I could graduate in 3 years was enormous. While I had many ups-and-downs during that time, I found that language-learning came fairly easy to me compared to many other people.

Understanding language acquisition as I do now, I know that one of the main reasons I was able to succeed in a French learning environment was because my mother tongue (L1) was very well-developed by the time I moved, so I mainly had to translate my new French vocabulary words into English. I was also very active in thinking about the differences between each of my languages and this helped me to clearly separate the similarities and differences between them. I found myself becoming interested in "cracking the codes" of different languages and so I later went on to study Mandarin in university. After that, I moved to Spain for a year and learned Spanish.

When people find out that I am able to speak different languages, they are always quite amazed and have a very positive attitude about my multilingualism. Bilingualism and especially multilingualism are generally regarded as beneficial and even highly-esteemed skills to possess, especially within the "adult world." However, once I became an ESL teacher working with bilingual and multilingual students in mainstream classrooms, I discovered that this positive attitude towards BMLs did not always exist when it came to children. In fact, I noticed that BMLs were often viewed as if they had a disability.

Looking at these students through a lens of "lack" seemed to be the dominant perspective from which many teachers operated from. They often worried about teaching BMLs because they could not understand how to help them access the curriculum. This was especially true if the students were "beginners" in the English language.

Now having worked in elementary and secondary schools in various parts of the world, I have found the trend to be very similar: the BMLs' proverbial glass is often half-empty. I firmly believe that this is not the fault of teachers, many of whom spend additional time and go the extra mile to support and reach out to these students. The real problem is that general education teachers have not been given access to valuable information about the learning trajectories and processes that this particular group of students will go through as they acquire English. Teachers themselves are in a sink-or-swim situation.

Some of the natural stages and phases a BML will move through can perplex and puzzle educators and many of the assessment and instructional practices that are known to work well with BMLs may in fact run counter-intuitive to a teacher's natural instincts.

There is a crisis in the education of bilingual and multilingual students. While the number of BMLs in English speaking classrooms is increasing exponentially, the way that we assess, work with and understand these students has not yet caught up. This puts a dizzying gap between teachers and their students. Even when teachers have the best of intentions, they find themselves consistently facing lack: lack of information, lack of time, lack of resources and lack of support.

Looking at BMLs from a deficit perspective rather than one which recognizes and values their bilingual or multilingual talents will not enable teachers to do their jobs effectively, nor will it allow students to be viewed as assets to their classrooms and learning communities.

That same high-regard that is given to bilingual or multilingual adults needs to ring loud and clear throughout our classrooms and be embedded within all of our teaching approaches and attitudes.

FACTS ABOUT BILINGUALISM AND MULTILINGUALISM

Trying to pinpoint a precise number as to how many bilingual or multilingual people there are in the world is an extremely difficult task. This requires a great deal of research from censuses in each country which ask citizens questions about the different languages they use. One researcher, Professor Francois Grosjean, a former psycholinguistics professor from *Neuchatel University* in Switzerland, has concluded that there are likely around 50% or a little more than half of the population who speak at least 2 languages in the world today. This figure is difficult to determine because of the fact that several countries do not ask any questions about language on their censuses, as in the case of Belgium and France, for example (Grosjean, 2014).

It is clear that bilingualism and multilingualism are growing phenomena around the world. As a result of globalization and the knowledge about its advantages, more people than ever are growing their language repertoires. The European Parliament has identified a need to promote language diversity in Europe, recognizing that languages are a critical aspect of identity and daily life and that language contributes to a strong expression of culture. In light of these values, they have created a language policy along with programs and resources to support this goal.

> *As part of its efforts to promote mobility and intercultural understanding, the EU has designated language learning as an important priority, and funds numerous programmes and projects in this area. Multilingualism, in the EU's view, is an important element in Europe's competitiveness. One of the objectives of the EU's language policy is therefore that every European citizen should master two other languages in addition to their mother tongue (Gyorffi, 2016, p.1).*

In the United States, there is also rising interest in creating bilinguals, with an enormous increase in bilingual education models. Programs offering content learning through 2 languages—English and another language like Spanish, Chinese, French and even Haitian Creole, have now exploded. From the year 2000, there were an estimated 260 bilingual education programs operating around the country. Ten years later, this number grew to approximately 2,000 programs and has shown no signs of slowing down (Wilson, 2011).

THE NATURE OF BILINGUALISM AND MULTILINGUALISM

Bilingualism, or the ability to speak 2 languages, has been a well-investigated phenomenon for several decades. Due to the fact that many countries have recognized the value of bilingualism as an essential skill rather than simply a beneficial one, extensive research has been done and has resulted in good understandings about cognition and language acquisition in bilingual individuals. In the European Union and within other bilingual countries, this knowledge is used to support the development of policies and programs with the aim to nurture bilingualism.

On the other hand, multilingualism, or the ability to speak 3 or more languages is still not widely understood simply because there has not been much research done in this area. Recently, because more and more individuals are arriving to English-speaking countries from linguistically-diverse regions where 3 or more languages are spoken, there is interest in better understanding them. As a result, there is now more research being done.

Bilingual and multilingual people are extremely diverse; not only across the languages they know, but also for how they use and express their languages. In countries where there are several languages spoken, like Kenya for instance, individuals are typically exposed to a regional mother-tongue alongside "official languages". In Kenya, the official languages are Kiswahili (Swahili) and English, both of which are used for educational purposes. These languages are also used for communication between people who speak different mother-tongues (or local languages). In many multilingual countries, individuals acquire a repertoire of languages which are based on a mix of exposure, need, and even around political decisions within the country. They tend to use their languages within specific contexts or situations where one language would be more practical, or perceived as more "appropriate" than another.

It is a myth that every bilingual or multilingual person has the same level of proficiency with each of their languages (Grosjean, 2010). In fact, most have varying degrees of fluency and literacy in their languages. For example, one person may have a high level of comprehension in one language but with only the foundations of oral fluency; another might be fully fluent and literate in two languages but without any literacy in their third. The way that individuals need to use their languages can dictate how developed that language will become.

Some individuals even use a mix of their languages at one time, depending on who they communicate with, so that they can best express what they want to say more concisely or even more emotionally. Multilinguals have the ability to sort through their languages, using them flexibly in different situations and with different people.

Bilingual and multilingual individuals' use of their languages can also change considerably over time (Grosjean, 2000). Lack of use, movement from one country to another, or even loss of a relative who helped to maintain the language can determine which language becomes more dominant for an individual. In the context of the education of BMLs in English-medium schools, large numbers of students are effectively "educated out of" their MTs in order to replace them with English over time. As a result, this produces *subtractive bilinguals*.

Subtractive bilinguals are created as a result of many factors, largely because of the widely-held, "dominant" view that English holds more importance than other languages. It also develops due to a lack in understanding about the benefits of bilingualism and multilingualism. Without adequate understanding of bilingualism and multilingualism and their development, subtractive policies within organizations and human services fields (e.g. education, family medicine and even psychology) continue to perpetuate this belief.

TYPES AND PROCESSES OF BILINGUALISM

ADDITIVE BILINGUAL:

This is where the learning of an additional language (L2) does not take away from, or replace the development of the first language (L1). The goal is usually for the individual to become a balanced bilingual.

SUBTRACTIVE BILINGUAL:

This is when the learning of another language (L2) takes away from the development of the first language (L1) and then begins to replace it. This can occur when individuals begin to assimilate into a "dominant culture" without continuing to grow or develop the L1.

BALANCED BILINGUAL:

This refers to an individual having fairly similar proficiency in both languages.

SEQUENTIAL BILINGUAL:

When an individual learns their first language (L1) and then learns another after the age of 3. This can occur when individuals are immersed into a new culture or language or are educated within a bilingual education model.

SIMULTANEOUS BILINGUAL:

Simultaneous bilinguals learn their two languages at the same time. This usually occurs when individuals are spoken to in one language by one parent and a different language by the other parent. Both languages grow simultaneously.

ADVANTAGES OF BILINGUALISM AND MULTILINGUALISM

Being a bilingual or multilingual individual has numerous benefits at the individual, societal and global levels. People who speak another language gain access to different cultures and diverse experiences. This can be a great advantage, especially in terms of the opportunities available to them. They are able to access a wider range of employment options, enhance personal and professional relationships as well as gain access to other networks within their own and global communities. Their often broad view of the world also contributes to the "cultural capital" of their society and country which means that they add further skill to the talent pool.

There has been a significant amount of research done in this area since the early 1900s; however, it was initially thought that bilingualism created a negative impact on language-learning and intellect (Konnikova, 2015). This perspective has changed considerably since then, largely amongst researchers and experts, and there has been extensive interest in understanding how language develops for bilinguals. This has contributed to the knowledge of its benefits. However, within the general population, there are still many myths about bilingualism and multilingualism which continue to be perpetuated. Some of these myths can include beliefs that:

- Bilingualism or multilingualism can negatively affect a child's intelligence
- Children really only have the capacity to focus on one main language at-a-time
- If a child attends school in English, it is important for parents to start speaking English to them in order for the child to better adjust
- The child's MT is not as important as English

Research has actually shown that speaking more than one language benefits the brain and other cognitive functions. It is important for professionals and parents alike to be educated about this in order to help encourage them to see the value of bilingualism and multilingualism; both for the short and long-term.

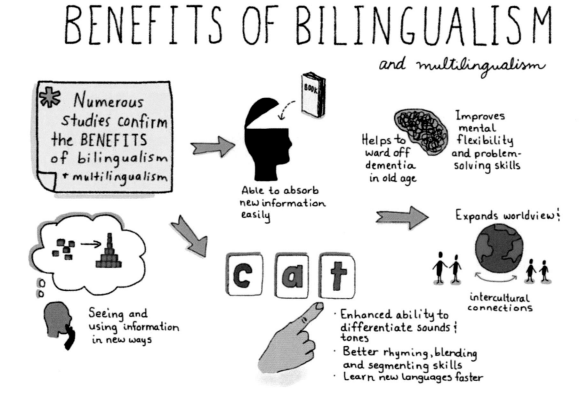

Bilingual and multilingual individuals have enhanced capabilities

What is the "Best" Model of Education for BMLs?

The question of how to best educate BMLs has been asked consistently over several decades. This has led to a great deal of research on the issue, with one particular longitudinal study revealing that bilingual education models produced the best results in academic achievement.

This specific study by Thomas and Collier (1997), examined student achievement over 11 years and with 42,000 participants. It highlighted many important findings.

All program models created fairly close results in their success up until around grade 2; then, students in bilingual education models made huge leaps forward as they moved closer to graduation. Transitional programs and ESL programs proved to be unsuccessful models for long-term student achievement.

While the benefits of bilingual education models need to be acknowledged and every effort should

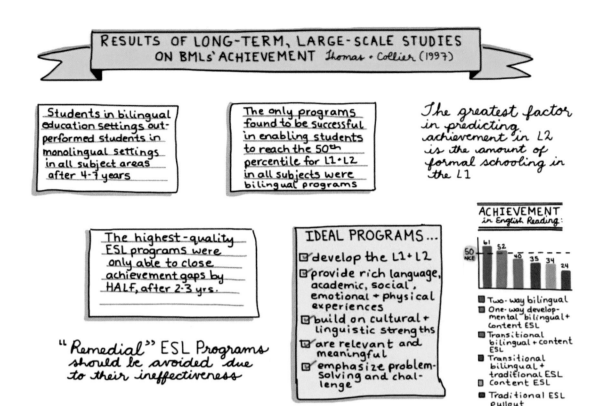

"One-Way" Developmental or "Dual Language Programs" support one main group of students to become bilingual and literate in both languages (e.g. getting Spanish MT students to learn English while supporting the maintenance of Spanish).

"Two-Way Developmental" or "Dual Language Programs" aim to build bilingualism and biliteracy amongst 2 different language groups (e.g. French speakers and English speakers are educated in both languages—their MT and the new language).

be made to offer such programs, the current reality is that there are relatively small numbers of bilingual programs available for large, diverse populations of BMLs in English-speaking educational settings. This means that most teachers will be meeting the needs of BMLs within mainstream classes. In this case, what can teachers do to ensure that BMLs reach their fullest potential? How can schools support students to reach graduation and have the option of post-secondary study?

Both Francesca and I have asked ourselves this question numerous times over the past decade. As educational consultants, we have been fortunate to work in a multicultural, international hub which has provided us with the opportunity to work closely with all kinds of BMLs and intercultural families. We have also worked closely with teachers in national schools as well as international schools, and with many different curricula. This has allowed us to see the issues surrounding the education of BMLs through a wide-reaching lens. As colleagues, we often sit with a coffee after work and find ourselves analyzing student cases and discussing them at length. Years ago, we set out to examine how best to meet the needs of these students in the context of mainstream education and we were delighted to find so much research done by experts in applied linguistics and psycholinguistics; but we soon began to realize there was an enormous knowledge gap between the more theoretical "research world" and the "practical world" of mainstream teachers.

We now know that the average teacher is given little, if any training or background in the basic issues surrounding BMLs, let alone up-to-date research findings from journals or conferences. With this in mind, we knew that it was not possible to expect teachers to become proficient in working with BMLs if they did not first have a strong knowledge-base about them.

As it turned out, our research led us to several golden nuggets that we have begun to apply in our own work with students and families, helping us to fully realize their impact and value for classroom teachers. As well, we have begun to understand how schools and teachers can better service their BMLs in mainstream classes, equipped with not only the right knowledge-base, but with a "toolkit" of high-impact instructional strategies to match.

ISSUES OF ASSIMILATION INTO THE DOMINANT LANGUAGE

It is essential that mainstream teachers have a strong working awareness of the issues that relate to the education of children from "minority" language backgrounds.

While teachers are well-intentioned, they are not always well-informed or given training in the issues that relate to dominant language assimilation or linguistic human rights. This gap in knowledge must be closed in order to assist teachers in understanding just how far-reaching the consequences of educating children "out of" their mother-tongue can be.

A large majority of teachers and caregivers from English-speaking countries are part of the "dominant" culture. They have received many benefits as a result of coming from a culture which validated their language as an "official language." Speaking the dominant language guaranteed them access to a broad variety of educational and career opportunities, often without their awareness of this advantage.

The same opportunities are not as easily afforded to individuals from minority cultures, mainly because their language does not have "official" status. This means that they have had to fit into other languages and systems of education as a result. Many were likely to have struggled academically, or might not have been able to navigate the supports that were available to them. They likely came to view their language as unimportant or simply, "street language" because of the fact that their parents received incorrect advice to "speak English" in the home environment. The perceived "status" of a language can have a huge impact on whether it is supported within a community, country or organization. "Low status" languages are vulnerable and can face extinction over time as individuals abandon them over "higher-status" languages like English, for example.

Dr. Tove Skutnabb-Kangas, a professor, researcher and expert in "linguistic human rights" has estimated that between 90-95% of the world's languages will become endangered or extinct by the year 2100 (2008). This not only leads to the tragic loss of languages but ultimately, cultural biodiversity. One of the factors that can help to ameliorate this statistic is educating parents since the "transmission of languages from the parent generation to children is the most vital factor for the maintenance of both oral and sign languages" (2008, pg.2).

Once children become educated in a language that is not their mother-tongue, or if they are not permitted to use their native language in school, the assimilation process begins. Their language is then at major risk of dying out at the family level, but also within that particular linguistic population as a whole.

Like parents, teachers and care professionals can play a huge role in helping the student and his or her family maintain their mother-tongue. Teachers can learn strategies for promoting and using the mother-tongue in learning situations. They can be a resource for parents by linking them to external language and cultural supports. They can also run information programs in order to help raise awareness across parent populations in their school. This can help parents to better understand these issues in-depth and can even help to reinforce the instinctual, intrinsic capacity of parents to care for and support their children in the most natural and comfortable way.

We will continue to explore the issues around mother-tongue support in greater detail in the following chapters.

PERSONAL STORY: ALICE

I moved with my family to London from Poland in 2000. I was already 11 years old at that time and I remember being so scared of going to school because it was in English. I didn't know much English, only a few sentences so it was totally new to me. The teachers at my school were quite good; they never seemed to make any issue about the fact that I didn't know English. Most of the children at my school were from different cultures and also didn't speak English very well. My teachers could see how hard I tried and always helped me but it wasn't enough to get me to "A Levels". I managed to pass the GCSEs (graduation exams) and left school when I was 17. I had a few jobs in high street shops and have worked up to being a manager of a lady's spa by taking other courses. I suppose if I was in Poland I would have gone to university to become a veterinarian but here in the UK, the standards were just too high for me. Who knows, maybe one day I can go back to school, but not right now.

LABELING AND IDENTIFICATION OF BILINGUAL MULTILINGUAL STUDENTS IN SCHOOL CONTEXTS

If you have ever tried to navigate the information on BMLs or English-language learning, no doubt you will have discovered the abundance of information on the topic, as well as an overwhelming number of acronyms that deal with different types of English-language teaching and learning. Whether it is ELL, ESL, EAL (or now BML), the list goes on. These labels represent different segments and models which focus on the teaching of English in various contexts such as: schools, language schools, foreign language centers, etc.

SPECIFIC REFERENCE TERMS AND CONTEXTS USED

ESL - English as a Second Language
Typically used in primary, secondary or post-secondary settings

EAL - English as an Additional Language
Often used in primary and secondary settings

ELL - English Language Learner
Used within primary and secondary settings in the USA and Canada

LEP - Limited English Proficient
Used within primary and secondary settings in the USA; used within the research

LOTE - Language Other than English
Refers to foreign language classes taught in Australia and some US schools

LBOTE - Language Backgrounds Other than English
Used in Australia in reference to government schools

EFL - English as a Foreign Language
Typically used in schools that teach English as a language class for students who speak a different primary language, or even in external language centers around the world

LM - Language Minority
A term often used in the research to describe individuals who speak an "unofficial language" of a region

---

What is very clear about these labels is that there is a definite need to update and refine them. The way we "brand" these students with outdated or often limiting terms like "ESL" or "LEP" keeps the focus on their lack of English.

One of the most common terms, "English as a second language" is often erroneously used with students who in fact, speak more than two languages. In this case, multilingual students are being placed into the same category as bilingual students and there is no reference given to the fact that they actually speak more than two languages. This masks extremely important information which should be passed onto teachers. Since there is a need to label and make specific reference to BMLs in regards to our work with them, it should be done in a way that accurately reflects their language repertoires.

Of course the use of labels for individuals should be used with caution. When we use the kinds of terms that can categorize individuals, we need to adopt definitions which offer positive perspectives.

Within our school contexts, this means terminology which affirms that bilingualism or multilingualism is a benefit. In doing so, we come closer to recognizing the value that bilingualism and multilingualism offers, not only in adulthood but also during childhood—a sensitive time when many BMLs can find themselves trying to fit in both academically and socially. We also need to understand that individuals can internalize their labels, and that the label itself holds incredible power in that it can contribute to the way the individual begins to view themselves (Rist, 1977).

A PLACE TO START: A COMMON LANGUAGE FOR BMLs

A common problem across mainstream schools serving BMLs is that there is a lack of consistency in program models, including the labeling and identification of students. Knowing what we know now, it is clear that a real reason for this comes down to misunderstandings about BMLs and a lack of solid knowledge about them. Because of this, many decisions are made and program models implemented that are not truly sound. Here are just a few examples that might be found within schools:

- There are no bilingual/multilingual specialist teachers on staff so students are assigned to the Special Education/Learning Support department by default
- BMLs are considered "ESL/ELL/EAL" students for a fixed number of years and then they are assumed to be "fluent" after only 2-3 years— as a result they are then "exited" from support before they are ready
- Schools may not identify BMLs because the child's parent has not disclosed information about their language background on forms or the school did not ask the right questions about the child's linguistic/cultural background
- There is no common understanding or language amongst educators around the world to communicate about BMLs

One of our former colleagues, a specialist with bilingual students in Australia, was a teacher within different education systems around the world. Some of these include international schools where BMLs made up large proportions of the student body. She described some of her challenges working across different systems and staff, as well as the issues with labeling and identifying students:

As a former EAL specialist, I've worked in Australia and within international schools. I've found that there is never very much in common with the way we identify, label or set up programs for BMLs across schools or systems. Within every position I've held, we would have to sort this out very early on in order to come together with working policies and procedures. Each person was used to very different definitions and models. In many situations, students who would be identified and provided services in one of my former schools would not have been eligible in another. This to me is a major problem. We need a common way to define and refer to our BMLs and a common way of understanding and supporting them.

Certainly there is a need to redefine our students and our work with them. If we start by comparing the definitions of BMLs across different countries, we can see many similarities and differences between them.

Some of these definitions make reference to specific cultural groups that reside within a region, like aboriginal people, for example. However, only the UK definition makes reference to the terms, "bilingual" and considers students learning "English and one or more other languages" rather than simply being "limited English," "second language," or "another language."

DEFINITIONS OF BMLs IN DIFFERENT COUNTRIES AND REGIONS

AUSTRALIA - NEW SOUTH WALES

"ESL learners are students from language backgrounds other than English (LBOTE) who are learning English as a second or additional language as well as developing literacy skills in English. They need to simultaneously learn English, learn in English and learn about English in order to successfully participate in informal social interactions as well as more formal and academic contexts (NSW Department of Education and Communities, 2014, p.6)."

Definitions go on to include individuals who are born in Australia as well as those who are migrants, refugees and international students. These students may have had prior schooling and literacy experiences while others may have had little or no exposure to schooling or education. They categorize students into 3 distinct phases of English proficiency.

AUSTRALIA - QUEENSLAND

"Students who are learning the English language while they learn the school curriculum are known as English as an additional language or dialect (EAL/D) learners (Queensland Government, 2013)."

Definitions can include Aboriginal students, Torres Strait Islanders, migrants (migrant heritage) and individuals born in Australia or other countries where English is spoken.

CANADA – ONTARIO

"English language learners are students in provincially funded English language schools whose first language is a language other than English, or is a variety of English that is significantly different from the variety used for instruction in Ontario's schools, and who may require focused educational supports to assist them in attaining proficiency in English. These students may be Canadian-born or recently arrived from other countries. They come from diverse backgrounds and school experiences, and have a wide variety of strengths and needs (Ontario Ministry of Education, 2008, p.5-6)."

English language learners can either be Canadian-born English language learners (e.g. Aboriginals, distinct ethnic Canadians, etc.) and Newcomers (immigrants, refugees, visa and international students).

An additional definition of "ELD" or "English Literacy Development" is provided to distinguish between students who "have significant gaps in their education because of limited prior schooling."

CANADA – BRITISH COLUMBIA

"English Language Learner students are those whose primary language(s) or language(s) of the home, is other than English and who may therefore require additional services in order to develop their individual potential within British Columbia's school system. Some students speak variations of English that differ significantly from the English used in the broader Canadian society and in school; they may require ELL support (British Columbia Ministry of Education, 1999, p.6)".

Definitions include: Canadian-born students, immigrants, refugees, ELL students with additional special needs.

USA – CALIFORNIA

"ELs (English Learners) come to California schools from all over the world, and from within California, with a range of cultural and linguistic backgrounds, experiences with formal schooling, proficiency with native language and English literacy, migrant statuses, and socioeconomic statuses, as well as other experiences in the home, school, and community. All of these factors inform how educators support ELs to achieve school success through implementation of the CA ELD (California English Language Development) Standards and the academic content standards (Torlakson, 2012)."

USA – New York

"Students whose primary language is a language other than English are often referred to as English Language Learners (ELLs). In New York State, under Part 154 of the *Commissioner's Regulations* (CR Part 154), limited English proficient students are: ...students who by reason of foreign birth or ancestry speak a language other than English and,

- either understand and speak little or no English; or
- score below a state designated level of proficiency, on the *New York State Identification Test for English Language Learners* (NYSITELL) or the *New York State English as a Second Language Achievement Test* (NYSESLAT) (New York State Department of Education, 2015)."

United Kingdom

"Bilingual students are students who have access to more than one language at home or at school. Typically, these are pupils who are living in England and learning in English and one or more other languages. It does not necessarily imply full fluency in both/all languages (Department for Education and Skills, 2012, p.2)."

With the dramatic movement of students and families around the globe, classroom teachers are in great need of new ways of speaking about and understanding BMLs in the context of a globalized, international community—not only within the boundaries of their states or countries. The common interest and concern in BML issues amongst teachers around the globe is already wide-spread, and still growing.

As we know, in more and more schools around the world, BMLs now make up the majority of the student population. This is proof that we cannot continue to operate as we previously did, believing that the needs of all these students will be met by one or two support teachers who will take on the responsibility of these students' learning. We need to have faith in the fact that the classroom teachers themselves are one of the greatest assets and resources their students will have because they consistently make a difference in the lives of their students on a daily basis. Their influence is profound, and so it makes perfect sense to amplify and extend this resource so that teachers themselves can become "experts" in this area. However, expecting that teachers can do this without the right training and internal support would not be sound, practical, or realistic.

A TEACHER'S EXPERIENCE: KAREN

I'm expected to teach more and more ELL students in my class each year but I feel like I'm floundering to tell you the truth. We don't have any professional development in this area and I never really know if what I'm doing is the right approach.

UPGRADING THE DEFINITION

Certainly there is a need for different regions to adapt their definition of BMLs to specific populations of students who reside there; however, the basic definition should include the terms "bilingualism" and "multilingualism" as the main terms of reference.

Primary and secondary school settings are distinctly different in nature to other settings where English is taught, like foreign language centers for example, so the definition needs to fit the environment where it will be used.

In light of these issues, we need to make a simple shift and tune-up our definition to one that not only amplifies our students' linguistic strengths but one which is more relevant, accurate and descriptive.

Defining our students as being "bilingual" or "multilingual" reminds us of their other language(s), culture and identity and brings these positive aspects to the forefront of our minds. Within the school context, full or "native-like" proficiency in English is a goal that BMLs are working towards. Within our schools and classrooms, we should also be promoting the development of students' MT or other languages and understand that learning English does not have to happen at the expense of these languages.

Recognition of students who use an English dialect other than what is considered "Standard English" in the academic setting or region is also essential within our definitions. Many of these students can find it difficult to cope with differences between their own dialect which is second-nature to them, and the more "formal" or "academic" one used within their school. These students too, can benefit from additional understanding and support from their teachers. They can be guided to learn about the concepts of "dialects" and how to shift between their own dialect and the "Standard English" dialect used within their school and other establishments.

A student's dialect, like a mother-tongue, also reflects their unique culture and identity. Since there is not enough awareness about dialects, there are common misunderstandings by many well-intentioned individuals who aim to help these students "lose their accents" or "speak proper English". By building an understanding around this, teachers can empower their students by validating and respecting their unique dialects.

Here are the upgraded definitions for the purpose and context of our school settings. We encourage teachers and schools to think about how they could adapt these to best suit their particular needs.

BILINGUAL STUDENT:

A bilingual student comes to the learning environment with varying proficiency in English and another language. They may have knowledge of another culture and traditions, as well as prior learning experiences through their mother-tongue. They may or may not have had prior schooling, or be literate in either language. Bilingual students may think in their mother-tongue and/or in English. They may be born within the country as citizens or may come from a foreign country as: immigrants, refugees, international students or expatriates.

MULTILINGUAL STUDENT:

A multilingual student comes to the learning environment with varying proficiency in English and 2 or more languages. They may have knowledge of another culture and traditions, as well as prior learning experiences through those languages. They may or may not have had prior schooling, or be literate in either language. Multilingual students may think in their mother-tongue/other language or in English. They may be born within the country as citizens or may come from a foreign country as: immigrants, refugees, international students or expatriates.

ENGLISH-DIALECT (ED) STUDENT:

A student who uses another dialect of English may have varied proficiency with the standard form of English used within the school context. They may be monolingual, bilingual or multilingual. They may have knowledge of other English dialects. They may have knowledge of another culture and traditions, as well as prior learning experiences through their dialect or other languages. These students may or may not have had prior schooling or literacy skills. They may be born within the country as citizens or may come from a foreign country as: immigrants, refugees, international students or expatriates.

DIG DEEP:

1. Why is it so important to view BMLs from a positive view-point rather than from a deficit perspective? What implications can this have on a student's language development?

2. Are there any students in your school who should be identified as BMLs but have not been? Why is that?

3. Why do you think a parent of a bilingual or multilingual child chooses to enroll their child in an English-only school?

BREAKOUT:

4. How does your school identify BMLs? What about those in need of extra support?

5. What kind of impact does your BML program or support have on students' English development? What about their overall academic achievement?

EXPLORE:

Explore the current definitions for bilingual/multilingual students that your school uses. Compare this definition with the upgraded definitions from this chapter. How do they compare? Does your definition use a "half-full" or "half-empty" definition? How could you rewrite it to be more descriptive, accurate and relevant?

[4]

The Mysteries of Language Acquisition

IN THIS CHAPTER YOU WILL...

- Learn why one's mother-tongue (MT) is so valuable
- Learn about CUP to explain how one's languages work together
- Understand why BMLs are often a misunderstood population
- Understand the two types of English language proficiency: BICS & CALP

GROUNDING QUESTION:

What do you already know about the development of one's first language (MT)?

One of the biggest issues we see as a result of teachers being uninformed about BMLs and second (additional) language acquisition is the inaccurate assessment and categorization of students.

In many cases, BMLs' language abilities are incorrectly assumed to be more advanced than they actually are. This is understandable. To the untrained eye, the child might speak like a native, often with the same accent, and they might have even have picked up the superficial ability to function within the classroom environment. Since many BMLs can do this fairly quickly, there is a tendency for educators to believe that a child has "caught up" to their peers and no longer requires additional support. Yet when these same individuals have to put more complex thoughts onto paper, or have to process higher order thinking skills and concepts, their weaknesses are likely to be revealed. This can compound if they are exited from support and monitoring because teachers perceive them to be "good" in oral language proficiency. As the child continues to struggle with challenging tasks, teachers begin to question whether this child is showing signs of a learning issue.

As educators, we tend to use "indicators of the obvious"—familiar signs and signals we get from our students about their learning which guides our teaching and assessment. These indicators let us know whether the student has learned or not-learned, and they carry clues that help us understand why a student might be struggling. Simple mistakes or omissions within a mathematical computation can indicate that the student has misunderstood the procedure, or a poorly-developed written piece can indicate that the student has not yet mastered the writing process. Our ability to look for these obvious signs and patterns is ingrained in us as teachers and we become very adept at responding to them.

We also come to expect specific errors within concepts and we try to interpret what they mean so that we can move the student ahead. This strategy is helpful in most cases. We innately know what kind of student errors are "typical" and "atypical". When we find a student's learning to be atypical, we seek out other opinions, specialist support or even refer the student for observation or external testing.

What many educators do not understand is that BMLs often experience subtle issues that affect their ability to process and recall information in English. This can mimic the symptoms of a learning disorder. In fact, looking at the numbers of BMLs overrepresented in special education or learning support settings, it is not a surprise to find that many have been diagnosed as "dyslexic," having "reading disorders," or even "language delays." In many cases, these diagnoses are made by other professionals who themselves are not fully aware of language acquisition in BMLs. As a result, they do not use appropriate educational or psychological tests to assess BMLs.

The information and tools in this next chapter will help you to build a solid, practical understanding of the typical development of a BML learning English. This information will take you to a whole new level of expertise so that you can understand and teach your BMLs with confidence.

CASE IN POINT

It is fast approaching the end-of-term and Year 7 teacher, Michael, is evaluating one of his BML's summative writing assessments.

Si-u arrived last academic year from Korea and has now had one-and-a-half years of instruction in English. He developed friends easily and learned to adapt to English more quickly than many other children he's worked with. Si-u is also one of the top students in Mathematics and Michael notices that he is very dedicated to studying.

Looking at Si-u's writing now, Michael is surprised at the level of the written work. It appears that Si-u's vocabulary has increased since the last assessment but Michael notices that there is not much meaningful content on the page. He can see a noticeable gap between what Si-u is able to express orally and what he is actually putting down on paper.

Michael makes a mental note to observe Si-u consistently during the next month to monitor for any potential learning difficulties. He has heard that students with gaps between their ability (ie: cognitive level) and independent achievement levels, can often signal a learning disability.

What should Michael do over the next month in order to gain more information about Si-u's learning?

LEARNING AND UNDERSTANDING THE IMPORTANCE OF THE MOTHER-TONGUE (MT)

What do we mean by "mother-tongue?" When we think of the term, "mother-tongue," we often think of the first language learned within one's family as an infant. This is largely true; however, Dr. Tove Skutnabb-Kangas has provided extended definitions of mother-tongue which are also important to consider. While we can think of the MT as one which is learned naturally, it is also true that individuals can adopt a new language and use it as their primary or working language in a way that is similar to their MT. This is important for us to understand as we move forward to explore language development and acquisition in further detail. "Mother-tongue" can also be defined as:

- the first language one learned
- the language one identifies with the most
- the language one is identified with as a native speaker by others
- the language one knows best
- the language one uses most

(Skutnabb-Kangas, 1984, 18)

In some cases, individuals may even have 2 MTs if they are raised as simultaneous bilinguals with 2 parents providing about the same amount of language input. That individual might later favour one of their languages over the other, especially if they tend to use one more than the other.

It is important to get as much information about your BMLs' language backgrounds as possible upon their entry to school. You need to be clear on the development of their languages and their proficiency in each. One's MT is not always clear cut, especially in cases when they are multilingual.

THE DEVELOPMENT OF OUR FIRST LANGUAGE

The acquisition of language is doubtless the greatest intellectual feat any one of us is ever required to perform. ~ Leonard Bloomfield

Learning to speak our mother-tongue is probably the greatest accomplishment of each and every human on the planet. Each language comes with its own vocabulary and grammatical system, structures, syntax and complexities but we are not even aware of these complexities because language seems to come to us so naturally.

By around the age of 4, a child will have nearly mastered the fundamentals of their language, and by the time he or she starts school, they will have consolidated about 80% of the grammar and more than 90% of the sound systems in their language (Finegan, & Besnier, 1989). How incredible is that?

Research shows that the length of time it takes for a child to develop language in their MT follows a predictable sequence; however, it is important to point out that there can be some variation in the age at which children reach each milestone. From the moment a baby is born (and even while in still in utero), it is exposed to, and surrounded by language. Babies come into the world with a built-in capacity for language so that they are able to identify and replicate all phonemic sounds for all languages. Noam Chomsky, considered the father of psycholinguistics, explained the concept of language development in children through his notion of the "Language Acquisition Device (LAD)" which later became his theory of "Universal Grammar." His theories, which are widely accepted, explain how children are able to learn language so quickly despite the fact that they are not specifically taught, nor do they learn through imitation alone. He believes that every human has the capacity for encoding the appropriate structure and rules of any language (Chomsky, 1957).

Very quickly, if a child has not been exposed to specific sounds, their ability to replicate them becomes more difficult later on. Montanaro (2001) states that there are basically only 2 stages involved in first language acquisition: *Pre-language*, which begins before birth and lasts until the age of 10 or 12 months; and the *Linguistic Stage*, which takes place from 12 months to 36 months. During these important times, babies take in everything they hear.

> *As children learn to talk, they go through a series of stages, beginning with infancy where they are unable to converse and do not yet understand any language. They go from babbling at seven to ten months old, to producing their first recognizable words six to twelve months later. Then within a few months, they combine words and gestures, and produce their first word combinations around the age of two. This is followed by the ever more complex, adult like utterances, as they become active participants in conversation, taking turns and making appropriate contributions. They begin to use language for a larger array of functions – telling stories, explaining how a toy works, persuading a friend to do something, or giving someone directions for how to get somewhere (Clark, 2003, p.16).*

MOTHER-TONGUE AND COGNITION

In most cases, MT speakers are not consciously aware as to what the grammatical rules of their language are, when they use them or why. If asked, they might say something like, "I don't know how I know, I just know." They may learn formal rules of grammar later on, but it is clear they did not need "instruction" in order to learn how to talk or construct sentences as a child.

We learn our MT with relative ease and without any direct "thinking" about it. Child development and speech and language research also shows us that humans master certain components of language within fairly consistent timelines. When an English MT child attends their first day of kindergarten at 5 years of age, they will have already mastered the language skills necessary for communication. They will have a vocabulary of approximately 5,000 words and will then begin to build up awareness of the written form of the language.

Acquiring our MT is also the first step that leads to the sophisticated way we learn to communicate with ourselves. When we reflect on something or have a running commentary in our heads, it happens in the most efficient and automatic way available to us and that is typically through our MT. This is our language of default because we use it for our internal dialogue as well as for thinking through abstract concepts and metacognitive processes (thinking about our own thinking or learning). Our MT provides us with our "thinking language". It is necessary that children have a strong MT in order to build age-appropriate cognitive processes (Bloom, & Keil, 2001). Once we have achieved linguistic competence, we then begin to use it for higher purposes. Language is power and we begin to realize this more fully as our cognitive processes give us the freedom to explore our world, develop understandings and manipulate concepts and ideas with relative ease.

In mathematics, the very basic level of logic begins with a "concrete" concept. A 4-year old child needs to count actual items to understand the idea of "more" or "less".

A 12-year old on the other-hand, can begin to work with more complex mathematical problems that deal with abstract ideas represented through language. They no longer need to have tangible objects in front of them to work with a concept or problem-solve. They are able to represent these tangibles in their minds abstractly and then organize, manipulate and process them step-by-step—all the while monitoring their thinking and decision-making often with internal self-talk. This kind of task would not be possible without the beauty of language. Take this problem for instance:

> *Adam is thinking about two numbers. Their greatest common factor is 6. Their least common multiple is 36. One of the numbers is 12. What is the other number?*

If you attempt to solve this problem, you will find yourself reading the information first and then interpreting it in order to clarify exactly what it means. You might have had to recall and retrieve what each of the keywords (greatest common multiple and least common multiple) were before you were able to figure out a specific process or strategy for solving it. Did you notice any self-talk going on at this point? As you were thinking about it, you were using your mental logic to organize and strategize. By the time you came up with the answer, you would have performed a hierarchy of mental tasks—word retrieval, interpreting, reasoning and mental planning. Then as you began working backwards or guessing and checking to come up with your answer, you started carrying out specific processes like multiplication or addition for example, until you narrowed down or arrived at the solution. You can see that this math problem has just as much to do with language and thought as it does with mathematics itself.

There is a complex relationship between language and our ability to think. Language is like a vehicle for thinking. It allows us to explore ideas, navigate through problems and organize and process information. If you did not have strong language skills in English, you could not have easily performed this problem. If you were a BML still learning the foundations of English and you were faced with this problem, you would likely have had to translate the keywords into your own MT first to really understand them. You might have also taken slightly longer to mentally analyze what the problem was asking (through your MT) before performing calculations to get your answer in the most efficient way possible. From this example, we can clearly see that language facilitates our mental processes.

You can understand how BMLs who are still developing foundational English proficiency might experience challenge and frustration with language-based tasks. They may not be able to "self-talk" in English fluently enough in order to interpret and process the information. They may resort to the easiest option and that can be to use their MT to translate the information and complete it. That is because their MT is their established thinking language.

Through our work in various schools, we have noticed some have an "English only" policy (complete with signs posted around the school) banning students' use of languages other than English. This kind of practice demonstrates a lack of awareness and understanding of the importance of the MT for students' optimal cognitive functioning and development. In this kind of environment, students can be placed at a disadvantage simply because they cannot yet perform complex mental tasks as fluidly in English as they can in their MT. If these students are expected to work as optimally and as quickly as their MT English peers, many will not perform well. This can then make very competent, intelligent students "appear" to have some kind of learning disorder.

Some teachers worry about over-relying on the child's MT, fearing that they will be missing out on opportunities to learn English. While it is understandable why they might think this, research has shown that these fears are unfounded (Butzkamm & Caldwell, 2009). Students experience the world through their primary language so it makes sense to make new information understandable to students in the most meaningful and natural way. The MT is a powerful tool that can support the "transfer" of concepts in one language to another. Language transfer also helps individuals learn how languages work and are organized (Cummins, 2001).

Language transfer should be considered an optimal tool for learning. What is learned in the individual's MT can be communicated back through English and then the reverse can also be true: what is learned in English can be shared through the MT. As the student begins to communicate a thought or idea from one language to the other, they begin to actively translate, reinforcing their vocabulary and linguistic flexibility.

Take a look at the example in the box below. Marco, a 10-year old MT Italian-speaker (who attends school in English), talks with his mother in Italian about what he learned in science class. Discussing the concept in his MT allows his mother to further expand his Italian vocabulary. This also enables him to form rich personal connections to the topic, making the learning more relevant and meaningful.

CONVERSATION BETWEEN MARCO AND HIS MOTHER IN ITALIAN

MAMA: So, what did you learn at school today, Marco?

MARCO: In science we learned about "composting" (says word in English)," but I don't know what it is in Italian. It's when you take dead leaves and vegetable waste and it turns into soil after awhile. Our teacher asked us to try it.

MAMA: Ahhh yes, you mean "concime". Don't you remember when we went to grandfather's house before; he made a compost pile behind the house? Remember he used to take all of the food waste there after we'd eaten? Then he used it to plant his vegetables.

MARCO: Yes, I remember. I didn't know about *concime* (uses the Italian word) at that time. Remember we took photos of grandfather and I picking all the beans from the garden? Can I look at them?

In this example, we can see how Marco brings his new knowledge back home and his learning (about composting) becomes more embedded in meaning as a result of the personal context that his mother provides through her discussion with him. Marco not only strengthens his Italian vocabulary, but the personal story he shares with his mother serves as a meaningful extension of his classroom learning. There is no doubt that the MT is a valuable conduit to support learning and language transfer, both of which contribute positively to a student's cognitive development.

This needs to be understood and practically applied in classrooms everywhere. In many cases, that will mean policies need changing and training programs for teachers and parents need to be implemented. Policies that undermine or undervalue the development of languages other than English need to be discarded. Signs in hallways saying, "English Only, " or teachers reminding students in school that the classroom is an "English Zone", need to be abandoned so that teachers can begin to add bilingual approaches to their teaching. Teachers should also cast aside any guilty feelings they may have about speaking to students in a shared language in order to support or scaffold their learning. Many teachers who do this often feel like they are "cheating" but the more they are educated about the benefits of using the MT to support student learning, the more they will come to promote it as the valuable asset it is.

COMMON UNDERLYING PROFICIENCY

COMMON UNDERLYING PROFICIENCY - "CUP"

Dr. Jim Cummins states that many skills can and do transfer between languages (Cummins, 2001). For example, once a person has learned to read in one language, they do not need to relearn how to read in another language. The individual already has knowledge about "reading" that they simply transfer over to their new language. The same is true for other skills, like concept learning. If a person knows all about water (agua) in their Spanish language, then there is no need to relearn what water is, they can simply transfer their knowledge to the new English word, water.

The "CUP" or Common Underlying Proficiency is like the unseen area of an iceberg—it holds knowledge that both (or all) languages can access. CUP demonstrates that languages work together dynamically, sharing information between them flexibly and fluidly.

The CUP theory also explains how one language supports the development of another and helps us understand why it might be easier to learn new languages after we have first acquired our MT.

LOOKING AT THE IMPORTANCE OF THE MOTHER-TONGUE FOR LEARNING:

Jim Cummins has outlined 5 key points to demonstrate how the mother-tongue is useful for educational purposes (2001). These understandings should serve as the foundations for policies and approaches that support BMLs' educational development:

1. Bilingualism affects children positively because they learn how languages work and can process them more efficiently. Research also indicates that BMLs gain more flexibility in their thinking skills.

2. The level of the child's MT can predict development in their other language since languages transfer between one-another and are interdependent.

3. Use of the MT in the school promotes the development of both languages and students are at an advantage when they are taught in their MT, especially if literacy skills are taught. When the MT language is undermined, or even rejected, its development is likely to decline.

4. Using the MT or other language in the classroom does not mean that the majority language (e.g. English) will suffer. Within bilingual programmes, the research has shown that the majority language is not affected when half the time is spent learning academics through a minority language.

5. Children's mother-tongues can be lost quickly once the majority language (e.g. English) takes over as the child's working language for education and socialization. Children can actually lose the capacity to communicate in their mother-tongue after 2-3 years. This can greatly impact family and cultural relationships.

HOW CAN WE MAKE USE OF THE MT IN THE CLASSROOM?

When students come to us from other language backgrounds, it is critical that we acknowledge their MT as a powerful tool which can help them keep their new learning going.

Even when students arrive and do not have any peers or teachers who speak the same language, their ability to access information through their MT still exists. Helping them with this is often a case of being open—perhaps in helping them access alternative resources like books written in their own language as well as Internet sites or various technologies, for example.

In order to learn concepts fully, it is essential that an individual *understands* to a high level. This is critical. Whether this happens through English or another language really does not matter. Either one can facilitate thinking and understanding.

Content-learning must not stop for students just because they are learning a new language. BMLs should be encouraged to use this valuable resource to help them engage in grade-level or year-appropriate learning.

While this might sound complicated, with the right approach it can be much easier than you think. Empowering the BML to use their MT in the classroom can make a world of difference to their learning.

PERSONAL STORY: NIKKO

I came to Ms. Francesca's EAL class when I was 15. My family moved to Dubai from Japan and I had to go into Grade 9 immediately with very little English. It was extremely difficult and I was always stressed out. One of the ways I was able to survive, and I believe to learn English very quickly was because I was allowed to use Japanese text books for all of my core subjects—science, social studies, etc. Even when we were learning *Romeo and Juliet* in English class, I was allowed to read it in a Japanese translation. Of course it was difficult for me to keep up with the discussions about the play but at least I felt confident that I knew the material and what was going on in the class. My parents were also happy when they saw me still able to use my Japanese language in my English school. My teachers were able to adjust my assignments so that I could always take extra time to complete them in English. For example, the other students would be doing an essay and my assignment was to do a poster to summarize the key ideas in English. It would take me a long time even though most of these assignments were shorter than what the other students had to do because I had to write the information in Japanese first and then translate it into English.

Japanese students at the *Universal American School* have regular mother-tongue reading sessions with parent volunteers.

A BML learns that both of her languages are valuable tools for communicating.

It doesn't have to be "English only" at this IB school. Teachers help BMLs connect to the *Learner Profile* through their mother-tongue languages.

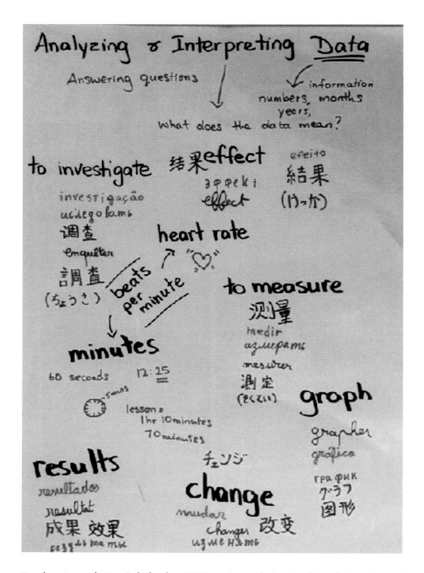

Teacher Amanda Ennis helps her BMLs activate their prior knowledge through their mother-tongues.

WHAT IMPACT DOES THE MT HAVE ON ACADEMIC SUCCESS?

In terms of academic achievement, what do we know about the role that a student's MT plays? Dr. Hetty Roessingh, a professor from the *University of Calgary* in Canada, was a high school ESL teacher for many years prior to becoming a researcher and professor. Her research provides great insights about BMLs which address the practical questions that many teachers have. In two very interesting studies (Roessingh 2008; Roessingh& Kover, 2003), she and her colleagues examined the educational success of BMLs who arrived to Canada as immigrants at different ages of arrival (AOA). She looked at student achievement on a challenging Grade 12 English diploma exam as well as the academic experiences of BMLs once they went on to university. These findings reveal fascinating information, much of which actually runs "counterintuitive" to typical logic:

> *An important distinction among the cohorts is that of additive versus subtractive bilinguals. Older arrivals are learning their second language through the lens of the first: fully developed at age-appropriate levels, with all the additional benefits of advanced curriculum knowledge in mathematics and sciences; metacognitive awareness and strategic competence, cultural capital, strong identity, and disciplined study habits. Although younger arrivals might have the edge in sounding good, they are nevertheless forever chasing a moving target as they struggle to catch up in English at the same time as they lose their first language. Most, it seems, never do close this gap. Those who arrive between the ages of 12 and 14 (i.e., junior high school) face other learning challenges. They may be in linguistic limbo for an extended period with neither language developing sufficient strength for the cognitive demands of high school (Roessingh, 2008, pp.92-93).*

SUMMARY OF THEIR RESEARCH FINDINGS

LATE-ARRIVING STUDENTS (15-16 YEARS OLD)

- Seemed to be able to "transfer" academic skills, knowledge and competencies to English
- Performed the best out of all the age groups on the exam
- Were able to do "more with less" in terms of transferring knowledge from their MT with a lower English vocabulary than expected because of their CUP

- In university, this group could no longer rely on their transfer skills because the expectations became much more challenging

STUDENTS WHO ARRIVED BETWEEN THE AGES OF 12-14 YEARS OLD

- Proved to be at the highest level of "risk" because they did not have enough proficiency in either their MT or in English
- They were thought to be "stuck between languages"
- Neither language was particularly strong
- Many were persistent in graduating and took extra courses during the summer
- Based on these studies, age 15-16 is a good age to immigrate provided individuals have a base proficiency in English (with a grade-equivalent of around 5.0)

YOUNGEST ARRIVALS 6-11 YEARS

- Were often perceived by teachers to have advantages due to good phonics, decoding skills and native-like proficiency
- These students constantly struggled to keep up
- They struggled to develop their academic language skills
- These students would have benefited from intervention in the early years to help them catch up before high school
- Younger arrivals or Canadian born immigrants were typically 2 years behind by grade 6

CANADIAN-BORN STUDENTS OF IMMIGRANT PARENTS ("GENERATION 1.5 STUDENTS")

- Consistently demonstrated a need for support
- Were identified as good candidates for academic intervention (e.g. "booster" classes)

BETWEEN THE COHORTS

- All students had a vocabulary gap compared to NS peers-as much as 2 years to 2.5 years but the 2 older groups were more likely able to cope using their existing CUP
- A strong link between academic vocabulary and academic success was identified—this should signal a need to focus more on vocabulary development

Once in University

- All students struggled with English proficiency at university: younger arrivals did not close their gaps and older arrivals were not able to support their learning through their MT
- Of the students who graduated from postsecondary education, many had low GPAs which became a barrier to further graduate studies

---

Does This Mean that all BMLs will Face these Trajectories?

As we all know, each *student* is unique just as each *school* is unique. While we have observed similar findings with BMLs over the years, we have also seen many successes—where BMLs have graduated from secondary school with high-level diplomas like the *IB Diploma*, for example. This shows us that it *is* possible for BMLs to succeed.

In many such cases, the difference is the implementation of a "whole school approach." This means support for BMLs is enhanced and all teachers have high-quality professional development to understand BML issues. These schools also support the development of students' MTs and provide flexible programs to meet students' needs in the right way, at the right time.

This research is valuable because it provides us with an understanding of the common challenges or pitfalls that BMLs can face at different ages and stages. Knowing about these potential problems can help administrators and teachers plan ahead to create more impact within their programs, timetables and instructional approaches.

Language-Learning Goals vs. Academic Language Learning Goals

There are different motivations for learning a new language, and this creates different end-goals for individuals. For example, if you were traveling to Italy for a holiday and wanted to learn a few survival words for getting around and ordering in restaurants, you would probably aim to learn about 10-20 new words or phrases to help you. Someone planning an exchange to Paris for a few months might take a beginner level foreign language class to learn the basics of French. They would want more intensive instruction because they would need to carry out conversations and interact in social situations almost immediately.

In the English school, the end-goal is quite different for BMLs. Whatever age they arrive to school, their goal is not only to get around or survive, they must be able to master English language skills to facilitate the academic and cognitive skills that will lead them to high school graduation.

This process of learning through English for academic purposes involves two goals: 1) gaining English proficiency to a high level of near-native fluency and 2) the ability to carry out complex, higher-order thinking processes in English. Success with these goals ultimately comes down to vocabulary.

For teachers working with BMLs, helping them reach both of these goals requires a solid understanding of additional-language acquisition in order to know the trajectory of "typical" English development as well as how to best support them at each stage.

How Second (Additional)-Language Learning Happens – Acquiring vs. Learning

Learning another language does not require an individual to return to the babbling stage since they have already learned how to "speak" through their first language or MT. Learning an additional language involves acquiring new vocabulary and understanding grammatical structures and pronunciation, for example. The school is an ideal environment for language-learning because it allows for numerous opportunities for individuals to engage with language naturally.

Learning another language tends to follow fairly predictable sequences and stages, many of which are similar to those of one's first language (Krashen, 1987 & Krashen, 1988).

According to researcher Stephen Krashen, individuals can learn a new language in two ways: through language acquisition and language-learning.

Language acquisition takes place when a learner unconsciously picks up or acquires new aspects of the language when the input they receive (e.g. speech from teachers or other children) is largely understandable to them. This is similar to how babies acquire their first language. During this process, the learner is concerned with "meaning" rather than "rules" or "correctness." Their goal is simply to be understood.

Krashen claims that individuals can learn a second language simply by absorbing what he calls, "comprehensible input." Comprehensible input takes place when the learner is able to understand the core meaning of the message but not all of it. It is just slightly beyond what the learner can interpret at their current level. Krashen believes that this is the most effective form of language-learning and in this way; individuals keep advancing their language development.

EXAMPLE OF COMPREHENSIBLE INPUT

Two kindergarten children are playing with toys on the carpet during free play. One child, "Tom," is a native English speaker. The other child playing alongside Tom is "Fergus," who is from the Philippines and is a native Tagalog speaker.

Tom looks over at Fergus who has a number of toy cars and trucks that he is playing with, and decides he would also like one. He says to Fergus, "Give me that truck," while pointing at the truck he wants. Fergus already knows the phrase "give me" and "car" but he has not yet heard the word, "truck." Despite this, Fergus picks up the truck and hands it to Tom and they both continue playing without interruption.

Since Fergus already had previous knowledge of the phrase, "give me," he was able to comprehend Tom's message despite the fact that he was not yet familiar with the word, "truck." He was able to gain full meaning once Tom pointed to the truck.

Since the kindergarten class provides many opportunities for natural language to take place, Fergus will continue to acquire new language in this way.

Can you think of other examples of comprehensible input?

Of course there are other forms of comprehensible input aside from speech alone. Reading content or watching videos, for instance, can also provide the learner with input that builds their language acquisition. In literacy, it is critical for the teacher to understand exactly what level the student is able to read at independently so that they can ensure the student receives the "right" amount of input and challenge (not too easy, not too difficult).

Teachers naturally provide what Krashen calls "roughly-tuned" input (vs. finely-tuned input) when they talk to their students (Krashen, 1985). They intuit what kind of language the particular student will need in order to understand and so they adjust their own language to roughly fit the needs of that student. It is similar to how parents communicate with their babies or young children. They modify their speech to the level they feel will allow their baby to understand. This is a natural form of "scaffolding".

With a more deliberate understanding about the importance of comprehensible input, teachers can make more of an impact in their BMLs' language development. Here are some ideas below:

IDEAS FOR AMPLIFYING COMPREHENSIBLE INPUT IN THE CLASSROOM

- Through *teacher-talk* which makes use of vocabulary slightly beyond a student's current level
- Vary the use of repeated/consistent language which students tend to hear again and again (replace with words or phrases that have similar meanings in order to give them repeated practice over time e.g. "Hand in your books..." can be replaced with, "I need to collect your books...")
- By pairing visual cues to support the message
- Using gestures or actions to imply the meaning of information
- Activating prior knowledge about a topic so students will have more context
- Use more academic language to give students access to higher-level vocabulary words (e.g. "We are going to compare..." instead of, "how are they different?")
- Be aware of the kinds of language you use in the classroom, do not "dumb it down" for BMLs but rather try to roughly match your language to the level of your student
- Replace difficult texts with those that cover the same content but are at students' levels of understanding
- Ensure all staff have access to student reading levels and English language levels since this will help them to plan learning activities that will best fit their needs
- Check back with students to ensure they have understood the information; modify your input if required

---

Language learning is another way for individuals to learn a second language. This kind of learning takes place in settings where more deliberate instruction about language occurs, like the foreign language class or mainstream classroom, for example. The learner is made more conscious about aspects of the language and more formal rules about it. Language learning typically involves correction of errors, memorization about vocabulary or grammar, and is primarily related to "textbook learning" or "pencil and paper learning" rather than through natural communication exchanges. Language learning on its own does not promote natural acquisition (Krashen, 1987; Krashen, 1988).

In the mainstream classroom, there are many opportunities for students to "acquire" language and "learn language." In effective classrooms, teachers ensure there are numerous opportunities for students to engage with one-another. Small group or partner-work ensures students have the chance to share their ideas through oral discussions that increase direct language feedback from their peers. Feedback sessions between students and teachers enable the teacher to provide more direct input to the student as well as assess their developing language skills. Academic tasks provide students with opportunities to apply what they already know about language. It is important to note that BMLs should not be "pushed" beyond their capabilities to attend to every error within their written work since it is not possible for them to know *or learn* all the rules of grammar or spelling at once. Having a specific focus over a sustained time period and then seeing steady improvement in that area will signal that it is time to move onto a new goal.

Teachers also need to make conscious efforts in their planning to include activities for students to gain language input in addition to *output*.

When teachers are skilled in creating language and literacy-rich learning environments for their students, they are more likely to create the kind of opportunities that will support their BMLs' continuous English development.

ACQUIRING THREE OR MORE LANGUAGES

Since the field of multilingual language acquisition is still very new, there has been relatively little research done in this area. We do know that children who are already bilingual are able to learn another language much faster and with greater efficiency (Safont & Jorda, 2005; Rivers, 1996). As well, multilingual children receive the same benefits that bilingual children do in terms of being more sensitive to sound systems in words, forms of words and sentence structures (Flynn, Foley, & Vinnitskaya, 2004).

Many of the processes involved in L3 learning are the same as L2 (e.g. requiring comprehensible input), but there is evidence to show that individuals who are learning a third language tend to use their second language (not their MT) when using transfer to support the L3 (Williams & Hammarberg, 1998; Clyne, 2003). This likely happens because individuals see the second language as having more similarities to the third language than their MT in terms of being "foreign." Even in cases where the individual's MT was more similar to the L3 than the L2, this still happened! This is an interesting point for teachers to note because it means that students might actually be more comfortable using their L2 in different learning situations instead of their MT, which also seems counterintuitive. In all cases, take time to talk with students about this and observe which language they prefer to use as a support for their English development across different circumstances.

When working with children who are simultaneous bilinguals (e.g. children who have learned 2 languages from birth and from both parents like a mother-tongue), we cannot assume that either of their languages function as an "L2" or "second language". In this case, both languages may serve to function as their mother-tongue. It is good practice to observe the student and find out more about how they use their different languages.

WHAT ABOUT SPEAKING?

In your work with BMLs, you might have noticed that there is some variance from one student to the next in terms of their ability or willingness to speak. Some start speaking almost immediately and are able to take risks or even initiate conversations with peers. Others are more cautious or reluctant and seem to require additional time before starting to speak. Both of these situations are quite normal and usually point to individual differences.

Some students may first go through a "silent period" of up to 6 months on average, before they make any utterance in English (Krashen, 1985). The silent period is a time for the learner to build up comfortability and competence with English and to observe from a safe distance before dipping their feet in. During this time, teachers should continue to involve students in the activities of the classroom, but should not place any pressure on them to speak before they are ready. Students who are not yet speaking can, and should participate in hands-on ways so that they can still demonstrate their learning and comprehension.

There are many factors that can influence a student's ability to acquire the new language. Having to take risks in speaking can often mean that the learner builds-up anxiety, or fears making mistakes, especially in front of peers whom they perceive as not being very forgiving. If the anxiety or fear is intense, it can create a "block" to the student's language acquisition. This block is coined, "the affective filter" by researchers (Krashen 1982). As we have already learned previously, many BMLs experience anxiety in one form or another so it is very important that teachers respond with understanding and supportive strategies every step of the way.

SPEAKING WITH AN "ACCENT"

It is a popular belief that an individual acquires English without an accent if they learn the language prior to puberty. While this is commonly true, it is not always the case. We have seen BMLs who retain an accent from their native language even when they have been schooled entirely in English (with native English-speaking teachers) from early on; and we have also seen some adults who manage to learn English later on and can pass for native speakers, without any foreign accent.

Francois Grosjean has explored possible reasons for this phenomenon with a leading expert on the subject for his popular blog in *Psychology Today* (2013). Through his research, he uncovered several possibilities as to why an individual might maintain a foreign accent. These can include: language interference-where an individual continues the habit of using the sounds from their first language when applying them to the new language; they may be unable to perceive the finer aspects of the sound-system in the new language or they can even be impacted by individual differences like motivation, for example.

In some instances, and especially within the context of education, parents can become set on the idea of their child speaking English without an "accent." This is an issue which reflects the perception that English spoken without a foreign accent is "better" than English spoken with one. This belief, still popular with many, needs to be changed to reflect a wider acceptance of different accents and the understanding that accent alone is not an indication of one's fluency, intelligence or proficiency with the language. Grosjean also reminds us that it is actually a more common phenomenon for bilinguals to speak *with* a foreign accent than *without*.

INTERESTING SPEECH PATTERNS IN BMLs

INTERLANGUAGE:
When a new speaker attempts to speak in the new language but is not yet fully proficient, they often apply language or grammar patterns which do not originate from any of their languages. It seems to be an "in-between" or "interlanguage" that fades away as they gain greater proficiency with their new language.

CODE-SWITCHING:
Code Switching is the practice of alternating between either 2 languages (or 2 dialects of the same language) during conversation. It usually occurs unconsciously between individuals who speak the same languages.

TRANSLANGUAGING:
Translanguaging, a term first used by the Welsh academic Cen Williams (1994) is "the ability of multilingual speakers to shuttle between languages, treating the diverse languages that form their repertoire as an integrated system". In other words, speakers of more than one language mix, use and apply all their languages in unique ways in order to fully express themselves and be understood.

LANGUAGE INTERFERENCE:
Language interference is a term to describe what happens when people apply knowledge from one of their languages to another. This knowledge may be phonological, grammatical, lexical, or orthographical. Usually, the speaker or writer tries to apply proper linguistic rules in the same way as it works successfully in the first language. This also shows evidence of language transfer.

LENGTH OF TIME TO LEARN ENGLISH

Most teachers are very interested in knowing how long it will take their students to learn English. Many schools provide "ESL programs" to students for about 2-3 years because they find that that is the average time it takes for students to be able to "speak like natives."

However, while many students can seem to speak like native English speakers after only 2-3 years, the perception that they have "learned English" is incorrect. What is actually happening is that students have managed to learn enough English to communicate and get along with their peers in social and classroom situations. They can begin and maintain conversations, respond appropriately to requests, retell information and participate in discussions within the classroom. They have picked up enough "high-frequency vocabulary" to use with ease. While this is certainly an accomplishment for BMLs, their goal of mastering English is by no means over.

If we contrast the kind of language that is required for the playground with the type of language needed for the classroom, we will find remarkable differences.

Social language can be learned very quickly by BMLs and many are so fluent with it that they can actually be mistaken for native speakers, especially if they also happen to speak with a native accent. This kind of social language proficiency can give a false-impression of English mastery to teachers and parents and sometimes, even to the learner themselves. Again, this goes against the natural grain of what teachers and parents would naturally assume.

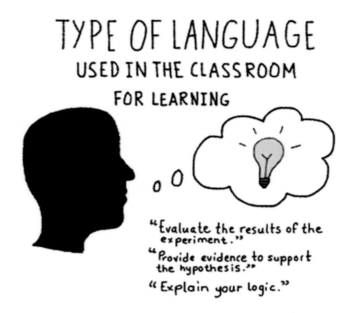

On the other hand, the language used in the classroom or academic setting is much different. It requires learners to know and use more formal vocabulary related to concepts and thinking. Learners are often exposed to this language when reading textbooks, through abstract-thinking tasks, for comprehending idioms or metaphors and writing essays, for example.

This kind of academic language places a heavy vocabulary burden on individuals because it first requires the knowledge of several thousand words in order to simply comprehend the input. Then, with their understanding, the learner typically needs to make more complex connections to the text or information. We saw this in our mathematics problem earlier and we can see it again with this example of an academic task:

> *Examine the work of graffiti artist, Banksy. Objectively decide whether he should be considered a criminal or hero.*

To answer this question, the learner must first decipher all vocabulary words in order to then perform the complex cognitive tasks of analyzing, evaluating and decision-making. Learning, as we know, involves a variety of linguistic and cognitive tasks.

If a student is not able to comprehend required vocabulary, then they face a major barrier in their ability to learn and participate in age-appropriate academic tasks. Jim Cummins first explained this distinction between social language and academic language back in 1979 (Cummins, 1979; Cummins, 1981a).

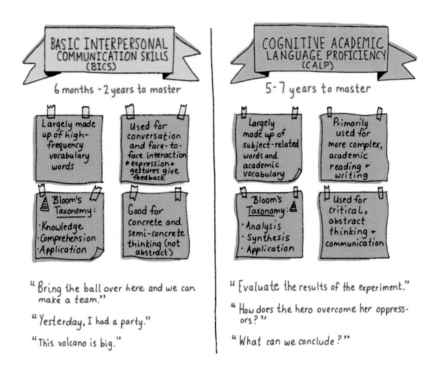

He called social language "BICS" (Basic Interpersonal Communication Skills) and referred to academic language as "CALP" (Cognitive Academic Language Proficiency). Cummins first noticed the difference between these two types of language while analyzing referrals and psychological reports for children thought to have had communication disorders (Cummins, 1981a). Many of the children in question had only been in Canada for 1-3 years and teachers and psychologists were not always aware that some of them were in fact, fairly new to English because they had typically acquired good social language (with some even possessing native-sounding accents).

As a result, both teachers and psychologists expected these students to perform well academically, believing that they should be able to handle academic tasks once they were fluent in social language. As Cummins began to research this phenomenon further, he discovered that BICS developed fairly quickly, usually between 6 months-2 years but CALP took much longer, taking between 5-7 years (at the earliest) to master. Later studies confirmed this phenomena and extended this idea further, showing that if a child did not have any prior schooling in their MT, it could actually take as long as 7-10 years to develop CALP (Thomas & Collier, 1995).

The life paths of BMLs can be seriously and detrimentally affected if they are assumed to need special education or learning support (Cummins 2008). A strong knowledge-base in the concepts of BICS and CALP is critical for all educators and professionals who work with or are in a position to make decisions about BMLs' education or development.

COMMON ISSUES RELATED TO BICS AND CALP IN SCHOOLS

There are numerous issues that can crop up when teaching staff and other professionals do not understand the differences between BICS and CALP. The examples below illustrate several situations that can arise and how they are often dealt with.

1. In many cases, BMLs who receive support in school are exited after 2-3 years-around the same time that CALP is developing. During this time, they will still require specific strategies and support to scaffold their learning to help them build their higher-order thinking through reading and writing.

2. Teachers often become confused when students (who seem to speak so well) struggle with reading and writing skills. They may not have consolidated spellings in their writing or they might demonstrate difficulties with reading comprehension, for example. Understanding that this is fairly typical development for BMLs can help teachers to feel secure with the knowledge that this is not an immediate signal of a learning disability. Using an "intervention" approach to teach specific strategies that help the child get over their hurdles is very effective and can often be done in brief "mini-lessons" and guided practice sessions.

3. Some schools use the practice of grade retention or "doubling" for BMLs who are below the level of their peers and who may be at "academic risk." This is a very inappropriate and unsound practice. Having the child repeat the same grade or year will not change the fact that they are still a bilingual or multilingual student who is likely to still have some challenges with specific aspects of language and academic development as a normal part of their development. This kind of practice views BMLs from a deficit perspective. Retaining them may result in a blow to

their self-esteem and confidence levels. Relationships they have developed with peers may also suffer. Many BMLs are quite bright despite the fact that they cannot always express their knowledge easily. Forcing them to repeat the same curriculum and learning activities can jeopardize their motivation and curiosity for learning. Differentiating the grade or year-level curriculum activities to match the level of the learner is a key strategy that will help BMLs be successful in their age-appropriate classroom.

4. Ensuring that you gather extensive background information on new students entering your school will help you to determine whether they are a BML. If the new student has good social language (BICS) they may slip through the cracks in being identified. Parents do not always fill out important background information about languages unless it is explicitly asked because they often assume their home language(s) are not relevant to the English school if their child already "speaks good English".

5. In most cases, using standardized tests to determine the IQ or whether the child has a learning or language disorder is not appropriate for BMLs. That is because these tests are "normed" on a different population and can give "false positive" results for learning disabilities, communication disorders or intellectual delays. Any kind of educational or psychological testing for BMLs should be done with caution by a qualified individual who is well-informed of BICS and CALP. As Jim Cummins has stated, "Failure to take account of the BICS/CALP distinction has resulted in discriminatory psychological assessment of bilingual students as well as other negative effects (Cummins, 1986, p.24)."

Understanding the natural course of second (additional) language acquisition of BMLs helps to set appropriate learning goals and targets for students. Know that the ultimate goal you are reaching for is to teach them how to think critically and create opportunities for them to communicate at the highest possible levels. Always teach your BMLs with the intention of getting them to think-not only to learn how to speak English.

When students are learning BICS, they pick up a great deal of the language through social interactions within the classroom and school-yard. They learn "survival phrases" quickly and then acquire other useful vocabulary and phrases for functioning within their environments. Much of this language is repetitive and used in the context of routines and regular activities. Feedback is easily available to the student because they can get multiple opportunities to hear the vocabulary words used within specific contexts. They can also improve their pronunciation because they are likely to hear words repeatedly, allowing them to focus on details. Within the school and classroom environments, there are multiple natural opportunities for students to participate in a range of social and academic activities that further develop their BICS. Classroom teachers can support students' language development in a variety of ways that connect the context to their learning.

In developing CALP, students often need support to understand and process more complex, content-specific vocabulary in order to be able to function and perform to their best ability. Often, they are expected to rely on textbooks and these texts can be well-beyond their independent reading levels, so comprehension is difficult. Students are also asked to write lengthier, analytical-style essays or assignments. This requires a student to spend a great deal of time preplanning their resources and ideas as well as taking additional time to edit their work. This can cause many students to feel overwhelmed. As a teacher, your job is to make the learning comprehensible to the student in the most efficient way possible. You can do this by differentiating the task, using alternative materials and even using the student's MT to support their learning.

CASE IN POINT

Using the scenarios below, how can we understand the implications for each child's:

- *Mother-tongue development?*

- *English development?*

- *Thinking (or cognitive development?)*

Louise is a 6-year old student from France. She has recently moved to London with her parents and they have enrolled her in an English-medium international school which also offers additional classes for MT French speakers. She also takes Spanish classes once a week.

Saleh is a 12-year old Kuwaiti boy who comes from an affluent family. Both his parents have been educated at the post-secondary level and his father has a good job with the government. Although both Saleh's parents have strong Arabic mother-tongues, they also speak English to an intermediate level. Both parents value education and want Saleh to become "internationally-minded" so they have enrolled him in an English-medium international school since he was in kindergarten. They also began speaking to him in English the year before he entered school so that it would not be a "shock" to him and so he would adjust well to the new English environment. At home, Saleh interacts with his maids who come from the Philippines. They have been with the family since Saleh was born and have taught him some phrases in Tagalog, although they largely speak English to him. There is also an Indian driver for the family who regularly interacts with Saleh and speaks a mix of Arabic, English and Hindi.

Asani is 15 years old and has recently moved to Sydney, Australia from her home-country, Japan. She has had only basic instruction in English while the rest of her studies have been in her mother-tongue, Japanese. She will be enrolling in a state school where the medium of instruction is English.

DIG DEEP:

1. How does understanding the differences between BICS and CALP make a difference on a school and classroom level?

2. Why do some BMLs' prior knowledge and true potential go unrealized in the English learning environment?

3. Approaches and identification of BMLs have been described as "counter-intuitive." Explain the reasons for this.

BREAKOUT:

4. Considering what you have already learned, what is the impact of BMLs not having a solid MT?

5. Share ideas or suggestions for making learning input "comprehensible" for BMLs. What are the most important considerations?

EXPLORE:

Examine your school policies and practices. Do they reflect good knowledge of the BICS and CALP constructs? If so, explain why and if not, discuss what needs to be done.

[5]

Vocabulary Development in BMLs

IN THIS CHAPTER YOU WILL...

- Understand the impact of vocabulary on BMLs' language and learning
- Understand how to assess BMLs using the *English Language Progression Map*
- Learn how to set short and long-term vocabulary and language goals for BMLs
- Understand important considerations for vocabulary instruction and programming

GROUNDING QUESTION:
What is your main strategy for teaching vocabulary?

VOCABULARY DEVELOPMENT – THE ELUSIVE "MISSING LINK" FOR BMLs

Looking back on our careers over the years, both of us have been fortunate to have worked with outstanding mentors and colleagues as well as having accumulated a wealth of experience in different segments of education. Despite this, we were surprised to learn how little we actually knew about the impact that vocabulary has on student achievement in school.

During our research for this book, we happened to stumble upon the vocabulary research of Dr. Paul Nation, an Applied Linguistics professor and researcher from the *Victoria University of Wellington* in New Zealand. He has spent his career researching many complex aspects of vocabulary development. While reading through his work, it became clear that a great deal of knowledge about the importance of vocabulary has not filtered down to schools and teachers.

A fascinating quote from one of Dr. Nation's books signaled that we were onto something very significant: "The ten most frequent words in English typically cover 25% of the words in any text and the 100 most frequent words cover around 50% (Nation, 2014, p. 13)."

Think about the impact of that for just one moment. What can that mean for our BMLs—many of whom struggle with mastering new English vocabulary? We became excited by the concept of "word frequency," and understanding how some words would be more important to learn (at different periods of a learner's development) than others. For example, it makes sense to think that brand new learners of English would get the maximum benefit from learning the most common words found in English.

This means we could begin to direct our instruction of vocabulary in a more focused manner in order to get targeted results for our students' language-learning.

As we continued our research to find out more about word frequency, we found that the acquisition of a specific number of words related to specific tasks that learners could accomplish with them. For example, we learned that with 8,000 words, reading the newspaper with good, unassisted comprehension is possible; while a novel can be read and understood with 9,000 receptive vocabulary words. Also, students in secondary school require 7,000-8,000 words in order to comprehend their text books (Nation, 2014). Such fascinating information!

We quickly discovered other key researchers who have also made significant contributions to this area of study, and some whose research was also particularly relevant for educators. We began to apply this information to our BMLs and developed a practical tool, the *English Language Progression Map* (*ELP Map*), to assist teachers and administrators in assessing their students' vocabulary development. In addition, this tool also helps teachers to analyze students' vocabulary-learning trajectories and predict any "trouble spots" that can crop up at certain points along a students' learning journey. In this way, teachers will better understand the bigger picture of students' language and vocabulary-learning progression while being able to understand where students are currently at. This allows teachers to be more informed about the kind of teaching and learning that their BMLs will benefit from at specific times. It will also help staff teams develop support models within their schools.

Many of us are not aware of the possibilities that exist for improving the vocabulary development of our students within our schools and classrooms. Considering the fact that many BMLs have only a limited number of hours where they are exposed to English and most of this time is through their teachers and peers alone, it makes sense then to maximize this time, harnessing the research and applying it to our practices.

Experts have known for a long time that vocabulary is the key to academic success. In fact, it has even been described as the "missing link" to student success (Biemiller, 2001).

We believe that vocabulary has become the missing link largely because teachers and other professionals are not made aware of the significant role that it plays in relation to BMLs' (and all students') success in language development, literacy and academics.

There is little to no knowledge base about what good vocabulary instruction looks like, or how to assess student vocabulary outside of traditional-style vocabulary tests common in many classrooms. While students do "pick up" new words naturally, it is much more complex than that. There are certain conditions that help to making learning new vocabulary words successful. In order to fully understand how vocabulary-learning happens, it is important to know more about the subject of vocabulary itself.

WHAT THE EXPERTS KNOW ABOUT THE VALUE OF VOCABULARY

- It is well-established that vocabulary is the strongest predictor of reading comprehension from grades 2 or 3 on (Biemiller, 2012, p. 198).

- But now, educators do virtually nothing before grade 3 or 4 to facilitate real vocabulary growth. By then, it's too late for many children (Biemiller, 2001).

- It has also been shown that grade 1 general vocabulary is a strong predictor of reading comprehension in grade 11 (Biemiller, 2001, p. 10).

- A substantially greater teacher-centered effort is needed to promote vocabulary development, especially in the kindergarten and early primary years (Biemiller, 2001, p.4).

- In recent years, we have seen a tremendous emphasis on the importance of phonics instruction to ensure educational progress. We also have seen that while more children learn to "read" with increased phonics instruction, there have not been commensurate gains in reading comprehension (Biemiller, 2001, p.2).

- Overall, I hypothesize that most children (90 percent plus) can acquire new vocabulary at rates necessary to reach "grade level" or near grade level vocabulary in middle elementary school, if given adequate opportunity to use new words and adequate instruction in word meanings (Biemiller, 2001, p.3).

- If we are serious about "increasing standards" and bringing a greater proportion of school children to high levels of academic accomplishment, we cannot continue to leave vocabulary development to parents, chance, and highly motivated reading (Biemiller, 2001, p.4).

- What native speaking children acquire through immersion, largely at home, ELLs must learn from their teachers. Words beyond the conversational domain (i.e. words that have Latin roots and that will increasingly appear in the informational texts children will encounter) also become central in children's learning needs, especially ELLs (Roessingh, 2013, p.278).

- There needs to be a strong focus on vocabulary learning for all youngsters. This requires a sustained, longitudinal effort (Roessingh, 2013, p.279).

- Early identification and intervention may hold the key to changing the slope of the educational trajectory, especially in the K-grade 2 range where there might be potential for accelerated acquisition of language and early literacy skills (Roessingh & Elgie, 2009, p.27).

WHAT IS VOCABULARY EXACTLY?

Simply put, vocabulary refers to our knowledge about words. Our ability to understand the words we hear or read relates to our receptive vocabulary, while our ability to actively use words appropriately relates to our productive (expressive) vocabularies.

We begin building our receptive vocabularies as infants and then start demonstrating our receptive understanding of language by responding to and following an adult's instructions. Even before a baby is able to speak, they can follow simple instructions like, "get the ball," or "come to mommy." The receptive vocabulary is like a word bank that allows an individual to understand the spoken and then later, the written word.

In contrast, the productive vocabulary (or expressive vocabulary) relates to the vocabulary words that one uses for speaking or writing. An individual does not actively use all of the words that are in their word banks; that will depend on what different situations and contexts require. For example, a person may know a word like "eschew" (to avoid something) receptively so that they understand it when hearing or reading it; however, they may not actively use it since it is not a word commonly used in typical conversations or within more general kinds of writing. On the other hand, if the individual was a professor of English literature who often uses more formal language, "eschew" could likely be a word in their productive vocabulary.

Most people have larger receptive vocabularies than their productive ones since they typically have more opportunity to hear and read words than use them. If you think about how many hours in a day people watch television, read, browse the Internet or listen to others at work or home, you can begin to get a sense of this. Contrast that with the number of hours the average person spends actively speaking or writing on a daily basis and you will see that it is much less in comparison.

An individual's ability to make regular "deposits" of new words into their receptive vocabulary banks will depend greatly on the amount of quality exposure to new words as well as their ability to recall them. As they engage in a variety of activities that promote the active use of these words, this in turn reinforces their understanding of these words.

In the context of our BMLs, we need to help them build their vocabularies by providing consistent and meaningful opportunities for them to: listen and read (receptively) as well as speak and write (expressively).

WHAT CONSTITUTES A WORD?

There are different ways that researchers count vocabulary words. It can be quite technical but throughout this book, when we use the term "word" in reference to number of vocabulary words, we are actually referring to a group of "word families." A word family includes the root word's inflected and derived forms, for example: like, likes, liked, liking, etc.

Since vocabulary is so vast with well over 54,000 word families in the English language (Nation, 2013), it makes sense to categorize words so they can be prioritized and dealt with purposefully. Researchers have grouped words by the most frequently-occurring, with the first 3,000 words being labeled, "high-frequency vocabulary," the second group, "mid-frequency words," ranging from around 3,000-9,000 words and then finally, the remaining words are "low-frequency words" (Nation, 2013; Schmitt & Schmitt, 2012). Low-frequency words are rarer words which begin from around 9,000 words and up.

High-frequency words are easy to hear and come across in the context of day-to-day interactions and within early reading materials, for example. BMLs that are new to English will begin to build up their vocabulary with these high-frequency words quite naturally. However, since many mid-frequency words tend to be context-related, they are not as easy for the learner to come across in typical conversations or interactions. Opportunities need to be created for individuals to gain exposure to these words through embedded academic study and reading, for instance.

Low-frequency words are the least likely to be encountered in typical day-to-day situations and conversations as they are more specialized and relate to more technical concepts and fields of work or study. Since many of these words do come up within particular units of study in the school curriculum, you will still find BMLs learning some low-frequency words alongside their "conversational English" or high-frequency words.

WHAT ELSE SHOULD WE KNOW ABOUT VOCABULARY?

Considering the positive impact that vocabulary can have on learning, what else do we need to know about it? To begin with, it helps to understand how many words native English children have in their vocabularies in order to draw meaningful comparisons to BMLs. Young native-speaking English children between the ages of 5 and 6 have approximately 4,000-5,000 vocabulary words; a 13-year old has around 10,000-11,000 words and a senior high school student would have about 14,000 words

(Nation, 2013). Both native speakers and BMLs acquire on average, about 1,000 vocabulary words per year (Nation, 2014; Biemiller 2011). An educated NS adult has roughly 20,000 words, while an educated bilingual adult is reported to have an average of 9,000 words. Although it is certainly possible for BMLs to grow their vocabulary to native-like levels, research has shown this is actually fairly uncommon (Nation & Waring, 1997).

A compounding challenge for BMLs is that they are often significantly behind in vocabulary compared to their NS English peers. If you consider the fact that NS students have arrived at kindergarten already knowing around 5,000 words, you can then appreciate the fact that there are going to be significant differences between what these two groups of students will be able to accomplish with their English language skills. During a BMLs' early years in school, the expectations are easier for them to attain, but later on as more advanced vocabulary is expected for reading comprehension, the early gaps in vocabulary begin to have an impact on the student.

A great deal of research has shown that BMLs are continuously "chasing a moving target" in order to fill their gaps in English vocabulary knowledge. Yet as they learn, the expectations keep moving ahead of them at a fast pace while many struggle to catch up.

This often means BMLs are working at the "frustration level" in reading tasks since age-appropriate texts are much too difficult for them to comprehend independently. This then creates a huge need for support in order to mediate the vocabulary gaps for these students, hence the reason why so many "ESL classes" or "pullouts" exist in schools. The problem with this is that much of the support is not targeted in the right way, so it fails to impact student achievement. For example, struggling BMLs should not need someone to "spoon-feed" them to keep up with the classroom work; they need to acquire specific learning and vocabulary strategies that will have high-impact at different stages of their development so that they can perform tasks largely independently.

For instance, teaching students how many subject-related words come from Greek and Latin roots (such as automobile and biography) can immediately give them an effective strategy to support their reading comprehension. These kinds of strategies are quickly and easily taught and students can begin to use them with good success, when reinforced.

We also need to recognize that "ESL" classes are not the only solution for meeting the needs of BMLs. When all teachers are educated in issues related to their BMLs, and when there is alignment and cohesion amongst the school staff in their knowledge base of these students, a world of innovative opportunities opens up that might not have worked before. For instance, classroom teachers can feel more empowered to provide specific teaching strategies for their BMLs. Counsellors and administrators can juggle the timetable in flexible ways and BML specialist teachers, if available; can support school administration in policy-making, training and implementation of key practices across the school. There are numerous ways to support student learning without simply relying on the traditional "ESL" support model. All support models should seriously consider vocabulary acquisition as an important starting place.

GETTING STARTED WITH VOCABULARY ACQUISITION

The *English Language Progression Map* (*ELP Map*) below is a chart which provides a rough overview of the path or trajectory of a BML's vocabulary, language and literacy development. In producing this tool, we have synthesized a variety of research constructs together with vocabulary numbers and literacy skills to give teachers a general idea of the number of receptive English vocabulary words their students are likely to possess at different stages of their learning path. It should be noted that like many other language development charts, this one is largely based on accepted theoretical knowledge rather than "precise" knowledge. Within our own work with students, teachers and parents, it has proved to be an extremely useful tool to help explain the language-learning path in a more concrete and practical way.

The value that the *ELP Map* can provide to educators is innumerable. First, it allows teachers to better understand the impact of vocabulary development and help them to identify where a student is along that trajectory in relation to their ultimate vocabulary goal. When teachers understand that vocabulary is the missing link for BMLs, it can help them keep the importance of vocabulary-learning at the forefront of their minds. Teachers can use the additional information, including the "Hallmarks" to inform them about student skills and behaviours which typically occur within a particular stage. Keep in mind that the hallmarks are not meant to be a total list or solid continuum of skills, but rather are a collection of "big ideas" that usually take place within that particular stage of vocabulary and language acquisition. There are many more skills which could be added but are not necessary for our purposes.

The main purpose of this chart is to help teachers and professionals understand the significance of the different levels of vocabulary and to help move students ahead with focused and meaningful strategies. Once again, this *Map* is a reflection of our research collected from multiple sources in the literature on vocabulary development, language acquisition and literacy, including our own work with BMLs.

Another purpose that this *Map* serves is to give educators a "common language" when making reference to their BMLs. For example, if a German MT student attends an English-medium international school in Hong Kong and his family later moves to the UK, the information that accompanies the student can be meaningful to his new teachers because it makes reference to language they themselves are familiar with and can easily interpret.

Currently, there is no standard way of operating when it comes to BMLs, either in relation to their identification or the language that is used to describe them. This *ELP Map* also aims to do that. Additionally, there is key information that signals potential "hot spots" along the bottom, within the *Literacy Progression* section. This means that well-researched phenomena like the "fourth-grade slump" (Chall & Jacobs, 2003) have been included to alert educators about potential issues that BMLs may experience. In these cases, teachers can be forewarned and can try to preempt these challenges through assessment, high-impact strategies, literacy-rich programs and the *right* kinds of supports.

This way of framing BMLs' development can have a tangible meaning for educators, parents, professionals and even the students themselves. That is not to say that teachers cannot use other English language proficiency charts to track or monitor more specific skills, but this can be done in addition to (or in conjunction) with our *ELP Map*. This is to better understand individual students' learning paths as they move forward in their education, as well as setting targets for vocabulary goals, identification of potential challenges or "hotspots" along the way. Additionally, examining BMLs' learning informs the planning of specific kinds of instruction and support.

English Language Progression Map (ELP Map)

6 months – 2 years — "words" = word families; MT = mother-tongue — © Alison Schofield & Francesca McGeary — 5–10 years

Stages with Approximate Vocabulary Sizes	FL 1 0-500 Words	FL 2 500-1,000 Words	FL 3 1,000-3,000 words	FL 4 3,000-6,000 words	TL 1 6,000-8,000 Words	TL 2 8,000-9,000+ Words	Extended Vocabulary for University
Frequency Band	High-Frequency Vocabulary			Mid-Frequency Vocabulary		Low-Frequency Vocabulary	
Language Acquisition Stages	Pre-production	Early Production	Speech Emergence		Intermediate Fluency	Advanced Fluency	
Key Hallmarks of Level/Stage	**HALLMARKS:** Possible silent period Developing simple receptive language May experience anxiety May echo words Slight comprehension Responds to gestures, visual and physical prompts All thinking happens in their MT	**HALLMARKS:** Uses one to two-word phrases Understands key words Relies on programmed phrases and expressions Responds to simple questions Requires cues from the environment to make meaning Thinks in their MT	**HALLMARKS:** Communicates in sentences for classroom and social interactions with 2,000-3,000 words Sentences often contain grammatical errors Requires context for learning situations but understands the "big picture" Begins to learn some content vocabulary Uses MT for thinking and translating words	**HALLMARKS:** Expanding vocabulary Mainly fluent speech Good overall comprehension Understands general English at 5,000 words Expanding content-related vocabulary Still has some challenges expressing ideas and higher-order concepts through English Fills in meaning gaps with their MT	**HALLMARKS:** Understands a wide range of conversation without support at 6,000-7,000 words Carries out fluent conversation across a variety of topics Has a base of academic vocabulary but not always enough May begin to "think" in English Challenges with idioms and figurative language	**HALLMARKS:** Speaks and understands with "near native" fluency Understands most written texts at 8,000 words Builds knowledge of technical/ low-frequency words Expresses higher-order thinking and abstract ideas through language with greater ease Better comprehension of "metaphoric language"	**HALLMARKS:** Fluent in several genres of literacy Able to use many language devices appropriately Accurately uses a range of subject-specific vocabulary words and low-frequency words Able to infer complex vocabulary word meanings from affixes
Literacy Progression	Phonological awareness Environmental print May write some words	Early literacy skills, phonemic awareness, concepts of print Writes words or simple sentences	"Learning to read" Developing word decoding and spelling skills Written messages can be understood despite grammatical errors	Transition to "reading to learn" Has most/all of reading and writing foundations Often needs support in target areas for writing May experience a "slump" in reading due to lack of vocabulary	Reads and writes for different purposes but not always on-level May have challenges with grammar, vocabulary and "metaphors" Concept of "passive voice" may be difficult	Can function more independently for higher-level assignments (research, projects, presentations, etc.) Literacy can still lag behind students' oral and listening proficiency	Works to master technical vocabulary and advanced writing skills

Can generally accomplish with relative ease

Up to 7 years old - Vocabulary Goal is Extended Vocabulary

	FL 1	FL 2	FL 3	FL 4	TL 1	TL 2	Extended
% per Level	4%	4%	14%	21%	14%	7%	36%
Cumulative %	4%	8%	22%	43%	57%	64%	100%

From 7 years old and up- Vocabulary Goal is TL2

	FL 1	FL 2	FL 3	FL 4	TL 1	TL 2
% per Level	6%	6%	22%	33%	22%	11%
Cumulative %	6%	12%	34%	67%	89%	100%

UNDERSTANDING THE ENGLISH LANGUAGE PROGRESSION MAP (ELP MAP)

We have chosen to label the stages in two different categories: "Foundational Language" and "Thinking Language". Foundational Language means precisely that—it reflects the base of vocabulary needed for acquiring the language we use for everyday communication and conversations. Foundational Language provides us with the elementary vocabulary that enables us to learn to read with (largely) high-frequency words. Individuals can still pick up vocabulary that is more advanced at this stage, like content- or subject-related words, especially if these words are repeated over and over in the students' daily routines and academic studies, for example. Generally speaking, however, students are not yet able to manipulate or use more advanced words for processing or expressing concepts in abstract ways through English. This is because of 2 possible reasons: either the child is not yet at the developmental age where they would be doing these kinds of complex cognitive tasks in their mother-tongue (e.g. around 11 or 12 years) or simply because they do not yet have enough of a vocabulary base to support higher-level thinking and abstraction in English.

Since Foundational Language is based on high-frequency words that make up day-to-day conversation, most students should be able to acquire these necessary vocabulary words fairly quickly. It is important to understand; however, that Foundational Language actually makes up a very small percentage of a BML's overall vocabulary-learning goal.

In contrast, Thinking Language relates to the language that students acquire in order to perform a wide-variety of higher-order thinking tasks and metacognitive processes. In this stage, students are building more advanced academic vocabulary which allows them to comprehend and communicate complex thoughts and concepts with greater ease. They are also more able to make inferences or "read between the lines" through their English language. They have acquired a good base of mid-frequency, subject-related words and academic words. They can now better "analyze," "evaluate" and "synthesize," ideas and topics using their English language.

ACADEMIC WORDS

The *Academic Word List* (Coxhead, 2002) is a list of the most-frequent 570 word families which are useful for a broad range of higher-level, academic subjects. This list of words is important for students' academic learning in school and especially for post-secondary preparation.

The stage, "FL4" presents a time of transition for students as they are mastering foundational language and moving towards the capability of handling more complex language and academic tasks. With 5,000 vocabulary words, students are able to understand most "general" English (Nation, 2013) but it is a time when students can experience a lag in their literacy and learning if they have not built up enough vocabulary to support strong reading comprehension. From our experience, this is where many BMLs seem to get "stuck." In some cases, schools cease support for BMLs around this time, since students often seem to be orally fluent in their English language proficiency. Also, they have usually mastered the basics of literacy and are beginning to be more confident in speaking and working independently. One of the biggest problems is that students can stagnate if they do not receive the right level of language input that allows them to move forward. This can easily happen, for example, if teachers do not ensure that BMLs continue their ongoing, independent reading with appropriately-leveled books, or if teachers assume that a student is more proficient than actually are due to their earlier success.

At FL4, BMLs' oral proficiency can often sound "native-like" and they can function well with the routines of the classroom. Since we know that this stage can have potential "hot spots" for difficulties, we need to plan effective strategies and supports well in-advance. Armed with this knowledge, schools can prepare students with the appropriate, targeted supports and strategies to help them make a smooth transition into Thinking Language.

After about 9,000 words, BMLs can and should keep improving their vocabulary with the right input and motivation. This is often a necessary goal for BMLs in secondary education who are setting their sights on post-secondary studies. There is no limit to how many vocabulary words we would expect students to gain at the Extended Vocabulary stage, but in comparing it with approximately 14,000 words that NS students achieve by graduation time; we can only recommend that more is better. Of course we know that this is not always a realistic goal for many BMLs, especially for those who have joined the English-medium school after 7 years of age or older. These BMLs must "race the clock" in order to ensure they reach the minimum goal of acquiring a vocabulary of 9,000 words.

The concept of "vocabulary coverage" must be understood in order to gain a firm understanding as to why 9,000 vocabulary words is an important number for BMLs. 1,000 of the most frequent words in English will account for about 80% of the words in a given text. In other words, 1,000 words "covers" 80% of a text (Nation, 2014). If you are a reading or literacy teacher you will probably know that understanding only 80% of the words in a text does not provide good enough comprehension for students—95% and above is the approximate target for ensuring solid understanding.

Nation suggests that having 98% vocabulary coverage is best because it leaves less room for comprehension problems (2013). For example, if a student understands 98% of their text then it means that only one word out of every 50 words will be unknown. The more words that are unknown to the reader, the more challenging comprehension will be.

Vocabulary knowledge plays a significant role in an individual's ability to read independently. It is essential that every BML's reading is monitored and they are given appropriate feedback and strategies to keep up with the demands of reading more challenging texts.

KEY HALLMARKS AND LITERACY PROGRESSION BY STAGE

Remember that these stages should not be thought of as "hard and fast" or exactly "precise," but rather should be considered "roughly-tuned," to make use of Krashen's term. If we have a good knowledge base about vocabulary and its influence on literacy and language-learning then we are already on the right track. Many of you will already be used to using traditional developmental language acquisition charts within your schools or districts and you will probably find a great degree of similarity between those and the one we have created, albeit without the focus on vocabulary words. We have looked at well-over 100 of these kinds of charts from different schools around the world and have found them to share many commonalities despite the different labels, terms and descriptors.

The *ELP Map* uses "big ideas" or most common behaviours that you are likely to observe or identify as occurring within a specific stage. Since vocabulary influences literacy development and thinking, we have also made reference to several of these important hallmarks.

To restate the purpose of this tool, it is to ultimately help teachers identify the English vocabulary levels of their BMLs in relation to their overarching goal and to better understand the trajectories of these students. Teachers can then apply a variety of key supports at the right time. For instance, enriching vocabulary instruction between kindergarten and around 7-8 years old can enable teachers to create numerous language- and literacy-rich learning opportunities within the school day in order to close those early gaps in vocabulary. Schools can also place a more deliberate focus on vocabulary-teaching policies and strategies across the school, planning for impact and preempting the "literacy slump" which can have a negative effect on BMLs' literacy development. Finally, having a shared and practical way of communicating about BMLs and their progress to parents, students themselves and other staff members provides a very holistic approach to supporting them.

FOUNDATIONAL LANGUAGE 1 (FL1)

STAGE	HALLMARKS:	LITERACY PROGRESSION:
FL 1 **0-500** **Words**	**Possible** silent period **Developing** simple receptive language **May** experience anxiety **May** echo words **Slight** comprehension **Responds** to gestures, visual and physical prompts **All** thinking happens in their MT	**Phonological** awareness **Environmental** print **May** write some words

At this stage, BMLs are building their receptive language skills and taking cues from the environment in order to understand what is happening around them. Comprehension is minimal so BMLs must infer what is happening around them from context. Some may not speak at all during this stage, and this is often referred to as the "silent period." This should be considered perfectly fine and quite typical since some students need to feel extremely comfortable before taking the leap into speaking. BMLs should be given plenty of opportunity to participate in activities without any pressure to speak, although teachers should always create situations where they can dive into speaking at any time.

During this stage, BMLs will rely heavily on performance-based tasks to demonstrate their learning by drawing, pointing, creating, labeling, etc. Depending on the age of the student, they may be able to perform academic tasks using their MT to bridge the language barrier. This should be encouraged. While this stage appears "less active," to observers, BMLs are actually taking in valuable information—they are learning about English sounds as well as print in and around their environment. This then serves as a foundation for speech production, phonemic and phonological awareness skills. BMLs can be supported with visuals, gestures and labels within their environment. They can also begin to write letters or even words, depending on their age and comfort level.

Keep in mind that BMLs may experience increased anxiety at this stage so it is important to provide them with a supportive and comfortable environment. Introducing them to a buddy who speaks their language can also help them to feel more relaxed and able to cope in their new environment.

FOUNDATIONAL LANGUAGE 2 (FL2)

STAGE	HALLMARKS:	LITERACY PROGRESSION:
FL 2 **500-1,000** **Words**	**Uses** one to two-word phrases **Understands** key words **Relies** on programmed phrases and expressions **Responds** to simple questions **Requires** cues from the environment to make meaning **Thinks** in their MT	**Early** literacy skills, phonemic awareness, concepts of print **Writes** words or simple sentences ·

At this stage, BMLs will have learned valuable key words and survival phrases like "yes" and "no," as well as how to ask for things within their immediate environment. They will likely know some formulaic phrases like, "how are you?" and "I am fine," for example. They can understand the big ideas with increased support through gestures and visuals, but they still rely heavily on environmental cues to aide their comprehension. Learning needs to be differentiated for students in order to enable them to access tasks comprehensibly.

BMLs are actively using their MT for thinking, so when possible, enable them to engage their MT for learning tasks. If BMLs are ready, they can begin to learn about English phonics and early literacy (i.e. reading and writing). A special focus on learning English vowel sounds should be provided as many BMLs have difficulties discriminating between the subtle sounds of the short vowels. Early reading and explicit interaction with text can serve as a springboard for further vocabulary development.

Older BMLs may benefit from accelerated literacy instruction to support their phonemic awareness skills and early literacy development, especially if they are already literate in their MT. Then they can begin to "transfer" their literacy knowledge into English. Older BMLs should not be left to "fend for themselves" when it comes to learning the phonemic system and basic reading skills. They need to be provided with a solid foundation in order to build more complex knowledge about the way words work in English. This can and should be compared and contrasted to the sound systems in their language(s). BMLs who already have an existing literacy base in their own language can often learn the early foundations of English literacy within a few weeks if provided with an intensive approach (e.g. 20-30 minutes per day for one month).

FOUNDATIONAL LANGUAGE 3 (FL3)

STAGE	HALLMARKS:	LITERACY PROGRESSION:
FL 3 **1,000-3,000** **Words**	**Communicates** in sentences for classroom and social interactions with 2,000-3,000 words **Sentences** often contain grammatical errors **Requires** context for learning situations but understands the "big picture" **Begins** to learn some content vocabulary **Uses** MT for thinking and translating words	**"Learning** to read" **Developing** word decoding and spelling skills **Written** messages can be understood despite grammatical errors

Within this stage, there will be a great deal of growth from the beginning when BMLs have around 1,000 words to the end when they will have acquired about 3,000 words.

During this time, BMLs are continuing to expand their bank of high-frequency vocabulary words through simple conversations, listening and social interactions. They are building up their oral language fluency and their sentences start to come together with a greater number of new words.

BMLs still rely heavily on context to comprehend at this stage but they are growing in their ability to listen and understand more of what is happening during lessons and activities. Routines and repetitive daily activities will seem much easier for them now but language-based tasks and discussions will still be very challenging for them.

Towards the end of this stage, their oral fluency increases although they are still likely to make frequent grammatical errors in both their oral and written expression. This is quite normal and to be expected.

BMLs will still be making connections to their MT (or even L2 if they are multilingual). Many will move through this stage fairly quickly because they are able to translate new English words into their MT or other language. Keep in mind that this kind of rapid acceleration can give a false impression to teachers (and others) that the student is mastering English to a much higher level than they actually are at.

With younger BMLs or those who may not have established literacy in their MT, it is important to *continuously* monitor the development of their phonemic awareness skills and word decoding skills in English in order to ensure they are solid. Older BMLs should also be monitored to ensure that they have gained strong early literacy skills in English. BMLs of all ages need a focused reading program to enable them to build a strong foundation of reading skills.

Special attention should be paid to reading comprehension skills at this point. Injections of focused literacy support should be used with BMLs who are struggling with word decoding at this stage so that they can be put on-track. Building fluency with writing is also an important component since it allows them to actively apply the vocabulary they have learned so far. Rereading and self-correcting their own writing (to the best of their abilities) will also allow BMLs to reflect on their ideas, knowledge of grammar and vocabulary. Teachers should scaffold the BML's developing writing by providing them with one or two focus points that reflect their stage of development. Do not make great efforts to over-teach complex grammar rules since many will be beyond the BML's natural ability level. Allow them to build up their writing skills with special attention to expression of their main ideas with words they already know. Encourage them to try and use new words when it appears that they are repeating the same words over and over. Teach them how to use a *Mini-Thesaurus* (or adjective list). Teach BMLs to apply punctuation rules and provide them with daily opportunities for reading and writing. Sit with them and give direct feedback on their work; be explicit in helping them grasp the differences between their language and English.

At times it may be difficult for teachers to hold back their natural instincts to "correct" BMLs' work, especially when there are numerous errors. Remember that this will be counter-productive since they may not even be conscious of what is going on even once you have explained the problem. It is a far better approach for teachers to focus on the main idea and have BMLs try their best to express ideas and concepts meaningfully.

Once you have given them one or two achievable goals to focus on in their writing, you can target those points to more actively "correct" and model with them. As the BML grows in their English proficiency, their ability to notice new grammatical rules in English will also grow and they will start to apply this in their writing if given opportunities. At that time, BMLs can benefit from explicit discussions around particular grammar features.

BMLs may get "stuck" on certain vocabulary words and can be seen to use the same words over and over even when they are ready to start extending their word usage. Teachers can scaffold and support BMLs by giving them word lists or the Mini-Thesaurus to select new target words for use in writing and speaking.

FOUNDATIONAL LANGUAGE 4 (FL4)

STAGE	HALLMARKS:	LITERACY PROGRESSION:
FL 4 **3,000-6,000** **Words**	**Expanding** vocabulary **Mainly** fluent speech **Good** overall comprehension **Understands** general English at 5,000 words **Expanding** content-related vocabulary **Still** has some challenges expressing abstract ideas and higher-order concepts through English **Fills** in meaning gaps with their MT	**Transition** to "reading to learn" **Has** most/all of reading and writing foundations **Often** needs support in target areas for writing **May** experience a "slump" in reading due to lack of vocabulary

This stage requires acquisition of a much larger number of vocabulary words from the mid-frequency band. It represents a transition phase, with BMLs still acquiring some foundational language and then be-ginning to use more academic language with support. They start to shift from "learning to read" to now "reading to learn." Again, this is the time when BMLs' oral fluency often mimics native-speakers and they can appear to be much more proficient in English than they actually are.

Between 4,000-6,000 words, BMLs have better comprehension and can read with greater proficiency. They understand oral English to a good level once they reach about 5,000 words. They will likely encounter and acquire more advanced content-based words based on their themes or units of study (e.g. volcano, precipitation, etc.). They fill in any meaning gaps in their comprehension with their MT and are still in need of some curriculum differentiation and scaffolding. BMLs will likely require support at this stage to cope with more advanced and varied vocabulary in texts. They also need encouragement and targeted strategies to support their writing skills so that they can apply more advanced and descriptive words. Practice is especially important for their developing reading and writing.

BMLs are increasingly expected to use reading for more academically-demanding tasks like extracting text for research, explaining facts in their own words and clarifying meaning. They should be given thinking time and opportunities to discuss their ideas with peers before writing in order to generate and stimulate their ideas. Teacher feedback sessions or conferencing with the student is very important at this stage in order to keep moving them along with the right strategies for higher-level reading comprehension skills (e.g. inferencing). Since BMLs now have a good base of vocabulary words to give them fluency in writing, they should be challenged to further improve accuracy, expand their word usage as well as receive guidance around specific genres of writing. It is critical to focus on reading comprehension strategies for all age groups, especially since this is around the time when the literacy "slump" (i.e. "fourth-grade slump") has been cited in the research.

THINKING LANGUAGE 1 (TL1)

STAGE	HALLMARKS:	LITERACY PROGRESSION:
TL 1 **6,000-8,000** **Words**	**Understands** a wide range of conversation without support at 6,000-7,000 words **Carries** out fluent conversation across a variety of topics **Has** a base of academic vocabulary words but not always enough **May** begin to "think" in English **Challenges** with idioms and figurative language	**Reads** and writes for different purposes but not always on-level **May** have challenges with grammar, vocabulary and "metaphors" **Concept** of "passive voice" may be difficult

At this stage, BMLs can typically handle more academically-challenging tasks. Context-based activities are still very helpful but learners now have enough vocabulary to begin using it for "thinking" about topics and abstract ideas through English. BMLs are more able to think in English with increased fluidity. Their verbal skills are fluent and can sometimes be even more well-developed than their written expression.

Since abstract thinking may still be a fairly challenging skill for many BMLs at this stage, they can benefit from teacher support to clarify meaning and to help them think through processes. For example, prior to writing, BMLs can benefit from "talking it out" or discussing what they want to say with another person in English. They also gain value from the use of graphic organizers to help them plot and structure their ideas logically so that their written expression is much more concise.

Weak literacy skills signal the need for focused strategy-teaching to help BMLs get over any bumps in the road. Specific writing targets and feedback can help them to attend to particular areas of need, especially in relation to grammar. BMLs should be given tools like vocabulary lists in order to help them avoid embedded habits like repetitive language or an over-reliance on simpler vocabulary words. BMLs will likely require intermittent support, depending on task complexity, in order to clarify their understanding of assignments. They will need more direct instruction in order to understand idiomatic and figurative language, especially "metaphoric language" and the "passive (vs. active) voice" which can be a point of confusion.

BMLs at this stage still need daily, focused opportunities for reading in order to build their continued exposure and proficiency with new academic vocabulary words and especially lower-frequency words. Daily writing is also critical. Since many BMLs still have gaps in their vocabulary development, literacy becomes increasingly important for their ongoing progress.

While support for BMLs is often discontinued at this time in many schools and school districts, it should still be noted that they will continue to require focused and targeted support for building ongoing literacy skills and for breaking down learning into manageable chunks. Differentiation continues to be required for many tasks, especially since grade or year-level texts can still be challenging for BMLs.

THINKING LANGUAGE 2 (TL2)

STAGE	HALLMARKS:	LITERACY PROGRESSION:
TL 2 **8,000-9,000+** **Words**	**Speaks** and understands with "near native" fluency **Understands** most written texts at 8,000 words **Builds** knowledge of technical/low-frequency words **Expresses** higher-order thinking and abstract ideas through language with greater ease **Better** comprehension of "metaphoric language"	**Can** function more independently for higher-level assignments (research, projects, presentations, etc.) **Literacy** can still lag behind students' oral and listening Proficiency

Students at this stage appear to be "near-native" in their oral fluency. They are now getting used to using their English language for more demanding academic tasks that offer little, if any context. Their vocabulary allows them to read more complex texts and respond to assignments with more advanced written skills; however, some BMLs may still struggle with clarity in written expression in English.

From around grade 9 (or year 10), there is a transition towards more "metaphoric competence" for speaking and writing (Roessingh & Elgie, 2009). This means BMLs must now be able to use abstract language more proficiently for higher-level communication. Curriculum activities like comparative essays and character analyses can demand that students not only be more precise with their language, but more "artful" in the way they begin to express their thoughts and ideas. Even for BMLs with near-native fluency, this can still be a particular challenge. This can mean that BMLs who had not previously required support for some time might again require help, explicit instruction and guidance to develop these skills.

BMLs will now be exposed to advanced English concepts that require an understanding of complex literary devices like: analogies, imagery and irony, for example. They will also be required to write more formal pieces of expository writing across subject areas. Additional practice with graphic organizers as well as explicit modeling and direct feedback while going over samples of good writing will help BMLs learn what a "quality" piece of writing should look like. This will also allow them to critique their own work. This can be very challenging and BMLs will often require coaching in order to get a better sense of how to improve.

BMLs that have arrived after 7 years of age (and have a minimum vocabulary goal of 9,000 words) should still be pushed to build up extended vocabulary with more low-frequency words. They will need targeted opportunities to do this and should even be encouraged to do "narrow reading" in their specific subject areas if they are to continue on to university. A continued focus on words from the "Academic Word List" (Coxhead, 2000) will support BMLs' reading and writing for graduation-type exams and post-secondary preparation.

EXTENDED VOCABULARY

STAGE	HALLMARKS:	LITERACY PROGRESSION:
Extended Vocabulary For University (technical and low-frequency words)	**Fluent** in several genres of literacy **Able** to use many language devices appropriately **Accurately** uses a range of subject-specific vocabulary words and low-frequency words **Able** to infer complex vocabulary word meanings from affixes	**Works** to master technical vocabulary and advanced writing skills

At this level, BMLs are advancing their vocabularies further through extended exposure to low-frequency words through their reading and curriculum content. They should now be more able to adapt their style of writing to specific purposes and infer meanings of new words they encounter more easily. BMLs can benefit from "narrow reading" in their particular areas of interest.

Some BMLs may still have written skills below their oral proficiency. In this case, every attempt needs to be made to ensure they have opportunities to advance their skills for reading and writing to strong levels.

Keep in mind that NS have around 11,000-14,000 vocabulary words when they enter university so all attempts to help BMLs acquire additional vocabulary and literacy skills will go a long way.

LANGUAGE ACQUISITION STAGES

Since many educators are familiar with these practical stages for language acquisition, these have been incorporated into the *ELP Map*.

APPLYING AND USING THE ELP MAP

One of the main purposes for using this tool is to assist us in goal-setting for each of our BMLs. Knowing where we have to get the student to in relation to where they currently are, will help us to better understand their longer-term learning trajectory.

After BMLs have settled in to their English learning environment and you have had numerous experiences interacting with them and observing their work, you will feel much more confident in your judgements of their proficiency levels. Afterwards, you can begin planning for the shorter-term—deciding on the kinds of support they will need, setting up classroom routines that maximize language and vocabulary development as well as the types of differentiation that will enable them to work independently.

Whole schools can also use this tool to gather data about all of their BMLs so that specific initiatives, school-wide programs, support models and scheduling can be structured to target student needs.

SETTING THE LONG-TERM GOAL

In some cases, there is a limiting factor of time for BMLs. Depending on when they have joined English-medium school, they may be pressed to acquire enough vocabulary to build up their CALP and reach the minimum number of words by graduation.

If the BML has recently joined the English-medium school and they are 7 years of age or above, then their vocabulary goal should be a minimum of 9,000 words. They should still, however, be encouraged to accelerate their vocabulary beyond this number if possible.

If BMLs are younger than 7 or have already reached this minimum goal (e.g. they arrive at 15 already having 9,000 words), then it is wise to help them grow their vocabulary levels further. Having an ambitious goal that approximates a native speaker's vocabulary size (with around 14,000 words) can be reasonable for many BMLs. This is especially true if they have access to strong teachers who understand techniques and strategies to support vocabulary development. These BMLs who began their English-medium education before 7 years of age have the advantage of more time to grow their vocabularies.

The tables at the bottom of the *ELP Map* shown below are guides to help you better understand the contributions of each vocabulary stage toward the overall vocabulary goal of a BML. First determine whether the BML has entered English-medium school before age 7 or after age 7. Use the appropriate table to reflect this.

Each coloured box corresponds to the vocabulary stage of the same colour on the *ELP Map*. For example, the blue box corresponds with the FL1 stage, the yellow with FL2, etc. If we imagine our BML has begun her English-medium education at age 8, then we would be using the second or bottom table (from 7 years old and up). The blue box or FL1 stage indicates that once the BML has mastered this first stage (and acquired around 500 words) they have met 6% of their overall vocabulary goal (i.e. 6% of 9,000 words). You can also get a sense from the size of the box itself that this goal is short so time spent at this stage will be relatively short. In comparison, the FL4 or orange box is much larger because it represents 33% of the BML's total vocabulary goal on its own and requires a more extended period of time to master. All stages are *not equal* in the time it takes to move through them or in the *number of words* they represent.

As the student moves from stage to stage, you can see their "cumulative percent" or increasing goal as they progress. For example, if our BML has mastered FL3 then they have already met 34% of their total vocabulary goal—first with 6% from FL1, 6% from FL2 and then 22% from FL3. As they enter the FL4 stage, we can see that this particular stage represents 33% of their overall vocabulary goal on its own but once they have mastered it they will already have achieved 67% of their overall vocabulary goal of 9,000 words.

This guide gives you a better sense of the mastery required along a BML's trajectory—not only in terms of the amount of progress needed for each individual stage but also for the extent of progress already made towards their overall vocabulary goal by all their mastered stages combined. Again, keep in mind that this chart is not hard and fast or meant to be exact. It is a tool that can give you a rough idea about your BMLs' vocabulary and movement towards their goal.

Up to 7 years old – Vocabulary Goal is "Extended Vocabulary"

% per Level	4%	4%	14%	21%	14%	7%	36%
Cumulative %	4%	8%	22%	43%	57%	64%	100%

*in this case, BMLs' vocabulary should reach into "Extended Vocabulary" but not necessarily 100% of that stage

From 7 years old and up – Vocabulary Goal is "TL2"

% per Level	6%	6%	22%	33%	22%	11%
Cumulative %	6%	12%	34%	67%	89%	100%

*it is preferable to help BMLs continue beyond TL2 whenever possible, however, TL2 is the minimum goal

Once you know the big-picture of your BMLs' backgrounds, long-term goals and current stages, you will be better able to communicate this information to students and parents. You will also be able to pin-point the short-term goals and monitor their ongoing progress through each stage more successfully. Understanding that a typical BML learns an average of 1,000 vocabulary words per academic year can help you realize whether they are making enough movement towards their long-term goals and if they are likely to reach these goals in the given timeframe. If you feel they are not making enough progress towards their goal then you should plan more focused and intensive instruction that helps them accelerate more quickly. This should involve more time reading and writing as well as extended opportunities to interact meaningfully with subject matter.

Schools must develop strong policies on developing student vocabulary. Teachers must be trained to understand how their instruction impacts student vocabulary learning. Quality instruction in subject areas, more intensive literacy practices and a targeted focus on vocabulary learning can allow BMLs to acquire a greater number of words. Even an additional 400 or 500 words per year can have a major impact on a BML's progress and movement towards their overall vocabulary goal.

ELP MAP CASE STUDIES

The sample case studies below help to illustrate the evidence and decision-making processes that teachers can go through to determine a BML's stage on the *ELP Map* as well as the long-term and short-term goals. This information can then allow a teacher to determine the kinds of support and targets the BML will need to keep them moving forward.

DETERMINING THE BML'S CURRENT STAGE ON THE ELP MAP

You should be able to identify the BML's current stage (FL1-onwards) by roughly matching their observable behaviours, work samples and skills with the "Hallmarks" from the stages. You should consider the following before getting started:

Observe the BML's informal and formal social interactions with both peers and other teachers to analyze their oral language and comprehension. Take notes and samples of the BML's speech so that you can check their length of sentences (e.g. one-word, full-sentence, etc.), vocabulary usage, grammar, etc.

Collect an assessment of the BML's reading skills (a "running record" is best if possible). A variety of student writing samples should be collected—both "prompted" (teacher-directed topic) as well as "free-writing" (self-directed topic) and collected over the span of one month. These samples should include informal topics (e.g. favourite sport or activity) as well as more academic topics (e.g. what was learned in science class or social studies). Formal writing about academic topics will provide insight into how the individual communicates more age-appropriate or cognitively challenging information with subject-specific vocabulary while free-writing can give you a better sense as to what the individual can write without constraints or guidance.

We would highly recommend cross-referencing your decision about the BML's stage with other teachers who are also working with them. This will ensure that there is some kind of "inter-rater agreement" so that accuracy is improved.

Once you know your BMLs' longer-term goals and then current levels, you can begin to look more closely at their specific needs and shorter-term goals.

STUDENT CASE STUDIES

CASE #1: Snapshot of Background Information – NASSER, 15 yrs. Old

Nasser is currently in Year 10 in an English-medium, independent school in London, England. He is 15 years of age. Nasser is originally from Saudi Arabia but his family moved to London where he attended a private school from 4 years of age. He speaks both in Arabic and English with his family and English exclusively at school. Nasser states that his main language is English and that he also thinks in English the majority of the time. Nasser admits that his Arabic is not very strong and that his literacy skills in writing are very weak. He is a bright student who consistently strives to do well in all of his classes. Nasser was diagnosed as having "dyslexia" when he was 8 years old and received additional support for literacy; however, his reading and writing are still behind year-level expectations in English. Nasser has plans to attend university to become an engineer when he graduates.

ORAL LANGUAGE AND COMPREHENSION:

- Nasser has very good oral fluency
- He has good comprehension of classroom content and conversation
- He often tries to incorporate more advanced vocabulary into his speech when explaining, discussing or debating
- He is often observed to use *too many words* to describe or explain something because he cannot use more concise language
- He does not always understand the full meaning of idioms and metaphorical language

---

READING ASSESSMENT:

- Nasser's reading assessment shows he is reading at an approximate Year 8 level (reading age 12)
- Almost all of the essential reading strategies were present
- Nasser did not have full comprehension of higher-level texts (especially non-fiction) because of their advanced vocabulary and word usage

WRITING ASSESSMENT AND VOCABULARY:

- Nasser's writing samples express a central topic that is easily understood
- He uses many vocabulary words that are age-appropriate
- His wording is often repetitive
- He over-embellishes his writing with descriptive words which are often used inappropriately (e.g. "the humungous, over-populated country")
- He is observed to use a range of "academic words" and subject-specific words in his writing
- All writing samples consistently reveal his independent levels to be around Yr.6 and Yr.7 level
- He still makes occasional errors with grammar (e.g. "air is polluted" instead of "air was polluted")

CURRENT STAGE:

TL1   6,000-8,000 words

LONG-TERM GOAL:

The long-term vocabulary goal for Nasser is to reach beyond 9,000 vocabulary words since he has 3 more years in secondary school and has been in an English-medium school since age 4. He also plans to attend university.

In regards to Nasser's MT development, both he and his parents do not feel it is important to work on developing his Arabic language now that his English has become his stronger, academic language. They are satisfied that Nasser has a basic knowledge of reading and writing in Arabic and that he is able to communicate with his family.

WHAT KIND OF SUPPORT DOES HE CURRENTLY REQUIRE?

Nasser is clearly able to comprehend and participate across the expected listening and speaking domains. He is still developing his knowledge and use of vocabulary and should receive focused "conferencing" sessions with the teacher in order to give him direct feedback and specific goals or targets to reach over a month at-a-time. Currently, Nasser does not do any reading aside from the novel or book that is assigned in his English class. This is also true for writing. The specific focused goals and strategies he will need for the short-term are:

- To be put on a daily, individualized reading program (with appropriately-leveled books); this should be monitored by the English teacher
- To receive focused feedback sessions for writing and to increase the amount of writing (monitored by the English teacher)
- To learn to structure writing according to genre (type) and features, using graphic organizers
- To learn editing skills
- To learn how to use more precise language for speaking and writing through modeling
- To learn more academic vocabulary words (from the *Academic Word List*) and technical words
- To learn specific strategies related to vocabulary words with Greek/Latin roots
- To increase his understanding of idioms and figurative language

Differentiation: Nasser will require differentiated reading for English since the assigned, year-level texts are likely to be too challenging for him to read independently. He may need written instructions clarified for comprehension.

NASSER'S WRITING SAMPLE:

Last week my friends and I traveled to Amarica. We traveled on one of the best airlines In the world, Emirates airline. we traveled together and we got upgraded to the first class luxury sweets. We were relaxed and enjoyed the comfortable cabins. It was amazing. As soon as we reached the humungus, over populated country we entered the air port. The airport was full and the people looked like ants crawling to find food. We exited the airport after some time. We were now hitting the busy roads where the air is polluted with gas that clogged up my throught.

After a few hours standing under the blazing hot sun, we found a taxi. The taxi transported us safely to our 6 star hotel. The hotel was extremely expensive, but worth it. We paid over $ 4,000 for 2 weeks.

We explored Amarica and visited many beautiful places such as statue of liberty and many museums that have spectacular antiques and ancient valuables.

At last and most unfortunately, we started to pack up and put all of our suvieners into our bags.

CASE #2: SNAPSHOT OF BACKGROUND INFORMATION - JAAKKO, 10 YRS. OLD

Jaakko is a 10-year old boy who is currently in Year 6 in an English-curriculum, school. He has recently moved to Dubai, UAE from Finland. Jaakko speaks Finnish as a MT and has previously only ever attended school in his local community. He has been in his new English-medium school for the past academic year.

ORAL LANGUAGE AND COMPREHENSION:

- Able to pick up the "big picture" of lessons in class; relies on visuals and environmental cues to support his understanding
- Typically uses simple sentences with grammatical errors
- Can provide some accurate answers to questions during class
- Can make the main idea of his messages understood
- Is confident in speaking socially with other children inside and outside of the classroom
- Can use some subject-related vocabulary words in context
- Often pauses for "thinking time" between words in phrases and sentences when talking
- Relies heavily on his MT to translate words, phrases and concepts

READING ASSESSMENT:

- He received intensive literacy support after one month of arriving and is now able to understand and apply the foundations for reading and writing (since he could transfer his MT literacy skills to English)
- Has strong word-decoding skills but needs some support for pronunciation at times
- Is reading at Level "L" in the Fountas & Pinnell reading levels (reading age 7 years)

WRITING ASSESSMENT AND VOCABULARY:

- Jaakko's writing samples provide very detailed descriptions and information about his topic using mostly high-frequency words
- He is able to apply several subject-specific vocabulary words to his academic writings
- He understands the S-V-O (subject-verb-object structure) in English

- He has very strong writing skills for his current level of English and has grasped most of the basic rules of punctuation and capitalization
- His writings are well-organized and well-written; it is clear that his strong writing skills are a result of "transfer" from his knowledge of writing in Finnish to English

CURRENT STAGE:

FL3 1,000-3,000 words

LONG-TERM GOAL:

The long-term vocabulary goal for Jaakko is to reach the minimum number of 9,000 words since he has recently joined his English school in Year 7. Jaakko should also work to maintain his MT (Finnish) through weekly classes.

WHAT KIND OF SUPPORT DOES HE CURRENTLY REQUIRE?

In Jaakko's case, he has just entered the FL3 stage, so the most impactful support he will need is to ensure that he has full comprehension and participation during class lessons. He has a great deal of anxiety and wants to get things "right" so this does impact his risk-taking at times. Since Jaakko is strong in his MT and has full literacy, he should be encouraged to use it to support classroom learning when needed. His goals for the short-term are:

- To be put on a daily, individualized reading program (with appropriately-leveled books); this should be monitored by the BML specialist teacher
- To receive focused feedback sessions for writing and to take part in daily writing (e.g. journaling) - monitored by the BML specialist teacher
- To learn editing skills
- To continue acquiring high-frequency vocabulary necessary for Foundational Language and literacy
- To learn more subject-related vocabulary words and their Finnish translations

- To build up confidence in speaking and listening within small groups and "buddies"
- To continue to maintain his Finnish MT and literacy in weekly classes

Differentiation: At this stage, Jaakko will continue to require differentiation of year-level reading materials. He should use his MT in situations where he needs to research or find out background information about a topic. Jaakko will also need to have written assignments and tests adapted to his level.

Visual supports are critical to helping Jaakko establish context for lessons. He should also have a designated "buddy" in his class that he can approach for clarification of information since he does not always feel comfortable asking the teacher for help. Jaakko can make use of translation tools and apps to support his vocabulary in both languages.

JAAKKO'S WRITING SAMPLE:

Spring Holiday in Finland

First morning in Finland when I woke up my friend's came to our house and asked if I can come outside and play with them.

After weekend I went with my friend's in my old school. For the lunch there was bean soup. After my school I went to my football training. In that evening we went in to sauna and after that we grilled some finn's sausages in our fireplase. It was yummy.   place

Nextday I went back to school again. That day was in Finland fool's day we called aprillipäivä. My teacher try to fool's us many times. It was funny.

On Thursday I spent my day at school again in that evening we spent with our family friend's we went in a

restaurant and have a nice time with them.

On Friday wie slept late. When we woke up I went out and I cyckled to my friend's house.   cycled

On Friday afternoon I left to visit my grandmother and I spent a night in there. My grandmother has a big dog, the dog's name is tatu. I love to play with him there was also my cousin Joona and we played a lot together.

On Monday I went to see my oldest grandmother she is 93 years old.

CASE # 3: SNAPSHOT OF BACKGROUND INFORMATION – ANU, 6 YRS. OLD

Anu is a 6-year old girl who lives in California, USA. Her parents are originally from India but she was born in the States. Anu is multilingual and speaks Hindi and Urdu at home and with relatives. Her parents both speak English well but they do not usually speak it together or with the children in order to make an effort to maintain their other languages. Anu is currently in Grade 1 in a public school.

ORAL LANGUAGE AND COMPREHENSION:

- Has good oral fluency and comprehension of conversation and class concepts
- Participates readily in discussions in small and large groups during classes
- Converses with ease with both adults and peers
- Demonstrates that she can learn and apply new subject-related words quickly
- Speaks in full sentences with occasional grammatical errors
- Asks for clarification of new words as she comes across them
- Is still learning many new, high-frequency vocabulary words

READING ASSESSMENT:

- Her independent reading level is Level " F" in the Fountas & Pinnell reading levels (reading age 6)
- Does not always understand the high-frequency vocabulary words required to advance her vocabulary
- Is still acquiring basic reading strategies, sight words and phonemic awareness skills

WRITING ASSESSMENT AND VOCABULARY:

- Foundational writing skills are being established; writing is still at an early stage but she is making consistent progress
- Attempts to use new words in her independent writing
- Does not always record what she wants to say accurately; cannot attend to all the elements of

writing at the same time as she writes (e.g. recording all the correct sounds in words, attending to spelling/punctuation, correct letter formations)

- Can typically express concrete thoughts or events but is more challenged to use her imagination to create her own stories
- Needs to discuss her ideas prior to writing
- Underlines words she is not sure how to spell correctly as she writes

CURRENT STAGE:

FL 3 1,000-3,000 words

LONG-TERM GOAL:

Anu's long-term goal will be to master vocabulary beyond 9,000 words since she will be in English-medium education for the next 11 years. Anu's parents are being encouraged to have her learn literacy in one of her other languages through a weekend class.

WHAT KIND OF SUPPORT DOES SHE CURRENTLY REQUIRE?

While her oral and receptive comprehension skills are enabling her to understand and participate in the majority of the classroom learning at her current level, Anu's immediate need is to gain mastery of phonemic awareness skills to ensure she gains a good beginning in the early literacy skills. She also requires further exposure and reinforcement of new vocabulary words. Her goals for the short-term are:

- To advance reading and writing skills through daily practice with frequent teacher feedback and modeling
- To increase vocabulary development through literacy-rich experiences within the regular Gr.1 classroom and "enriched literacy" in an after-school class for BMLs
- To learn spelling skills and strategies

Differentiation: Anu requires differentiation for vocabulary, especially for mathematics tasks and worksheets which are more language-based. She needs some tasks broken down into smaller parts and can take longer for writing tasks. It can help her to receive shortened tasks at times. For writing tasks, she can benefit from "talking it out" prior to writing and to use specific graphic organizers for planning her work. The teacher can engage Anu's MT at times in order to help bridge her concept and vocabulary learning.

ANU'S WRITING SAMPLE:

There was Donkey but nozebras a log tim ago. all the time the Donkey were workig. they went to a wies man. the wies man let them.

There was Donkey but nozebras a log tim ago. all the time the Donkey
were workig. they went to a wies man. the wies man let them.

How should we think about Vocabulary Programming in our Schools and Classrooms?

Within the natural school environment, there are plenty of opportunities for BMLs to acquire language through content learning and social interactions. "Vocabulary Programming" in our case can simply mean that teachers become more aware of the things that have an impact on BMLs' vocabulary development and they work to emphasize these within their teaching approaches, scheduling and learning activities.

In most good schools, teachers are already carrying out quality work with their students but often it is not as targeted as it could be for BMLs to reap the maximum rewards.

For example, guided reading and individual reading programs are typically implemented in primary school but once students become independent readers around the end of grade 3 or year 4, these programs are often stopped as students are then expected to self-monitor their own reading. While this is often fine for NS, BMLs definitely need more time with leveled reading to ensure they consolidate their literacy and reading comprehension skills.

As well, teachers can increase the amount of peer interaction and "talk time" during learning activities so that their BMLs have more opportunity to actively use and apply their language skills purposefully. When teachers are more aware of the powerful impact that specific activities and practices can have on a BML's success, they can be more deliberate in their planning, scheduling and in the teaching approaches they decide to carry out.

Several years ago, we were asked to carry out teacher-training in a school that had a student body made up of 100% bilingual and multilingual learners. They were taught exclusively in the English-medium. Although the teachers all had a university degree, they had not been through any formal teacher education. Many of them reported that their students had been going to the school for years and were still not actively speaking much English. As we visited these teachers' classes, we began to understand why. The model of instruction was a "stand-and-deliver" approach where the teacher would talk for the majority of the lesson and the students were passive listeners. The quality of the teacher-talk was low and usually involved explaining the worksheets rather than engaging students in rich discussions or interaction. However, after some modeling the teachers learned how to use more effective practices that allowed students more time to discuss and work with their peers. They also learned how classroom discussions could prompt students to share and participate through language.

Teachers began to notice remarkable changes quickly—in fact, one teacher was so shocked to hear her students "speaking English" she thought a miracle had taken place! These students had acquired

English passively through the years but since they were never expected or enabled to actively apply their English, they appeared to be "lazy" and "incapable". Providing students with the right kinds of quality learning experiences under the right conditions is essential for nurturing their growing language and literacy development. This may even require only simple adjustments to already-established programs and schedules to help BMLs receive the maximum benefits.

The diagram below illustrates the opportunities that contribute to vocabulary and language development within the school environment. Many of these are acquired through natural interactions which are embedded in quality comprehensible input. Understanding this, we can see that the recess or "break times" in the school day are often just as important as classroom learning.

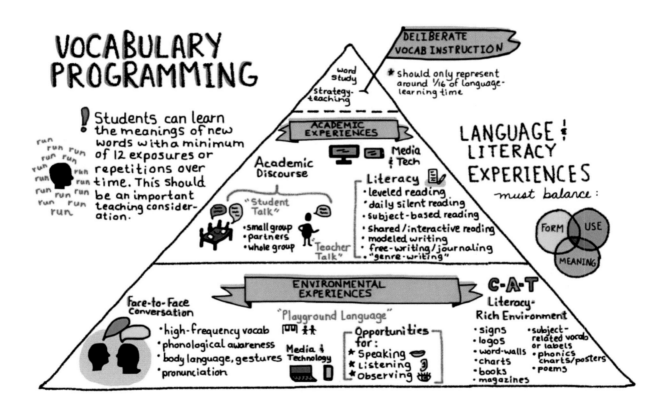

How can you use this information to structure your lessons or create more focused opportunities for BMLs to grow their language and vocabulary?

POINTS TO CONSIDER

- A special emphasis on accelerating vocabulary development for early primary/elementary students is essential in order to "fill the gaps" with vocabulary words which BMLs have likely not been exposed to. From what we see in the research, this time period can be especially critical for students' long and short-term academic success. More time and energy should be invested in considering and developing language/literacy programs for these students.

- Since most BMLs are shown to learn early literacy skills like phonemic awareness and word decoding fairly easily, there should be more "monitoring" at this stage instead of intensive supports from "ESL" classes, etc. BMLs struggling with early skills can usually benefit from targeted support with a quick, "intervention-style" approach over a short span of time in order to catch up rapidly.

- There should be more training and development for teachers to understand how to teach specific reading comprehension strategies for students (e.g. "making pictures in your head," "questioning," "context clues," etc.). Many BMLs can learn phonics easily but teachers should not be fooled by good word decoding. Running strong reading programs, like "guided reading" can be very beneficial for building strategies that support students' reading for meaning.

- Schools should move away from the notion of "entering" and "exiting" BMLs from their student support registers for 2 reasons:

  1. This does not allow schools to be flexible with their support teachers who are often "assigned" to ESL or classes for a fixed amount of time and;

  2. Bilingualism and multilingualism can be a lifelong journey and so BMLs may need support at different stages along the way. In some schools, if they have already been "exited" then they may no longer qualify for or get access to additional support. However, if all BMLs are identified throughout their school years, then all teachers (including subject teachers) will be aware that these students can experience periodic struggles with the curriculum or with the English language at times. This does not necessarily signal a learning issue or a need for long-term support.

- Support models should make use of the knowledge of BMLs' vocabulary stages and should tailor supports to what BMLs will need to gain greater vocabulary for oral and written proficiency, reading comprehension and written expression. Schools should be aware of the numbers of BMLs they have at different stages and should understand the significance of those numbers for school decision-making.

- Administrators and support teachers should dedicate their resources and time more flexibly depending on the needs of their particular BMLs. For example, if teachers know that the stage, "TL4" represents a major shift for students from "learning to read" to "reading to learn" then this is an area where BMLs are likely to need a great deal more support to help them develop key literacy strategies. As well, BMLs in the previous stage should be given specific instruction in reading comprehension and vocabulary strategies in order to better prepare them for the following stage. Extra focus and attention for specific supports can be given to these BMLs (e.g. to develop strategies for interpreting and responding to "academic language").

- Schools with a large or majority population of BMLs often have a small number of "support" or "ESL" teachers to meet the needs of a very limited number of students. Support is usually prioritized for the group perceived to have the highest needs (e.g. the "beginners"). This kind of approach is not an effective use of resources because it ignores a large number of BMLs within the school who also require support. Instead, resources should be maximized throughout the school using a flexible, "consultative approach." This can allow the support teacher to meet the needs of students and teachers in a variety of ways. For example, support teachers can meet with class teachers to plan and differentiate lessons to fit BMLs; it can include training sessions for teachers in a target area (e.g. reading comprehension strategies for BMLs), it may even involve the support teacher going into a class to "team-teach" for a specific topic or unit. Thinking outside-the-box rather than doing *what has always been done* can enable higher-quality support for BMLs and teachers across the school.

- Literacy programming should be an utmost concern to school administrators and teachers. Literacy is one of the essential keys to success for BMLs so schools must have enough books and resources to provide solid programs. Leveled readers (for young readers) and graded readers (for older BMLs) should be available for all ages. All students must be on a leveled/graded reader and receive some kind of monitoring to ensure that they are following-through and continuing to make progress. Schools must also ensure there is enough time in the schedule for literacy tasks and vocabulary development. Since vocabulary development is interconnected with literacy tasks like reading and writing, this needs to be a major focus in schools. Schools must adopt daily silent reading (for 15-20 minutes) along with regular writing activities—not only for "genres" or curriculum activities, but writing that emphasizes free expression (e.g. like journal writing, for example) so that BMLs' growth can be measured. Opportunities for individual feedback must also be offered and "reading and writing conferencing" or "writer's workshops" are solid approaches to this.

- Since BMLs typically get good exposure to high frequency words through general conversations and interactions, teachers should give more focus to learning the mid-frequency words. These words are high-utility and also help to build a mature vocabulary for the BML. There are numerous mid-frequency words for individuals to master. BMLs will also gain exposure to several low-frequency words within their subject or topic areas but since these words are much rarer words, there needs to be a more direct focus to help master these through strategy-teaching.

- All teachers (including subject teachers) must be aware that many English words are comprised of Greek and Latin roots. When students are taught how to decode these word parts (e.g. bio- ; photo-; pre-, etc.), they can begin to understand the patterns and become more active in building meaning. This can have a positive impact on BMLs' reading comprehension skills.

- Late arriving BMLs who do not have any knowledge of early literacy should not be faced with a "sink or swim" situation. There should be provisions for these students to receive instruction in the basics of English reading and writing so they can learn to read and then have a solid foundation moving forward.

- Schools should consider that older, more proficient BMLs might also require support even after they have developed CALP in English, especially as they move to gaining mastery with "metaphoric competence" in the secondary school. Students who are preparing to go on to university need special attention and focus on vocabulary, especially with academic words and low-frequency words for their specific areas of study.

- BMLs who arrive late to secondary and who have at least the first 2,000 high-frequency words in English can be accelerated by learning all of the words on the *Academic Word List* in conjunction with ongoing leveled reading. This will allow students to better cope with their textbooks and language used in class while at the same time, still addressing their ongoing literacy development from their current levels (Nation, 2014).

Ensuring your BMLs encounter a wide variety of vocabulary words should not be left to luck. Now that you understand the importance of developing their vocabulary, as well as how to better understand their individual vocabulary levels, you will be able to structure your school policies and class instruction to maximize learning opportunities. This can include: natural acquisition from oral language, a literacy and language-rich environment, individual reading and writing programs, academic discussions and even incidental learning, to name a few.

DIG DEEP:

1. How does understanding these English language vocabulary trajectories "change the game" in regards to the education of BMLs?

2. In 3-4 key points, how could you summarize Dr. Biemiller and Dr. Roessingh's perspectives and research on vocabulary development?

3. Why can the stage, "FL4" also be referred to as "Thinking Language?"

BREAKOUT:

4. What have you learned about vocabulary development that you didn't know previously? Why is vocabulary development the "missing link" for BMLs?

5. Considering the fact that many BMLs are not thriving in schools today, how can applying knowledge about language acquisition and vocabulary development turn that around?

6. How can a teacher implement daily routines to support their students' ongoing vocabulary development?

EXPLORE:

Think about how vocabulary is taught in your school. What else do you think is needed in order to ensure students are reaching their vocabulary goals?

[6]

Issues and Identification of BMLs

IN THIS CHAPTER YOU WILL...

- Learn how to identify potential BMLs and gather information from parents
- Understand different types of BMLs and how to support them
- Better understand refugee issues
- Develop a strong knowledge base around procedures for BMLs suspected of having special needs
- Understand the complexities that relate to psychological/educational testing with BMLs

GROUNDING QUESTION:

From your experience, what kind of diversity exists within any random group of BMLs?

If you have already been working with BMLs then you will likely have noticed the extensive diversity that exists within this population. In order to best meet the needs of BMLs, we need to fully understand each student's unique profile. This is usually accomplished through an extensive review of the child's background, typically with information provided by the parents.

In schools where this information is not gathered, BMLs can easily slip through the cracks with their teachers not even aware that they speak another language. Through the years, we have noticed that many private schools have a stated policy to accept students who already speak English proficiently. In one such case, we conducted a literacy survey of 430 elementary students in an international school. Our goal was to screen children who might be in need of literacy intervention.

We first completed a background and language questionnaire to better understand the profile of the students. Interestingly, we discovered that 87% of the students we profiled spoke an additional language(s) with their parents or caregivers. In the majority of these cases, the children came from expatriate, mixed-culture families where parents spoke a range of other languages, often in addition to English. Interestingly, the majority of the student body were BMLs (without any awareness by the school) despite their policy.

How could the school have made such an error? In most cases, students had come into kindergarten with some level of English already. If they joined the school later on, they were able to slip through the net because of a lack of proper intake procedures at admission.

Since students had already acquired good BICS level English, they were assumed to be much more proficient than they actually were. Of course, we probably do not need to tell you what happened several years later: Teachers were wondering why their large body of students were not performing well in literacy-based tasks while they had previously performed very well.

Our first question when meeting the school management about this issue was, "What percentage of your students are identified as bilingual or multilingual learners?" The staff answered, "Around 15%." You can imagine their surprise in discovering what our student background survey revealed.

This kind of scenario is actually much more common than you might realize. How did we identify at least 87% of students as BMLs when the school had identified only 15%? In this case, the school did not have correct procedures in place nor did they ask the right questions to identify the linguistic backgrounds of students upon admission.

When the first cohort of students in the school reached Grade 4 (Year 5), the staff were puzzled as to why the literacy results suddenly seemed so low. Understanding what we now know about vocabulary and comprehension, we can infer that these students had gained early literacy skills fairly easily but when they had begun to make the switch to "reading to learn," which required greater vocabulary and deeper reading comprehension skills, these students began to struggle.

The first order of business any school should put on their agenda is to find out exactly who their student body is. Part of this process includes identifying potential BMLs so that the school can begin to prepare their staff and educational programming appropriately.

In this chapter, we will explore identification and diversity issues within the BML population. We will also learn how to address more complex concerns and questions that teachers may have about BMLs with special needs, including refugee students.

IDENTIFICATION OF BMLs

Depending on your school and whether it is a private school or public (government school), your procedures for registering new students will be slightly different. You could have a secretary or admissions officer who collects information from parents at the time of enrollment, or you may even have a teacher perform that role. In any case, schools must ensure that they get access to the *right information* about students. While it is sometimes clear that a student comes from a home where English is not spoken (e.g. because the parent does not have full proficiency or they may have an accent in English), there are many scenarios where children go unidentified. Gathering the right information from the parent is the best place to start and it is important that schools have very specific procedures for this information-collection.

STEP 1: GATHER INFORMATION ABOUT STUDENTS WITH THE "PARENT INTERVIEW"

The first step to identifying potential BMLs is to ask the right questions. Have the parent complete the *Parent Interview Sheet* for each child. This is an important step in uncovering the child's linguistic and cultural background, as well as their prior schooling and medical history. This information is invaluable since it can allow you to learn more about your students, identify potential BMLs, and then begin to understand what kind of support they may require. This simple procedure should be streamlined within your school, and supervised by one of the teaching staff (ideally the BML specialist). This will ensure that the school is collecting adequate information for identifying potential BMLs (or students with any other concerns). This procedure should not be left to the admissions officer, registrar or secretary alone since they are not trained to know what to look for.

Sometimes it can be easy to identify potential BMLs simply because their parents do not speak English fluently, or because the parent has indicated on the form that their child has another language(s) in their background. In other cases though, parents are reluctant to indicate their child may be a BML because they might feel there is a negative connotation to speaking other (non-dominant) languages. This can be especially true if they think their child will require extra support. In some cultures, extra "help" can be viewed negatively or is something they may feel embarrassed about.

It is important then that schools ask specific kinds of questions that can be used to potentially identify any BMLs. Questions like: nationality, language(s) spoken by child, languages spoken by mother/father, list of prior schools attended (note countries the student has lived in, and the language-medium used in prior schools) should be asked of all parents.

Be sure to gather information about the student's full language repertoire, not only whether they speak English or not. For example, asking parents to provide information about their own language(s) can also give valuable information about what language(s) your student is exposed to. Even in cases where parents speak another language in addition to English but their child does not directly speak it (just has access to hearing it), there may still be some level of acquisition by the child. This information is worth noting in the students' file.

In another situation, a child may have acquired their parent's foreign accent in English and this should be noted, especially because it can impact some BMLs' ability to pronounce and differentiate between letter sounds for reading and writing purposes. For example, a child of an Arabic-speaker may pronounce the English short "o" sound (as in "octopus") as "oo" (like "mood"). Similarly, in French, the "th" sound (as in "thick") does not exist, so it may be replaced by a "z" (like "zebra") or "s" in other pronunciations. While the child may have their parent's accent but not speak their language directly, it *may* still have an impact and should be noted. However, keep in mind that the presence of an accent does not indicate an individual's proficiency with a language.

Once you have noted from the *Parent Interview Sheet* that the child is a possible BML, it is important to carry out a detailed but succinct interview with the parent to ensure all pertinent information is gathered. In some cases, this can be done in conjunction with an interpreter if the teacher does not speak the parents' language, or if the parent does not speak English.

PARENT INTERVIEW SCENARIO

TEACHER:
Thank you for talking to me today, Mrs. Morelli.

MRS. MORELLI (MOTHER):
Thank you.

TEACHER:
I want to ask you some questions about your daughter. I would like to find out more information about her so I can find the best way to help her in the classroom.

MRS. MORELLI:
Yes, thank you.

TEACHER:
Can you tell me what language you speak to Maria in at home?

MRS. MORELLI:
I speak in English to her. When we put her in English school, my husband and me speak in English to her. This is what her kindergarten teacher tell us to do.

TEACHER:
Okay, thank you. What language do you and your husband use to speak to each other?

MRS. MORELLI:
Together we are speaking Italian all the time but you know my husband travels so much now. He don't always see his children, maybe now just on the weekends because they are already in bed when he get home.

TEACHER:
So does Maria ever speak with you or your husband in Italian?

MRS. MORELLI:
No she don't speak much but I know she and her brother understand. When we go to grandparents, they speak with them. A little but not like they should be. But you know now English is very important. Nobody speak Italian here and it is very difficult to keep the language for them. Everything in English over here so now Maria and Dominico are becoming English. Even me, I am speaking English all the time now.

TEACHER:
Did you learn English in Italy?

MRS. MORELLI:
Yes, both me and my husband we study English in university and little in secondary school so we are okay.

TEACHER:
And do you or your husband speak any other languages?

MRS. MORELLI:

Yes both me and my husband speak Spanish, we used to live in Spain for two years after our marriage. But now we don't speak any, only if we meet our Spanish friends. And children they don't know about any Spanish.

TEACHER:

So do the children speak any other languages?

MRS. MORELLI:

No.

TEACHER:

Thank you. I also have this form for you to complete, if you don't mind. This will give us all the information about your children's educational backgrounds. I'll just let you complete it and then I'll come back to read it over with you.

What did this brief interview reveal?

Whenever we work with children who come from bilingual or multilingual backgrounds, we must always try to gather as much information from the parents as possible. Of course this also means questioning parents about their own language backgrounds and familiarity with English in order to get the full picture. This can be uncomfortable for some parents so we need to keep that in mind.

At this time, you are also likely to discover parents' beliefs about education, learning English and their connection to their own cultures and language. In some cases, as in the example above, you may also find that parents have been given inappropriate advice about speaking and maintaining their mother-tongue.

Asking parents to report on their own language backgrounds can be a very sensitive issue, especially for those who already possess some proficiency with English. Some families may even speak another dialect of English that is different to the Standard Dialect used in Western schools and education settings. Some may not be aware of the differences between these dialects.

As with any sensitive issue, it can be challenging to communicate without causing offense. Throughout the interview process, it is important to keep the parents' perspective in mind and appreciate that:

1. They may not have an accurate understanding of their own proficiency levels in English
2. They may not understand that their dialect of English is not the standard dialect spoken within the "dominant culture"
3. They may hold beliefs that having a good level of English reflects on their intelligence
4. They may feel that their proficiency in English will not allow them "entry" into the dominant culture they are living in

You may also want to have an interpreter present during the interview if you feel that the parent may not be able to fully express themselves comfortably. This might not be necessary, but should be considered to ensure they have the opportunity to give you as much information as possible through their dominant language.

In the parent interview with Mrs. Morelli above, she mentioned that she and her husband speak English to their children the majority of the time. It is clear that this was at the recommendation of Maria's previous teacher, who clearly did not understand the benefits of immersing a child in their own mother-tongue. This kind of recommendation is not only incorrect, but can be damaging to a child's developing linguistic abilities. It is evident that Maria has now become a subtractive bilingual since English has now become her main language and has taken over her Italian.

After the interview, you need to review the *Parent Interview Sheet*. You will then start to gain a much better idea about whether the new student should be identified as a BML or not. Be sure to clarify any information you are unsure of.

The next step is to do an initial interview with the student.

STEP 2: GATHER INFORMATION ABOUT STUDENTS THROUGH THE "INITIAL INTERVIEW"

New students need to feel welcomed and above all, safe. It is a good idea to start out asking their name and ensuring you get it right. They can teach you the proper pronunciation and this kind of interaction can be fun and release tension for the student.

If you can communicate with the student in their MT, it is a good idea to do so. This can mediate possible anxiety and can allow you to gain as much information as possible. If you feel it is appropriate later on, you can ask the student to switch to speaking English if possible so that you can get a sense of their language proficiency. Finding out all you can about their background and education, as well as their interests and family will help you to build rapport. You can also tell them a little bit about the school and what they might do and learn there.

This is an important time to make the child feel secure and help them understand or predict what school will be like for them. Of course the level of conversation and discussion you will have with them will vary, depending on their age.

If there is another student who speaks the same language in the school, preferably in the same class, it is a good idea to introduce them. If not, then you can still choose an appropriate buddy from the student's class who might best fit the role.

Remember that the first interaction with the student will help them to build rapport. It will also help to shape their impression of their new school. You will gain valuable information about the BML at this time, learning about their educational history and personal experiences. Of course you would also find out a great deal about their language preferences and proficiency during this time. This information should be noted and shared with others working with the student.

STEP 3: ASSESS THE STUDENT'S LITERACY SKILLS IN ENGLISH AND THEIR MT

One of the most important things you can do as part of an initial assessment of a new BML is to collect information on their writing and reading levels. It may not be appropriate to do this at the same time as the *Initial Interview* with the BML, but it can always be done later on, once they have had enough time to settle into school.

Doing an initial reading assessment and taking a writing sample is important information to be collected either in the student's MT language (if they do not yet speak English), or in both the MT and English if they already know some English. Have a translator give you information about the BML's MT writing sample (if you do not know their language), and find out whether the level accurately reflects the approximate age of the student (e.g. appropriate mental age or cognitive level). They may also be able to tell you about any specific issues with the BMLs' writing (e.g. they used outstanding vocabulary; they seemed to have many spelling problems, etc.). This is very important to make note of.

If the BML has attended school previously, try to get them to write about a topic they have learned about at school-something they are already familiar with and can share information about easily. This will provide you with a better understanding about their academic knowledge and how they are able to make use of reasoning, more advanced vocabulary and even the level of their writing. You can later have them translate the same piece into English if they are able.

If the BML has not been in school previously, you can get them to draw a picture and see if they know how to write their name. If you think they have knowledge of literacy you can have them try to write about something they already know a great deal about. For example, maybe they know about a particular animal, a sport or a tradition. This can prompt more descriptive, thoughtful and organized writing and can better reflect their cognitive knowledge. Asking them to write about something simple, like their family or what they "like" will not always give you the best insight into the level of their thinking or reasoning skills.

After collecting the writing samples, this information should be analyzed and shared with other teachers involved with the BML.

In some cases, the initial assessment you do may not be totally accurate. Since BMLs are in an unfamiliar, perhaps slightly stressful situation, they may not perform to the best of their ability. As a result, it is important to give them time to settle in and then reassess their reading, writing, speaking and listening and vocabulary later on.

In the case of refugee students or new immigrants, they may need much longer to settle-in since they can experience culture shock. As a result, it will not be appropriate to assess them until they are comfortable with the routines of the classroom. The amount of time that could take should be based on observations of the BML. It can be difficult to make predictions about how long that can take. There may be other social/emotional issues to address that are more important. Ensuring that you assess the BML under the right conditions is vital in getting an accurate picture of their skills and abilities.

STEP 4: OBSERVE THE STUDENT IN DIFFERENT ACTIVITIES AND SETTINGS

This step is important in providing you with information that can highlight how the BML is settling-in to their new school and class. Observations can be done by the regular class teacher, specialist teacher or counselor. Teachers should take notes on BMLs' language use, their ability to interact with other students as well as their participation in lessons. Any other significant behaviours should also be noted.

STEP 5: MAKE A DECISION ABOUT IDENTIFICATION

Once you have made a decision and have carefully identified the student as a bilingual or multilingual learner, be sure to collaborate, cross-check and share this information with your team members.

Use your collected information and student data to determine their vocabulary stage and set some short and long-term goals for them. It is important to have additional input from others when setting these up.

You will also need to get in-touch with the BML's parents and keep them updated about your observations, identification and support. Invite them to a parent education session and share information about bilingualism and multilingualism. Offer suggestions about how they can best support their children's MT and English acquisition at home.

Be sure to provide parents with a consent form that will inform them that their child may receive a variety of additional supports at the school.

LEGAL FORMALITIES

In some schools or school districts, there are particular policies and procedures for identifying BMLs based on legal guidelines. Additional (standardized) language proficiency tests may also be required, especially in the US.

The results of these tests are used to determine what level of support BMLs are legally entitled to within their school. In some cases, this is determined for a specified number of years (e.g. 3 years) based on funding or other factors. In some countries, there are caps on how long a BML can be given extra support, or specific criteria around when they should be "exited" from programs. In many cases, these guidelines are not always sound, especially since we know that BMLs go through specific stages where they may need more support than at other times. This can mean BMLs are exited around the same time they are transitioning to CALP and as we know, this is the time when many are in need of more support, not less.

HOW LONG BEFORE BMLs NEED TO BE "EXITED" FROM SUPPORT?

As mentioned, this question is more appropriate for specific places or school districts where certain laws govern school procedures and policies for BMLs. In our opinion, BMLs should always remain on the BML register of the school even if they are not actively receiving support. Why? Because the development of bilingualism and multilingualism is an ongoing journey, often taking many years and spanning across a student's school career. BMLs can (and likely will) require varying levels of support at different stages of their development. Even BMLs with advanced levels of English proficiency can require support to cope with the increasing demands of the curriculum at later stages. The nature of support they require may change. For instance, students may require assistance from time-to-time in order to acquire specific skills like: reading strategies, exam preparedness or advanced writing skills, for example.

The research shows that even BMLs who have attained high levels of language proficiency in English may still struggle with academic vocabulary or more advanced writing skills. Recognizing this fact within your school's policies will allow you and your team to deliver support to BMLs whenever you feel it is needed and in the most flexible and impactful way possible.

All teachers and pertinent staff within the school should be aware of identified BMLs. They should receive access to information about BMLs that will help them differentiate their curriculum to better meet students' needs. Also, making staff aware that a particular student is identified as a BML can help them better understand why that student may struggle at any stage of their learning trajectory.

THERE IS NO ONE "TYPICAL" BML: UNDERSTANDING DIVERSITY IN BMLs

Within our own practice, we have found it helpful to extend our descriptions of BMLs further in order to gain a greater depth of understanding about their profiles and specific needs. Factors such as: MT literacy, traumatic experiences or special needs can play a significant role in a BML's learning.

We know that BMLs are an extremely complex population who cannot easily be described in general terms. Knowing this can help educators dig a little deeper into BMLs' backgrounds in order to gain a better insight into the factors that can affect their learning. This will help to plan supports, set priorities and focused goals. It can also help you to tap into resources and external services or advise parents about their child's language and learning.

Our initial assessment of BMLs should include as much background information as possible. From there, we can make sound decisions based on the bigger picture. We can consider the BML's prioritized needs, even if they are outside our own area of expertise.

We should always feel empowered to consult with other colleagues and professionals. They may be inside the school or even work as external practitioners. They may be able to provide alternative perspectives or advice about particular BMLs.

We have noticed patterns within the wider BML population. These patterns have led us to identify a few prominent "types" of BMLs that have stood out. By recognizing the different types of BMLs, we are not aiming to "categorize" or "label" them, but are simply trying to gain a better focus of their needs and ultimately, find out what works best for them.

Since BMLs' particular needs can often come across as elusive to teachers and professionals, it is important to help demystify aspects of their language and learning as much as possible. It can be common for some BMLs to be referred to special education because teachers have simply not understood their underlying issues that relate to language acquisition. In many cases, these issues can explain why BMLs are "not progressing."

Through our work, we have observed BMLs displaying one or several of these characteristics: they are MT literate or have no MT literacy; they may be considered a young BML, they might have practical language proficiency, be a BML with special needs, come from a background where they have had no/disrupted schooling or they may simply have another English dialect. Having access to, and knowing all of this information can help you to better understand and observe a BML's specific learning or behavioural needs, both inside and outside the classroom.

MT Literate BMLs

MT Literate BMLs have typically developed a strong grasp of their MT and have achieved the foundations of literacy in their language for at least 2-3 years after kindergarten (around 8 years of age). They know how to read and write. These students have an advantage because they can use their MT and literacy knowledge to support their developing English language and concept learning. Depending on their age, these BMLs might even be able to independently access learning materials about class content in their MT. This can have a very positive impact on their in-class learning, especially if they are at an early stage of foundational English. These students can transfer their knowledge of literacy once they already know what reading and writing is all about in their own language. These BMLs should continue their MT language learning while in the English-medium school, even if it is only through a weekend or after-school class. This can also help put them on the right path to becoming a balanced bilingual.

No MT Literacy

BMLs with *No MT Literacy* have a foundation of oral language in their MT which can pave the way for vocabulary transfer from their MT to English. This can greatly support concept learning in the classroom, especially once they translate new words into already-known words in their MT. They may have previously had some level of early literacy exposure in their own language but it was not continued, often as a result of moving either from one country to another or from their MT-medium school to the English-medium school.

English literacy may take longer than it would for a *MT Literate* BML, especially because of the fact that they need to learn the basic concepts of literacy, like: phonemic awareness, word decoding, concepts of print, etc. that they do not already have active knowledge about through their MT language. These students are *learning literacy* and *about literacy* for the first time.

It is helpful to educate parents about the importance of continuing their child's MT and MT literacy. If possible, the BML should be encouraged to develop their MT literacy through additional classes, summer programs, or even through parent instruction. BMLs with solid MT proficiency in their oral language may feel the disadvantage of not being able to read or write in their MT later on, especially if they want to return to their country of origin or work in a bilingual environment.

YOUNG BMLS

As we have already learned, *Young BMLs* who came to English-medium schooling around early primary can be adversely impacted in their MT language development, especially if they were exposed to English extensively (e.g. at school and at home) as compared to their own MT. Since these BMLs do not have the advantage of solidifying their MT to a strong level before being fully immersed in the English-medium school, this can be a detriment to their academic learning. While their MT English peers have already solidified around 4,000-5,000 vocabulary words which are constantly being reinforced and expanded upon (in kindergarten and early primary school), the *Young BML* is continually trying to catch-up.

If their MT is not continued within the home environment, then this can create even more of a challenge for them. While the gap between the *Young BML* and their NS peers might be perceived to be smaller (since the learning expectations are not as challenging at this stage), we know that these early years are critical for vocabulary development. These BMLs may seem to pick up early literacy concepts and conversational language easily but they can experience an observable lag in their literacy once the information becomes more complex later on.

It is essential that parents receive education about the importance of continuing the MT in the home and if at all possible, continuing them onto MT literacy instruction. This can help to build a strong vocabulary foundation for the English language to "hook" onto. Some people may wrongly suggest that the *Young BML* should not learn their MT literacy until after they have mastered English literacy, but learning literacy for a child who is already achieving typical language in their MT is actually the next logical step for them.

As a result of so many erroneous beliefs and practices about *Young BMLs* (e.g. young children learn English better; discontinuing support once the student seems orally fluent, etc.), it is important that these BMLs get put onto the "right track" immediately. Ensuring teachers, parents and other professionals have the right access to quality information about *Young BMLs* and their language development is essential in order to put an end to misinformation about this particular group of BMLs. An intensive vocabulary focus along with language and literacy-rich environments (both in English and the MT if possible) are necessary elements for providing the solid foundation that these BMLs require.

PRACTICAL PROFICIENCY

At the same time as we discuss the importance of the MT, we must also identify a very complex BML. This is the student with *Practical Proficiency*. From our own experience, we have noticed these students often come from very multilingual environments where different languages may be spoken or heard on a daily basis. The student may not necessarily have *one dominant language* that is identified as their MT, but might operate very functionally using the *full variety* of their languages.

This BML's language repertoire may perfectly support them within the context of their own culture and home country; however, once taken out of that context, their individual languages may not demonstrate typical, age-appropriate norms when comparing them to other speakers of the same language(s) within the new context or environment.

In this case, there is potential for the individual to build on their language(s) further. Parents can be encouraged to help their child gain greater mastery in *at least one* of their MT languages, carefully considering the language(s) they want to nurture or the language that could be the most useful (or meaningful) for the child within their new community. For example, if the child already had some basic knowledge of Hindi and two other languages which are not widely spoken in their new country, the parents might decide to have their child focus on mastering Hindi. There could be more opportunities for growing this language, especially with numerous Hindi-speakers in their community.

We have also observed other students who fit within this group, although their situation is quite different to the previous scenario. These are BMLs who have not had the opportunity to gain a solid grasp of their family's MT language, or any other language to culturally-expected, age-appropriate norms. To be clear, it is not that these students are *incapable* of learning their MT for any reason; it is simply an issue with the amount of MT exposure they have had access to. These BMLs can use their language functionally and purposefully within day-to-day contexts but they do not yet possess the expected proficiency levels in comparison to same language peers their age. These students have good potential for further mastery of their language (and literacy) but they must first have greater exposure and opportunity to use their language(s).

Parents should be encouraged to pursue new language-learning opportunities for their child but they must be approached gently about this often-sensitive issue.

Schools and professionals must also be extremely diligent in understanding these BMLs' unique issues. In many cases, they are referred to special education because of potential language and learning disorders. If they undergo standardized or psychoeducational testing, they can easily receive "false-positive" diagnoses for language disorders or learning disabilities because these tests are not designed for this unique student population.

Expatriate families also need to be aware of the importance of consistency in maintaining their language(s) while abroad. Many families move frequently between countries where the dominant language can change and education in their own MT is not always available. As a result, children may switch back and forth between English and another language(s) and this can create challenges for their developing language(s), especially if they are not solidifying at least one language as their MT.

Again, education is of vital importance. Parents need to know the value of their own MT, and should have opportunities to learn more about building their child's language abilities. Bilingual school programs (e.g. MT/English) are an excellent solution for this. They provide students with the opportunity to develop language and literacy skills in both languages and without the need to choose one over the other.

Within the classroom, since it is common for these particular BMLs to be highlighted for special education because of perceived learning or speech and language disorders, teachers need to take a very close look at BMLs' early language development through interviews with parents and caregivers. This can give the teacher or professional a better sense as to whether the child has had enough opportunity to develop a strong MT. If not, then the perceived learning challenges may point back to this issue.

If parents are not able to support their MT within the home or there are no other opportunities for the BML to further develop their language(s) for any reason, then it is even more important that they receive strong vocabulary and literacy support to help them gain a solid working language in English. Over time, the BML can then build up English as their main thinking language. This will provide them with a foundation for their complex cognitive and learning experiences. These BMLs will need consistent and ongoing monitoring throughout their education to ensure that they continue to develop solid English language and academic skills.

BMLs with Special Needs

BMLs with Special Needs can exist across an entire spectrum, from giftedness to intellectual disabilities. These special needs must be diagnosed by a psychologist or physician and the BML will likely require some form of accommodations or modifications to their educational program. In most cases, this is done through the *Individual Education Plan* (I.E.P.). Most diagnoses fall into one or more of these categories:

- Medical and physical disabilities (cerebral palsy, epilepsy, etc.)
- Behavioural disorders (autism, anxiety disorder, obsessive-compulsive disorder, etc.)
- Cognitive (intellectual disabilities, Down Syndrome, giftedness, etc.)
- Learning disabilities (reading disorder, dysgraphia, etc.)
- Speech and language disorders (auditory processing disorder, speech delays, etc.)
- Multiple (mix of disabilities or disorders)

In many of these cases, teachers are faced with the more subtle task of trying to differentiate whether their BML is not making progress because of their level of English, or because of an underlying learning disorder. We will discuss this in greater detail further on in this chapter since there are many important considerations, not only for the teacher but for the school, parents and other professionals as well.

BMLs can also be above-average in intellectual ability or have other outstanding talents (e.g. music, arts or science) in one or more areas. It is known that BMLs are often under-represented when it comes to being identified as "gifted or talented" as well as qualifying for additional programs or learning opportunities (Aguirre, 2003). Teachers need to look beyond language and cultural barriers in order to uncover BMLs who may have unique, untapped potential that should be nurtured. These BMLs should have equal opportunities to extend or deepen their learning through differentiated instruction, learning contracts or special programs if available.

For any BML attending a government or public school who has a diagnosed special need, there will likely be specific federal/state/provincial policies that outline policies and processes for identification and provisions for them. Teachers can often feel overwhelmed when it comes to implementing IEP goals in the classroom, so chosen goals should be realistic, manageable and should be the skills that will have the most impact in the shortest amount of time. For example, if the general goal is to "increase the BML's reading levels," this will need to be more clearly defined and broken down to fit within specific time-frames. In this case, the teacher could focus on 1-2 skills per month and try to make steady progress to mastery-levels in that amount of time. They might instead focus on having the BML first master "identifying letter sounds" and then have them work on building simple "c-v-c" (consonant/vowel/consonant – *cat*) words with these letters until they demonstrate mastery. Then, they can have the BML learn about "long and short vowels" to build onto that skill later on, using it to help them decode more complex words, for example. Goals and objectives should always be succinct and should be given the right amount of focused attention and time; otherwise the paper they are written on will be wasted. Sometimes 5 or 10 minutes per day is all that is needed to focus on a specific goal or objective. The key is to be focused, use available resources and create impact that can be transferred to independent learning.

No/Disrupted Schooling

Typically when we speak of BMLs with *No/Disrupted Schooling*, we are referring to those students who have come from war-torn countries or are refugees or migrants. In any of these situations, BMLs will likely need a good deal of time to settle into the new, unfamiliar environment of the school before being expected to start learning intensively. We will learn more about refugee issues later on in this chapter, but for now it is important to know that these BMLs will require more involved emotional supports that can be provided by teachers, counsellors and even other students as buddies within the class or school.

A thorough interview with parents or guardians is important in order to fully understand this BML's unique experiences when it comes to their social, emotional and learning skills. Finding out how much, if any schooling the BML has had (especially in regards to literacy and mathematics) is important. They will likely need intensive literacy and mathematics support in order to gain a basic foundation.

English Dialect

BMLs who speak with another *English Dialect* will require specific support to help them recognize the similarities and differences between their own dialect and the Standard English which is learned in the school and other formal environments. It is important to honour these BMLs' dialects and recognize it as a link to their identities and culture. They should have opportunities to use their dialect flexibly within the school environment and should also be encouraged to advance their Standard English with some instructional techniques, specifically those that focus on developing academic vocabulary words.

Diversity within the BML Population

MT Literate	No MT Literacy	Young BML	Practical Proficiency	BML with Special Needs	No/Disrupted Schooling	English Dialect
Characteristics These students have established literacy skills in their MT up to a *minimum age of 8 years* (sometimes more depending on the number of years they spent in MT-medium education). They possess various levels of English language.	*Characteristics* These students have established their MT to age-appropriate oral levels, but have not yet developed the foundations of basic literacy in that MT language.	*Characteristics* These students have had a good foundation in their MT oral language, but have not had much (or any) literacy instruction in the MT yet. They come to the English medium environment between the ages of 3-7 years.	*Characteristics* These students may have either: 1) *several languages in their repertoire and with various proficiencies;* 2) *some functional MT language skills but not fully-developed to age-appropriate levels.* Proficiency/(ies) may be practical for daily life but not yet fully developed for academic purposes.	*Characteristics* These students have varying levels of English but they also have an identified special need. For example, a BML student may also have autism, Down Syndrome, a learning disability or even giftedness.	*Characteristics* These are students who have never attended school, or who may have had disrupted schooling due to war, trauma, poverty, etc. They may or may not be refugees. They do not have much exposure to academics. They may have had some exposure to English with varying levels.	*Characteristics* These students may or may not speak another MT. They may have varying levels of English and have had exposure to a dialect that is different to the Standard English being used at school. They may struggle with academic English and switching between dialects.
CONSIDERATIONS: **May require** literacy support to develop foundational skills **Should use** their MT to support their English and concept learning (transfer) **Should have** opportunities to use their MT literacy in class (for projects, readings, writing, etc.) **Encourage** them to continue their MT literacy-learning **Needs** to understand similarities and differences between English and their MT	*CONSIDERATIONS:* **May require** intensive literacy support for foundational skills **If there is** another student who speaks the same language, they can be encouraged to translate when required, or to work together with the student in their language **These students should be** encouraged to develop their MT literacy through literacy classes	*CONSIDERATIONS:* **These students need** an intensive and rich vocabulary focus **Parents should be** encouraged to continue speaking the MT at home **May** initially pick up phonics easily but may have some lags later on in the elementary school which can mimic a learning problem; intervention may be necessary **Help** students develop and maintain links between English and their MT	*CONSIDERATIONS:* **Clearly** understand language repertoire **Educate** parents in the value of the MT(s); refer families to MT classes or providers **Will benefit** from *ongoing,* intensive English literacy and vocabulary support **Additional** time and support to explain, understand and express concepts **May** *seem to have* other learning issues and can obtain "false positives" for LDs or language disorders	*CONSIDERATIONS:* **Create** an IEP that has long-term goals and shorter objectives **Select** a few of the most high-impact skills to focus on accelerating then move onto others **Gain** support and recommendations from colleagues and other professionals **Provide** plenty of opportunities for repetition and over-practice of skills in context **Break** skills/concepts into smaller chunks	*CONSIDERATIONS:* **Provide** them with social and emotional support to cope with the new environment over time (ie: a buddy) **Be aware** of emotional "triggers" in school **May have** *PTSD* **Link** the family to external services **Provide** intensive literacy support to teach early literacy skills and concepts once settled **Build** cultural and personal connections **Explicitly** teach routines, schedules	*CONSIDERATIONS:* **Honour** the student's home dialect and see it as a reflection of their culture and identity **Help** them recognize differences between their dialect and Standard English **Teach** them how they can switch between their dialect and the Standard dialect for academic and social situations **Provide** ongoing support for vocabulary development

CASE STUDY STUDENTS

STUDENT 1: DEMIR

✓ MT LITERATE

SUMMARY:

- Turkish
- Age 8
- Family has immigrated to England
- Turkish MT with some knowledge of English
- Attended private school in Turkey
- Has age-appropriate literacy skills in MT
- FL3

- Demir is reported to have good MT language and literacy as per his previous school reports; he has received excellent grades in all his subjects
- Demir had regular English-language classes twice weekly in Turkey but still has some gaps in phonemic awareness skills and vocabulary
- There are no students who speak Turkish at his school
- He will be receiving short-term literacy support in order to fill in the gaps in phonics and reading comprehension skills as well as some vocabulary instruction
- He is enrolled in external Turkish language classes once weekly

STUDENT 2: HASAN

✓ **NO/DISRUPTED SCHOOLING**   ✓ **NO MT LITERACY**

SUMMARY:

- Somali
- Age 15
- Family has refugee Status in Australia
- MT is Somali, also speaks some Arabic
- Disrupted schooling history, no MT Literacy
- FL1

- Translator has reported that Hasan has well-developed oral language in his Somali MT and some basic knowledge of Arabic
- His family has been referred to a community organization that supports refugees, as well as a Somali Community Association
- He has never attended formal school
- He seems to have some signs of Post-Traumatic Stress Disorder (PTSD) and will take part in a group therapy session at a refugee center
- The BML specialist teacher has been supporting Hassan in understanding scheduling and has set him up with a buddy who also speaks Somali and English
- He attends mathematics and English support classes to accelerate his learning, specifically for BMLs at school
- The teaching team has met to determine the priorities for Hassan which will include: settling in, accelerated learning for math and literacy in his specialist classes
- He will attend MT literacy classes at the Somali Association once weekly
- His progress will be monitored and the BML specialist will adjust support inside and outside of the classroom as required

STUDENT 3: PRITTI

✓ **PRACTICAL PROFICIENCY**   ✓ **YOUNG BML**   ✓ **DIALECT**

SUMMARY:

- Age 10
- From India
- Family has lived in a few different countries (Saudi Arabia, Egypt and UAE) before immigrating to Canada
- Speaks a mix of: Hindi, Guajarati and English (Indian dialect) and some exposure to Arabic
- Received some early literacy in Gujarati and English (alphabet only) before moving from India
- Was educated in English-medium schools but in different curricula/ education systems (one British, one American school)
- FL4

- Pritti's parents have reported that English is the main language spoken in the home, but that Pritti can also understand and speak some Gujarati (her parents' language) to relatives, including some Hindi which was widely spoken in her community in India
- Her parents spoke a mix of Gujarati and English to her prior to her joining kindergarten, but once she went into English-medium kindergarten, they began speaking English to her the majority of the time
- She attended kindergarten in English while in India and then continued English-medium education in the other countries; Arabic was learned as an additional language through ongoing lessons in school
- Pritti speaks an Indian dialect form of English
- She has a good base of literacy skills but reads and writes below grade-level

- She is near grade-level for mathematics
- She will require literacy support to accelerate her reading and writing skills in English
- Pritti's parents are not interested in continuing her MT development, they are satisfied with maintaining her oral language through the home but want her dominant language to become English; they are willing to invest in having her take additional classes or have a tutor

UNDERSTANDING BMLs WITH SPECIAL NEEDS

Identifying *BMLs with Special Needs* can be a complex and sensitive issue. Unless a BML has obvious cognitive or physical concerns within the classroom it can be challenging for a classroom teacher to put their finger on whether the learner's "lack of progress" is a result of their level of English language proficiency, a learning disorder or even both.

Research as far back as the 1970s (and mainly from the US), shows that many BMLs are over-represented within special education departments in schools. This is a growing concern, largely because it signals a problem in identification and placement of BMLs who may be inaccurately or inappropriately assessed and diagnosed. This then becomes an issue of human rights.

The under-representation of specific cultural groups in special education should also be questioned, since it may mean there are some students who genuinely need special education services who are not receiving it. For example, in US schools, Asian-American students are under-represented in special education settings. Both situations of over-representation and under-representation require a need for clearer and more specific guidelines for teachers and other professionals to follow when dealing with students who may potentially have a learning issue or special need.

REASONS WHY BMLS ARE OFTEN MISDIAGNOSED AND REFERRED TO SPECIAL EDUCATION

- Teachers do not have adequate training to distinguish between typical language acquisition processes in BMLs and disabilities (Zamora, 2007)
- There is a lack of effective instruction for BMLs within mainstream education classes; there is also an absence of pre-referral interventions (Shepard, Linn & Brown, 2007)
- Interventions are used inconsistently or sporadically (Klingner & Artiles, 2003)
- The assessments used are inequitable and/or inappropriately used with this population of students (Shepard, Linn & Brown, 2007)
- Even BMLs who have been placed in special education services can suffer negative consequences and can actually perform worse over time (Wilkinson & Ortiz, 1986)

CASE IN POINT

Ana is now in Year 5 at her school in England. She has been at the school for the last 3 years since moving with her family from Spain. She has had some additional support from a specialist teacher who was providing her with small-group, content-based support. However, her teachers are now concerned that she is not progressing at the same rate as the other BMLs in her English language development, and that she is not able to easily retain information she has previously been taught. Since Ana is generally a shy student and still reluctant to speak much in large group situations, it is difficult for her teachers to understand whether she is not understanding or simply choosing not to participate.

Ana's parents have not indicated any difficulties with her health, early development or social/emotional issues. They speak Spanish at home together and report that Ana has several interests she is pursuing outside of school, such as dancing and swimming. When asked about her language-level in Spanish and if it seems typical for her age, her parents report that she is speaking with a well-developed vocabulary in Spanish and even knows how to read and write as a result of attending additional Spanish classes outside of school. They are not concerned about her learning or development at this stage, however, they have spoken to Ana about her views of school and she has reported that she does not like school and that she feels she has no friends. Her parents feel that she is not motivated at school, likely because things do not "come easy for her". They are fine with the school taking action to further explore her learning challenges and have even offered to take her to a private psychologist for an assessment.

What should Ana's teachers do next? Should they refer her for the psycho-educational assessment with a psychologist? Is it warranted?

KEEP IN MIND...Typically when a BML does not thrive in the classroom environment, it often indicates:

1. The teaching and learning environment is not meeting their learning needs (e.g. they are not encouraged to use their MT in the learning process, learning is not scaffolded enough to meet their needs or they do not have access to additional support).

2. There are other root causes of the BML's challenges which do not relate to their actual ability or potential for learning. These can include cultural and linguistic differences that can have an impact on a BML's information processing, comprehension, ability to recall or retrieve information as well as their ability to sustain attention and follow instructions.

3. The BML does in fact have a special need which is impacting their learning and academic progress.

The solution for 1) and 2) is to improve the teaching and learning to reflect the specific needs of BMLs. Since BMLs are expected to adapt and conform to the expectations and culture of the school, community and new country, it can often be a case of "too much too fast". Instructional approaches should make use of the BML's MT in order to help them cope with the language barrier.

If the BML does have a special need, they will need to have access to specific accommodations and modifications as well as an *Individual Education Plan (IEP)* to target specific goals and objectives.

A PRE-REFERRAL MODEL FOR IDENTIFYING BMLs WITH POTENTIAL SPECIAL NEEDS

If a teacher suspects that a BML may have a learning disorder and wants to further explore the issue, they should first follow these 5 steps:

STEP 1: Parent involvement is key to helping teachers understand the BML's cultural and linguistic background as well as their relevant health and medical history. Teachers should ensure this information is collected prior to the observation process. Possible medical conditions which could be contributing to the BMLs learning or behavioural challenges should be ruled out, especially problems with vision and auditory acuity.

STEP 2: The teacher should assume that the lack of progress does not have to do with the student, but with the teaching or learning that is not meeting the BMLs' needs. At this point, the teacher should gather as much information as possible, through observation of the BML in the classroom context and in a variety of learning situations. Then, over a few weeks or even months, they should create new learning opportunities for the BML, developing more creative approaches for them to demonstrate their learning. For example, allowing them to use their MT during content learning, providing them with translation tools, applying more whole class, group or pair discussions to work out problems; allowing them to demonstrate a concept being taught through hands-on activities (and then assessing how well they understood the concepts) will provide good information about their learning. Assessments should include authentic means such as: anecdotal observations, oral assessments, performance tasks including use of the MT for writing or communicating about a topic or concept. Responses to specific instructional approaches can be more closely examined through a "dynamic assessment."

DYNAMIC ASSESSMENT

Dynamic Assessment (DA) refers to a test-intervention-retest situation where you work with a student on specific, targeted skills in order to:

- Make direct, quick impact in one area
- Gain further information about the student's ability to learn
- Allow students to demonstrate how they learn in a more controlled situation

---

When teachers are concerned about a BML's progress or ability to learn, they should select a specific skill to isolate and work with through a DA. For example, if the teacher observes through an oral reading situation that their BML is not able to grasp decoding of 3 letter words (CVC words), then this observation would serve as the initial test. The teacher should make note of these observations and follow-up to work with them at another time for the "intervention." In this situation, the aim is to focus and teach these skills, observing the student's accuracy rates, their style of learning, rate of learning, etc. Then, after this intervention phase, the teacher will retest the student on the skill to assess their learning. This is a more natural, reliable and informative way to assess BMLs when there are initial concerns about their ability to learn and absorb information. There is also flexibility to teach them in different ways and then observe their responses to the varied approaches. DA should be used by teachers who are concerned that their students are "not learning" or "not progressing" since it provides much more detailed and valuable information to work with.

STEP 3: Specialist teachers working with the BML should support the classroom teacher to create an optimal learning environment within their classes. They too should gather more information through observation and direct interaction with the BML over time and then share this information with the class teacher. This will give a better sense as to whether the BML experiences difficulties within certain tasks, teachers, classes or subjects. A more formal team meeting is required to share information about the BML as well as to ascertain whether specific changes to the learning environment or instruction is all that is needed or whether further steps should to be explored.

Any in-school specialists or consultants (i.e. special education teachers, psychologists, etc.) should observe the BML in the natural learning environment over a sustained period of time and within a variety of learning situations. They may work with the BML through dynamic assessment. They should take notes and build on already-existing data. They should assist the teacher through their professional recommendations to help them improve the teaching and instruction for that BML.

STEP 4: The BML's progress should be discussed at a referral team meeting made up of key staff and/or involved specialists. This meeting can include a senior member of the administration such as the principal or deputy-principal of the school, school counselor or school nurse (if necessary). Teachers should be open to and provided with additional support from more experienced teaching staff to help develop and design a learning environment that will maximize the BML's progress.

STEP 5: Finally, after a thorough and exhaustive process based on evidence, classroom observations and data-collection on the BML's responses to instruction and differentiation, there should be very clear signs as to whether the child has benefited from the recommendations and interventions. If there are still concerns after this point, then the student should be referred for additional assessment from a qualified, educational psychologist who understands issues related to BMLs and second (additional) language acquisition.

TESTING AND ASSESSMENT

Traditional assessment procedures are inappropriate for accurately identifying BMLs with special needs, and often misdiagnose "bilingualism" as a disability (Figueroa, 2000).

The over-representation of BMLs in special education provides evidence that testing procedures simply cannot differentiate between a disability and bilingualism as a cause of learning difficulties (Figuerao 2000; Figuerao & Hernandez 2000; Valdez & Figueroa 1994).

Most psychological assessment tools currently used to assess learning disabilities were originally designed for native English speakers. This means the assessments are linguistically and culturally-biased if they are used with a population that is different to the one they were originally meant for. For example, if a math question asks a student a question about "dimes" or "pennies" but the student comes from a country that does not have dimes or pennies or has never been exposed to these concepts, it is highly-likely that they will get the question incorrect. In this way, many tests are not accurately measuring BMLs' real knowledge or potential. Despite this, standardized tests and assessments are still being inappropriately used with the BML population. Even when translation or interpreting is used with BMLs during the assessment process, this has been found to negatively impact and discredit both the reliability and validity of the standardization. Therefore, the resulting diagnoses based on these test results are not valid (Sanchez-Boyce, 2000).

In the US in 1979, the court case *Larry vs. Riles*, saw a judge order an injunction against using any IQ tests that did not take into account the linguistic background and cultural experiences of the BML being tested. These students could not be placed in any special education programs based on IQ tests that had not been officially approved by the court (Valdes and Figueroa, 1994).

In our experience working with BMLs, it is very common for us to see these learners over-represented in special education services. Many have educational psychology reports with a resulting diagnosis of "dyslexia" or some related learning disability. In almost all of the cases we have seen over the years, these BMLs have improved significantly with the right interventions. In many of these cases, BMLs were still at the foundational stages of their English language proficiency and had achieved good oral fluency, often causing the psychologist to mistake them for a native speaker.

It is important for teachers and other professionals to understand that the normal phases of second (additional) language acquisition can mimic a learning disorder, especially because a BML's written work and processing skills may appear to be problematic in comparison to their oral language proficiency. Being aware of this important consideration can help teachers and professionals examine BMLs' issues with open eyes.

In the case below, a 5 year-old multilingual student was referred for a psychoeducational assessment. The psychologist was aware that the child had 2 mother-tongue languages (shared with each parent) and had only attended English-medium school for the past year. The student had already acquired some BICS in English with approximately 1,000 receptive words.

Despite knowing this background information, it did not appear that the psychologist had considered the student's language background to be very significant in explaining why some of these scores might have been low in comparison to a native English speaker of the same age. After the testing sessions were completed, the parents had a meeting and were told that their child was considered "at risk" for dyslexia and other learning disorders if they did not follow-up on the recommendations.

REASON FOR REFERRAL:

████ was referred to us by his school for full evaluation of his cognitive abilities and academic levels. Both his school and parents have concerns.

████ finds it difficult to pay attention when the teacher is speaking and is also significantly behind his peers in language-related skills. Moreover, he has challenges following instructions and recalling messages. He also has difficulties responding appropriately to *"WH" questions* (who, what, where, when, etc.). He does not yet differentiate colours and has not yet acquired all letter sounds. He also struggles with maths concepts as well as spelling and early reading skills.

Based on these results, the following is recommended for

1. A hearing and vision test
2. Further assessment with a Speech and Language therapist in order to evaluate his language skills (both expressive and receptive) and to support him with comprehension and articulation.
3. Tutoring/1-1 Learning Assistance for Literacy, Maths and Writing

Sections of a 5-year old, multilingual child's educational psychology report

Many BMLs do have gaps in their English language, this is normal. As a result, this often translates to low scores and "false positives" for learning, behaviour or communication disorders on a variety of standardized intellectual and achievement tests.

It is very important that psychologists and teachers understand that learning/language disorders should only be diagnosed by a qualified psychologist or speech therapist who understands BMLs and the problematic use of standardized tests for this particular student population.

This option should only be explored *if there is no other reason* to explain why the individual's learning is below the expected levels. If the student is a BML, then one potential reason for their low achievement is already known.

When BMLs are tested with tools designed for native-English speakers, they often show these "false-positives" for learning or other types of disorders. These tests do state that they are not suitable for use with BMLs in their administration guides but if the psychologist or therapist is not cautious or does not ask the *right questions* during their initial parent consultation, they may very well overlook the fact that the student is not a native-English speaker. Their test results may be unreliable or even falsely point to the presence of a learning disorder.

In our previous example with the 5-year old boy above, the psychologist's full report showed extremely low scores in all of the *language-based* areas; however, the *performance* tasks highlighted average scores. This certainly makes sense: because he is still developing the foundations of his BICS, he scored well-below the expected norms. He was more successful with the "hands-on" or "language-reduced" sections of the assessment. The psychologist interpreted these results as she should for a NS English child. This then triggered a set of recommendations to the parents that indicated their child was at risk for learning and language problems if he was not given academic and speech/language therapy. You can imagine how these parents felt receiving this news about their 5-year old boy who had only been in school for one year.

BMLs should not be tested in English with tools for native English speakers. Sometimes classroom teachers or specialists who refer a BML for psychoeducational assessment are aware of this and ask the parents to have the child assessed in their MT instead. Figuerao (2000), states that it may also be inappropriate for bilingual students to be assessed in their MTs. Since they have now been educated or instructed in another language other than their own MT, even if they are tested in that MT language, the results can also be skewed.

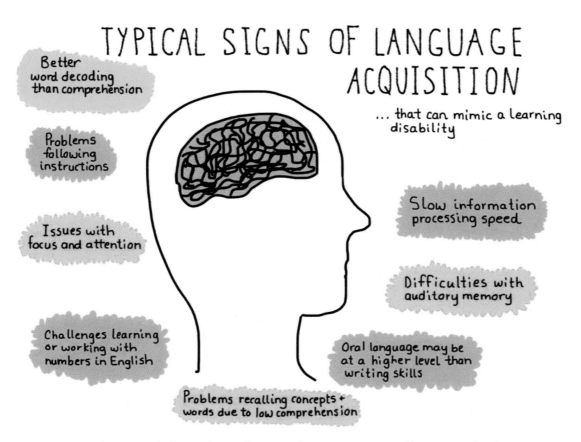

TYPICAL SIGNS OF LANGUAGE ACQUISITION

... that can mimic a learning disability

Better word decoding than comprehension

Problems following instructions

Issues with focus and attention

Challenges learning or working with numbers in English

Problems recalling concepts + words due to low comprehension

Slow information processing speed

Difficulties with auditory memory

Oral language may be at a higher level than writing skills

Caution must be exercised when making judgements about a BML's potential language and/or learning issues

This presents a dilemma. If a mainstream classroom teacher suspects that a BML is not progressing as they should and they would like to know how best to understand whether it is simply their level of English language development or whether it could be a learning disability—how should they proceed?

Caution is needed before moving forward with a battery of pscyho-educational assessments. Hudspath-Niemi & Conroy (2013) report that many educational psychologists over-rely on BMLs' test scores. This can cause them to narrow their perspective without carefully considering the broader context of the BML's profile. Since BMLs are not easily understood, test scores alone are not likely to capture the full picture of their knowledge and experience which contributes to their learning. They cite Rhodes et. al (2005, p.167) who provides a powerful perspective on the practice of cognitive ability testing with BMLs:

> *The few current cognitive ability measures normed on culturally and linguistically diverse populations 'do not account for varying levels of proficiency in two different languages that mark bilingual students as distinct from native students or English-only speakers'. Therefore, the goal of intellectual evaluations should be on the process of learning about the student's cognitive strengths and weaknesses rather than obtaining a score. Even when administration procedures are modified, assessment tools are carefully selected, and interpreters are used, the validity of cognitive ability test results is questionable.*

They also provide suggestions for assessments that are more-appropriate for bilingual and culturally-diverse students. While non-verbal tests may be more cultural-fair or unbiased as compared to others, they are not always able to assess the full range of cognitive skills that are often needed to build a broader profile of the learner. *The Kauffman Assessment Battery for Children* (KABC-II) is recommended and is reported to be more flexible in terms of the ability to select test items that are appropriate to the learner as well as having reduced language.

Also advisable and reliable is the use of "dynamic assessment". As already mentioned, this is when an assessor will test a BML initially and then apply a "test-teach-test" approach (Hudspath-Niemi & Conroy, 2013). After testing the individual, they will teach a specific skill(s) and then make observations about how quickly the individual was able to learn along with their accuracy rate and other important observations. Psychologists may also wish to use this approach within a variety of learning conditions in order to gain a better picture of the BML and their learning. They can then report their findings in a narrative format.

NON-VERBAL TESTS	KAUFFMAN ASSESSMENT BATTERY FOR CHILDREN (2ND EDITION, KABC-II)
<ul><li>More culture-fair; but still have some cultural bias</li><li>Less discriminatory</li><li>Do not provide a complete picture of the student's potential</li><li>Can evaluate: fluid reasoning, visual processing, short-term memory, processing speed</li><li>Cannot identify issues with: comprehension, auditory processing, long-term memory, retrieval</li></ul> *Suggested Tests:*<ul><li>*Universal Non Verbal Intelligence Test (UNIT)*</li><li>*Leiter International Performance Scale Revised*</li><li>*Non-Verbal section of the Differential Ability Scale (2nd Edition)*</li></ul>	<ul><li>Test of cognitive ability for children between the ages of 3-18</li><li>Reduced verbal instructions and responses</li><li>Culturally-related test-questions can be eliminated</li><li>Test items that relate to verbal ability of the student can be eliminated</li></ul>

WORKING WITH REFUGEES

When working with BMLs who may be refugees, or those who have experienced war or trauma in their home country(s), it may seem extremely daunting at first. These BMLs will need a very nurturing approach to help them adapt to their new environment, culture and language.

Some suffer from long-term effects like physical or health-related issues and in some cases, disabilities due to injury or even malnutrition. Many will come with emotional scars that can only heal over time.

In one of my pre-service teaching assignments, I had my first experience working with refugees who had come to Canada to escape war-ravaged Afghanistan. During a parent-teacher interview where we sat with the father and a translator, we learned that there were 10 children in this family between the ages of 7 and 25. All of them, along with the mother, lived in a house close to the school. The father opened up and told us how his 25-year old son had never known what it was like to be a child because of all the strife he had experienced in his life. He also shared how his younger children had been shot at while trying to walk to school. Yet as this father was speaking about such traumatic and violent incidents, I could not, in my reality, imagine how anyone could come out of such an experience and still remain fully-functioning and in "one piece."

I thought about his child in my class. He was 12 years old and one would never have guessed that he had ever experienced this kind of trauma in his young life. He was high-achieving, extremely motivated, sporty and popular with the other students. He seemed to be well-adjusted and dedicated to learning. He never missed a day of school.

From this experience, I began to understand the significant role that school plays in the lives of refugees and traumatized children. School is predictable; it is safe and provides daily routines, structure and time for play. Above-all, there are caring teachers who make enormous impact through their kindness and by creating opportunities for these children to simply *be* children.

For these students, school can be a place where they start to heal from their emotional traumas. Positive experiences can start to take over traumatic ones.

Despite this, learning can still be very difficult for many refugee students due to the amount of stress they may be actively coping with and recovering from. It is a good idea to link families with appropriate support services within the community. These agencies will be able to offer resettlement services, life skills, support groups and counseling.

Children who come to school after experiencing traumatic events can find it very difficult to cope and concentrate on learning tasks. Some may have witnessed violent acts or even deaths of loved ones. They may still be processing these situations. Knowing how to approach students who have experienced these issues can be uncharted territory for the average classroom teacher.

REFUGEE EXPERIENCES

The refugee experience is dramatically different from the immigrant experience. While they may have some similar experiences when settling into their new country, refugees have often experienced extreme circumstances which can *continue* to be life-changing and traumatic. Immigrants typically choose to move to their new country and so they plan and prepare for their move and new experiences in advance. They have had the opportunity to organize themselves, make necessary arrangements and have closure. Immigrants usually have the option of returning to their home country if they choose to. In contrast, the refugee's experiences can include the following:

- Individuals may not have had a chance to deal with, or wrap up their personal business, often because they have to flee quickly; this can leave them feeling deeply unsettled and upset
- They may have lived in substandard conditions within refugee camps, sometimes for years at-a-time without basic needs, proper nutrition or medical treatment
- Education of children may have been disrupted or non-existent
- Individuals and families may have experienced trauma, loss or extreme hardship; especially related to death or disappearance of loved ones, personal property or homes
- They may have witnessed extreme or violent incidents which can leave them emotionally and psychologically traumatized and that can continue to affect their daily life, even once they are settled into their new country (e.g. post-traumatic stress disorder-PTSD)
- Children may have been separated from family members, or may have been left on their own for long periods of time
- They may feel overwhelmed, anxious or confused once they have arrived in their new country
- They may experience deep and lasting sadness knowing that they are not able to return home because of continuing strife

BC Ministry of Education, (2009)

For a teacher, the main thing to understand is the current needs of the BML in the here and now. Most children are surprisingly resilient and can move forward towards a new life if they are well-nurtured and feel safe.

When the new BML arrives at school, it is important for key school staff to make contact with the family to reinforce that the school is a caring and safe place. This is best done through an interpreter if you cannot communicate with them through English or another language.

While it is not your role to "counsel" the family or child about their ordeal, simply providing a listening ear along with a nurturing environment can help give them confidence and trust in the school. This will be one of their biggest, initial needs.

Keep in mind, children who have experienced upheaval and trauma need a consistent, predictable environment before they can even begin to learn effectively. How long it takes a child to adjust can depend on their emotional state. They may be able to follow class routines and participate in predictable events, but it may take them quite some time until they are entirely settled and able to learn and function more independently. Remember that each BML will be different so it is not always easy to predict their trajectory for settling in.

Some may also have difficulties letting their guard down, in cases where they may have had constant "fight-or-flight" reactions to dangerous situations. These BMLs may also have strong reactions to specific kinds of "triggers" that bring back harrowing memories or make them feel unsafe. For example, hearing shouting, being in a dark area, seeing police or firemen in uniforms or even hearing loud noises like fire alarms can trigger memories and lead to extreme reactions. Teachers need to be aware of any possible occurrences of these triggers and prepare the BML carefully, well in-advance. This can be an ongoing process.

There are many things that the school can do to alleviate unnecessary stress on the BML and build trust over time. Providing BMLs with a buddy who can sit beside them, take an interest in them and offer assistance is a good place to start. This can help the student feel secure and build up a sense of belonging over time. If there is a buddy who speaks the same language as the new BML, this is ideal. If they can relate to someone from the same linguistic or cultural background, they may be more relaxed and better able to understand what is happening around them. This can also serve as a "buffer" for their stress.

If the BML can forge relationships quickly, this can positively impact the time it takes for them to settle in. It may also be wise to initially pair them up with a same-sex buddy, especially because some BMLs from different cultures may not be used to mixing with peers of the opposite-sex.

They may take a long time to initially orient themselves to the routines and procedures of the school. They may not have any prior experience with toilets, pencils, technology or even the concepts or sitting down and paying attention in class. Above all, they need to have teachers who are patient, kind and understanding. If teachers themselves do not have prior experience working with refugees, they should try to find a colleague who has. This can better help them prepare, as well as give them further suggestions and ideas.

CASE IN POINT

Ashkir is a Somali boy who has recently arrived to Australia with his aunt and sister. He is 9 years old and has never been to school. Both of his parents were killed in conflict and he and his sister have directly witnessed a great deal of violence. They have recently settled in Melbourne and have been registered to attend school in one week's time. Ashkir's teacher will be Mrs. Warburton, a very experienced primary teacher who has been teaching for the last 18 years. Mrs. Warburton has other Somali children in her class and there are more throughout their school. She has taught many refugee children with good success, and so she is set to prepare herself and her class for their new arrival.

What kinds of things will she do to prepare for Ashkir's arrival into her class? How will she be able to support his smooth transition considering the traumatic events he has experienced?

HELPING NEW REFUGEES

New refugees will take time to adjust to the environment and feel safe before they can begin focusing on learning. It is important to understand some of the processes they may go through, and how you can support them within the school and classroom.

ACCULTURATION/ORIENTATION

Students are new to the school environment. They need extensive orientation to help them feel safe (a major priority), as well as build up rapport with a few of the students in their immediate environment. They need time to observe, absorb and learn about what happens at school, without any additional pressure. Many students will experience "culture shock" and will need time to adjust. A supportive and nurturing approach is required. Engaging parents as well as external support staff can help the student during this transition time.

- Teachers need to understand the full background of the BML, including any potential "triggers" they may have
- Provide a welcoming environment but be sure not to overwhelm them
- The new family should be received by a staff who is trained in handling refugee students, or if this is not possible, teachers should ensure they can speak to parents (or use a translator) about the experiences their child will have at school, stressing their safety and security
- In some cases, it may be wise to "transition" the student to school slowly, a few hours at-a-time until they feel comfortable
- Prepare your class for the new student before they arrive and remind them about how to be welcoming and how they might support the student (allow the students to offer their own suggestions around this)
- You can provide "child friendly" information about the new student to your class, especially if they are likely to need a lot of support from the teacher and other students around them; it is helpful to "frame" the situation for students without telling them too much information
- Have one or two reliable "buddies" pre-selected and help them fully understand their role before the new student arrives; ensure you choose children who are sensitive and kind and can help the student work out issues like: where to find the toilets, how to wash their hands, where to keep their belongings, etc.
- Make arrangements ahead of time for how you will handle the student's "triggers"
- You may wish to have a teacher or counselor do some "intervention" with the student (alone or with a small group of students) by giving them time out of class if necessary to simply play or unwind (e.g. drawing, playing, arts/crafts, etc.)
- Continue to provide positive social praise to the new student; help them see you are happy to have them in your class and at school
- Keep a close eye on the student since they may not realize that they cannot leave the school or classroom at first
- In the beginning, you may want to keep pictures of important things close at-hand: toilet, food, water, important activities or events, etc. in order for the student to communicate immediately if they need to
- Learn a few words in the student's MT to build a connection with them; try to educate yourself about the culture of your new BML so that you can better understand them
- Ensure the family is linked to external support services that are available in the community

- Try to introduce them to other students who may be from the same place or speak the same language
- If same-language peers are present in the class or school, have them translate messages to the student when necessary, or simply share something with them in their language (e.g. provide positive praise)
- You may need to keep in close communication with the translator so they can speak about any concerns or information about the student's general progress to the parent/guardian directly. Parents may worry a great deal about the student in the beginning so it is helpful to reinforce that the student is doing well, making friends and settling in, etc. It is also important to let them know if the student has had any emotional upsets so they can help them cope with this

ESTABLISHING ROUTINES

An important part of the student's school experience will be to learn the general routines and follow them independently. Routines, structure and boundaries help children feel safe since they create predictability and feelings of security. As the student learns the routines of the school and begins to feel more comfortable, they will then start to build up confidence and trust, letting their "guard" down.

- Ensure you have a visual schedule in the classroom with clearly-posted pictures of classes and activities that the student can follow
- Keep their buddy sitting close to them in case they need support with something
- Continue to provide positive praise to the student
- Monitor the student's success with the routines over time
- Students who are not yet able to follow routines are not settled so keep their activities short and hands-on in order to build up their stamina and engagement
- Hands-on activities are essential for these students so try to make every lesson as hands-on as possible
- Students may need some cultural or social skills awareness, especially around customs that may be unfamiliar to them (e.g. how to greet, personal space, routines around eating, etc.)

Settling-In

Students who have "settled" are able to follow the basic routines of the school and classroom. They are more able to focus their attention for prolonged periods of time. They interact with teachers and students in the classroom and also participate in the regular class and school activities.

- The student may not rely on their buddy as much, however, they may still be helpful; at this stage, you may want to extend this role to other willing students
- The student will now be more responsive to instruction and learning in general; they may be better able to absorb information
- They will likely be able to handle more expectations placed on them in terms of assigned tasks, learning activities, classroom roles, etc.
- Students may benefit from intensive support for foundational literacy and mathematics at this stage
- You can begin some initial assessments at this stage and then continue ongoing monitoring of the student, their social and emotional development as well as their language development

It may be necessary for a member of staff (e.g. teacher, counselor, BML specialist) to provide initial "intervention" to refugee students who are not yet settled in the school or classroom. Intervention can simply mean providing more individualized care and attention, monitoring and follow-up of the BML over an initial period of time. Then as the child begins settling, and are more able to take risks within the classroom, they begin to trust their teacher and develop bonds with their peers. The term, "intervention" in this case can simply mean "helping students settle and build trust". This can be done in a variety of ways, either individually or even in a small group setting if appropriate.

Encouraging the child to play or interact with you cannot only enhance their language skills, but it can also help to establish trust and relationship-building. Remember that a teacher is not qualified to deliver therapy, but they can be an excellent support to students through compassion, positive interactions and encouragement. In many cases, routines, freedom to play and interact with other children in a nurturing environment provides the foundation for healing which many refugee children need.

THE REFUGEE EXPERIENCE

What it's like after arriving to a new country...

Refugees and families may have experienced trauma, loss or extreme hardship; especially related to death or disappearance of loved ones, property or homes
- BC Ministry of Education (2009)

WHAT PEOPLE THINK IT'S LIKE

WHAT IT'S REALLY LIKE

Refugees need time and support to help them cope with their new country, culture and surroundings

DIG DEEP:

1. Why is the "parent interview" so important?

2. Do you feel all BMLs at your school are correctly identified? Why or why not?

3. How can understanding the different "types" of BMLs support you in your teaching practices?

4. What issues are at the heart of the controversy surrounding the use of psychological assessment tools with BMLs?

BREAKOUT:

5. What are the approximate numbers of BMLs in your school as a whole? Within your class, could you easily identify the different "types" of BMLs?

6. Have you ever worked with BMLs who were refugees? If so, share your experiences. If not, how would you feel about it?

EXPLORE:

Do a mini-audit in your school to see how much information you have access to in regards to your BMLs. Select one BML and see if there is sufficient background information gathered about them in order to fully develop a strong understanding of their learning profile. If not, what information is missing? What steps do you think need to be taken in order to ensure the right information is collected about students?

[7]

Optimizing Learning

IN THIS CHAPTER YOU WILL...
- Understand the importance of getting instruction "just right" for your BMLs
- Learn how to decrease the effects of the "language barrier"
- Learn the importance of maintaining high-expectations and academic rigor for BMLs
- Know how to efficiently plan and differentiate learning for BMLs
- Understand how to differentiate assessments to fairly represent what your BMLs know

GROUNDING QUESTION:
How are you currently differentiating your learning content for the different levels of BMLs?

Once you know your BMLs and fully understand their language abilities and goals, you are well-equipped to begin planning effective instructional activities that engage and challenge them. We *do* want to challenge all of our BMLs, even those who may still be in the early stages of learning English.

BMLs who are not yet fully-proficient with English may feel overwhelmed by their attempts to access the grade or year-level learning content. Imagine a class of BMLs struggling with learning materials that are 2-3 years beyond their current independent ability. It is not sound, fair or reasonable, yet this is a common, daily occurrence in many classrooms. Text books and other similar materials which are well-beyond the levels of many BMLs often form the basis of instruction.

It is unfair to believe that teachers are deliberately setting their BMLs up for failure when they do not adapt the learning for them. Many teachers are perfectly willing, yet not trained or experienced enough to know where, or how to begin this process.

In order to compensate for this difficulty, some teachers lower the bar, or reduce the expectations for BMLs as a natural way for them to make the learning easier or more accessible. As a result, BMLs can feel under-challenged, bored and can even disengage from learning. We need to remember that BMLs have a language barrier, but they are still intelligent and have a desire, just like any other student, to participate, be independent and ultimately, succeed.

> *Children are frequently disenchanted by overly-simple activities which are designed to suit their language level but are often way below their cognitive potential and therefore fail to provide a challenge. In presenting a cognitive challenge, we aim to keep the learners engaged in the activity. Children need to be challenged; they are capable of a high level of thinking if encouraged to do so (Puchta, H. & Williams, n.d., p.7).*

Getting the balance between the "right" level of language input along with the "right" level of academic challenge can be a tough one for many educators. However, it is something they can learn to do effectively with some practice.

One particular difficulty facing most teachers of BMLs is the issue of struggling readers. Since it is common for a large proportion of BMLs to function below their grade or year-level for independent reading, they typically struggle with textbooks, selecting appropriate library books, reading assignments and even doing homework. Despite this, many are still expected to complete assigned tasks—often with much greater time and effort being invested as compared to their NS peers.

This illustrates how learning is not always equitable for BMLs and how challenge often extends far beyond what is independently possible for many. Tasks that are at the "frustration level" are a far too-common experience for BMLs simply because teachers have not differentiated the learning tasks to "level the playing field for them". In many cases, this is a problem with teachers not being sure how to differentiate or not feeling empowered to adapt BMLs' educational programs.

One of the most frequent conversations we tend to have with parents of BMLs is around the issue of difficult assignments and homework. Parents notice their children are struggling with assignments that are well-beyond their independent ability levels. Tension and frustration often lead to battles between parents and children once homework time comes around. Parents report they end up sitting with their child for hours just to help them get the work done. This kind of situation not only devalues the learning activity but also provides the teacher with an inaccurate assessment of the BML's ability.

With the right techniques and practice, learning how to differentiate lessons so BMLs can independently access and participate is not difficult. It simply requires good knowledge about their literacy and English proficiency so that you can break down your main lessons to create new "entry points" for them to join in and access the learning independently.

Sometimes this is achieved by engaging their MT to help them understand. It can also include adapting the language of the task to the level of the BML. At times, it might even make use of alternative reading materials. In any and all situations, differentiation must allow the BML to keep their thinking moving forward. Just because they are not yet fully-proficient with the English language does not mean their learning tasks and level of intellectual challenge needs to be easier.

In this section we will look at how to maximize academic learning for BMLs while helping teachers learn to "work smarter" with their planning and classroom activities. As a teacher, you should aim to create "high-impact" so that you see better results with reduced planning time and overall effort. You may have heard of the 80/20 rule which states that 80 percent of your results come from 20 percent of your efforts. We can easily apply this principle to teaching. Key routines and day-to-day activities have a major impact on how your BMLs are learning (or not learning), so maximizing this can make a world of difference.

Being able to create this kind of success in the classroom relies heavily on teacher expertise and know-how but can really only come with a strong knowledge base about your BMLs and their levels.

THE NEED FOR INCREASING TEACHER EFFICACY AND EXPERTISE: WHEN INSTRUCTION FAILS TO REACH THE BAR

The bottom line is simple: we cannot expect teachers to provide the best quality of education to BMLs if they have never received appropriate training or guidance in best practices. What we already know from the research is that teachers are not being given the right support or access to quality professional education programs about BMLs. This affects their understanding and application of second (additional) language acquisition and corresponding teaching strategies.

Not only are BMLs left to sink-or-swim in many situations, but teachers can also be left to fend for themselves in the classroom—often finding themselves in over their heads.

THE "EMBARRASSMENT" AND THE "HYGIENE"

In the article, "Embarrassment and Hygiene in Schools," teacher and researcher, Ronald Mackay, describes his experiences working with teachers and BMLs in the Arctic regions of Canada. These students were from an Inuit (aboriginal) community and attended English-medium school, although their mother-tongue was "Inuktitut". After observing many student-teacher interactions in this setting, Mackay questioned whether certain kinds of interactions could be contributing to a lack of success for BMLs.

He started to notice a common pattern of what he coined, "embarrassments," which took place when a teacher's lesson took an unexpected, downward turn. This could involve students remaining silent and disengaged from the lesson, having poor levels of participation, offering incorrect responses or an inability to produce written work, for example.

As a result of these unexpected responses from students, teachers would begin to struggle but still attempt to repair the embarrassments by applying a variety of "hygiene" tactics. This could include attempts to save the lesson by thinking aloud for the students, dictating notes to students or substituting easier assignments, for instance. The teachers' attempts to maintain their lessons immediately lowered the level of challenge and expectations for students.

In one example, the teacher explained the expectations for the learning task and provided instructions to all students. Their assignment was to complete a written composition about a ghost story they had read previously. The teacher began by writing the title on the board and then asked students to get started on independent work. As the teacher began circulating around the class, she soon observed that the majority of the students had only written the title and a few sentences down. She then realized that she needed to address the issue with all students. Notice the style of conversation between the teacher (T) and the students (S) in this excerpt of the interaction below:

> ...T: *There was a man and a woman who were friends. (T writes this on the board; Students copy.) Were they just friends? (pause)*
>
> S1: *Marry (pause)*
>
> T: *OK. They wanted to get married. (T writes this on the board; Ss copy it into their notebooks.) Did*

> *they? Did they get married? (pause)*
>
> *S4: No money (pause)*
>
> *T: No, they didn't get married; they couldn't get married because they had no money. (T writes this on the board; Ss copy)*
>
> *T: So? Do you remember what happened? (pause) Do you remember the story...?*
>
> *Mackay, R. (1993, p. 32-39)*

McKay notes that it was clear from the transcript that the teacher's original assignment had been extremely diluted and simplified. As students responded with inadequate responses and information to her questions, she began to fill-in the answers herself and recorded them onto the blackboard. All the students were then required to do was simply copy the teacher's notes into their books.

Since these students had fallen-short in their linguistic ability to cope with the assignment, the result was a lesson outcome that was much different from the original, planned objective.

WHAT "HYGIENE" PRACTICES DO TEACHERS USE TO "REDUCE" EMBARRASSMENTS?

- "Reasoning" or thinking aloud for the students
- Asking and answering questions themselves to point the discussion in a specific direction
- Reducing language from "academic vocabulary" to simplistic words and phrases
- Substituting more complex tasks to low-level "busy work"
- Reducing question complexity to allow simple "yes" and "no" answers from BMLs
- Dictating notes to students
- Asking BMLs to "copy" from the board
- Using fill-in-the-blank worksheets
- Taking over the lesson by reading aloud or asking other students to read aloud to quicken the pace or compensate for low-level reading skills
- Soliciting ideas for writing from the whole-class instead of encouraging more challenging individual work

WHAT COULD THE TEACHER HAVE DONE TO REPAIR THE LESSON WHILE STILL MAINTAINING THE EXPECTATIONS?

- She could have stopped and asked students to work with a partner or within a small group to see if they could retell the story together
- She might have spent more time "working with" the story *as they were reading it*, breaking it down into chunks so that they could better understand the meaning and vocabulary. She could have had them complete a "story map" to record details about the plot as well as "character descriptions" within groups (to ensure that students were able to fully comprehend the information and the context for learning)
- She could have used an alternative text that was more suited to her BMLs' level and culture so they could better engage with it while still extracting the major themes and storyline
- She could have incorporated more authentic discussion about the content of the book so that BMLs could "pull in" their own ideas, opinions and experiences
- She could have focused on engaging them more with the story while clarifying any challenges with vocabulary or theme

As we all know, being prepared and ready for anything to happen in the classroom will allow teachers to ride the ups-and-downs with confidence. This requires a level of competence that only comes with experience and practice as well as extensive insight into the particular needs of your students.

What comes across very clear from the research and from our own personal experiences is that teachers need greater understanding of how to "pitch" learning tasks to different levels, while still maintaining the integrity of the learning expectations as much as possible. To achieve this, we need to balance the level of challenge so that BMLs are stretched, but not frustrated, beyond what they can perform independently.

THE LANGUAGE BARRIER

It is essential to remember that BMLs must continue to keep up with age-appropriate learning as much as possible. As the BML moves forward in their learning, they are also developing their English skills by repeated interactions with relevant vocabulary and with opportunities for writing and speaking to others. As the BML performs their daily activities in the mainstream, English school, they are consistently stimulating their language growth with comprehensible input and opportunities for output.

If you have ever visited a foreign country, you know how difficult it can seem to get the information you need and to perform activities of daily living without speaking the language. In order to cope, you try to use all of the resources around you—gestures, survival phrases, signs, dictionaries, maybe even Google Translate. In this situation you are experiencing the language barrier but you know that you are able to get around it with the right tools and resources available to you. While this can be a tedious process at times, the motivation you have for getting the information you need, or getting to where you need to go, keeps you going.

Teaching BMLs is a little like that—it is easier if you first try to tap into their innate motivation to learn so that it helps to mediate the "language barrier". BMLs can learn in a multitude of ways but it takes some knowledge and creativity on the part of the teacher to learn what works and why.

The teacher's job then, is to essentially help BMLS overcome the language barrier that can first appear to be a "disabling force," and to help them engage with their prior knowledge. They should also help them connect with the curriculum in order to perform meaningful learning activities. This is often done with differentiation and in some cases, even curriculum modification.

WHAT THE ACADEMIC LEARNING EXPERIENCE IS OFTEN LIKE FOR BMLs

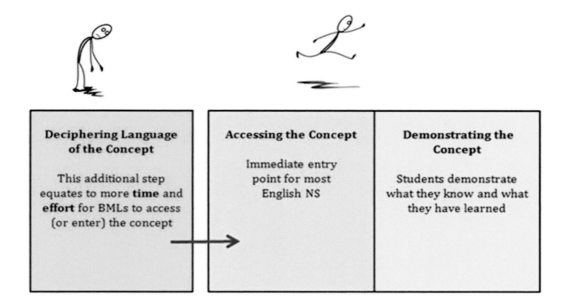

Deciphering Language of the Concept	Accessing the Concept	Demonstrating the Concept
This additional step equates to more **time** and **effort** for BMLs to access (or enter) the concept	Immediate entry point for most English NS	Students demonstrate what they know and what they have learned

BMLs often need more scaffolding to help them bridge the language barrier; NS typically access learning immediately

If we look at the diagram above, we can better understand how the language barrier impacts BMLs. When they spend too much time "deciphering language" by trying to understand oral or written information related to the concept, they may easily reach the threshold for frustration and exhaustion. For instance, when they are required to read background information on a topic or learn a large number of vocabulary words at once, this can be extremely labour-intensive and time-consuming. Then, by the time they have understood the basic information and central ideas of the concept, they may feel overwhelmed before even getting to *work with* the central concept. Keep in mind they also have the additional pressure of simply trying to "catch up" to their NS peers.

In comparison, NS peers, typically have immediate access to the central concept with relative ease. They are able to move fluidly, working with concepts and ideas or the real meat and bones of the learning.

This is the barrier to learning that BMLs frequently face in classrooms and which, in many cases can severely limit their progress before they even begin. However, this can be successfully ameliorated by understanding how to adapt and scaffold the content learning to the specific needs of the student.

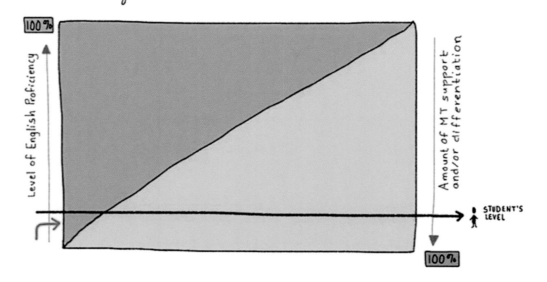

Teachers must help bridge BMLs' language barrier by filling in the gaps with their MT and/or differentiation

All teachers must aim to "level the playing field" for BMLs. A good way to conceptualize this is through the diagram above. Look at the small section in purple on one side and the larger orange section on the other. Imagine that the purple section represents the BML's level of English language proficiency. The orange section on the opposite side represents the relative, perceived "gap" that the BML has as a result of their "language barrier." This relates to their ability to access the age-appropriate curriculum content. In this case, if a student has begun learning English and is working within the FL2 stage, there is still a great deal of "proficiency" (i.e. mother-tongue proficiency) that this BML possesses under the surface. This proficiency can help to bridge the gap for the BML by supporting their academic learning in English. Then as their English proficiency increases (the purple area increases), there is less of a gap (the orange area decreases). This means that the student will likely be less reliant on their MT and will require less support/intervention from their teachers to bridge that gap.

Helping BMLs bridge the gap in the easiest way can include reading and accessing background information in the MT or additional language(s). However, in cases where the BML's proficiency in their MT is not strong or if they do not have literacy in that MT, the teacher will need to apply more differentiation to the learning activities to help them bridge that gap. This is the job of all teachers.

Since BMLs can be faced with the difficult task of deciphering the "language" of the task before even getting to the task itself, this can eat away at the time they could be using to work with the actual concept (or content). Ensuring that you plan tasks and learning activities that match BMLs' language ability will help them to better cope with academic challenge.

COMMON WAYS TO DIFFERENTIATE
for BMLs

RESEARCH
* provide more time to locate resources
* allow students to work in their MT or in MT groupings
* provide alternative texts with the same content (e.g. texts that match their current reading level)
* provide notes/expectations/assignments ahead of time and get them to spend more time on understanding what they need to do
* support students in preparing for research with graphic organizers to give structure

PROJECTS
* allow students to work in their MT or in MT groupings
* adjust the expectations to reflect what the student CAN do (e.g. reduce number of sections if it would take them much longer; have them focus on a specific area)
* support the student to plan and organize the components
* consider the time needed to complete the project and adapt as needed
* consider alternatives to presenting information orally if necessary (e.g. PowerPoint, pre-recording a video or audio, presenting as part of a group or presenting to the teacher privately)

MATH + SCIENCE
* provide essential vocabulary for concepts (have students translate them into their MT if possible) and give them access to these words for tests or assignments
* teach essential vocabulary for working with word problems (e.g. "less than", "difference between..." etc.)
* allow students to work in English or their MT
* have math and science word walls
* use "authentic assessments" or performance tasks to assess learning

☐ square
carré

÷ divide
diviser

TEACHER-TALK

- add more visuals, notes, gestures + expression
- have another student or buddy summarize
- always introduce lessons with the main ideas to help BMLs build the bigger picture first
- check back for comprehension
- keep teacher-talk to a minimum + have students do more of the talking

WRITING TASKS

- provide tools: adjective lists, editing checklists, etc.
- allow students to write in their MT (use a staff or parent to translate)
- accept "developmental" English and focus on the message/content
- allow students to talk before they write (e.g. think-pair-share)
- use graphic organizers to lay out/organize ideas
- accept shorter/reduced writing for lengthier or more complex tasks (especially if the individual needs more time to understand the task)
- change format from written task (e.g. to poster or slideshow)
- teach students to focus on 1-2 writing goals at-a-time

BRAINSTORMING

- encourage students to think in their MT
- allow students to work in their MT groups
- enable students to use drawings, diagrams or labels to record thoughts/ideas

READING • LITERATURE

* ensure comprehension!

- read in the MT (texts, books or Internet)
- provide similar content with accessible vocabulary (alternative texts)
- summarize the main idea for students and create a "story map" for ongoing use and reference
- watch the movie (if available) and stop periodically to take notes/add drawings to the story map
- find a "SlideShare" presentation to support understanding
- summarize and clarify chapter events with students
- use chapter summaries to condense key pieces of information
- have groups of students work together to summarize, discuss and share their understandings for specific chapters or sections
- provide contextual information for students (e.g. help them understand any relevant cultural info, background or vocabulary)
- engage students in rich discussions before/during/after readings

Using the "Levelings" Approach to Plan and Carry out Quality Lessons for BMLs

Having spent a great deal of time supporting teachers in their planning for BMLs through their units and lessons, we have seen many conscientious and caring teachers burn out as a result of their enormous efforts. While it is important to try and strike a balance between the learning (curriculum) expectations and your BMLs' ability levels, you must acknowledge that you can never be able to attend to, or focus on everything in your program. It would be impossible.

The key is to focus on differentiating just enough so that you help the BMLs access the lesson information and then enable them to respond and demonstrate their learning in a way that suits them best, and in a way that allows them to be stimulated and stretched. One of the secrets to working with BMLs is to learn how to cut away at the excess language or learning expectations in order to get to the heart of the learning.

We have often seen teachers become overwhelmed working with BMLs because they either think they have to create numerous extra lessons for students or that they must spoon-feed them through difficult tasks. These situations are not optimal for the teacher or the BML.

The trick is to keep things as simple as possible, and harness your efforts at the planning stages. Then, you can take the time to carefully think through your learning objectives and how to make big impact by having you and your BMLs work smarter.

If your BMLs have functional MT literacy, do not waste time helping them understand difficult textbooks; instead, leverage their MT (remember, it is one of the greatest assets BMLs have) and simply get them to read background information in their own language. They can even access resources online and take short notes about what they have learned. In this way, the BML is more independent and productive and can access concepts in a much more efficient way than you would have ever been able to teach them through a difficult textbook or written resource.

In order to help you in your planning, we have come up with a simple framework to guide your unit or lesson planning for your BMLs. We call it the "LEVELINGS Approach" and it is simply a memory aid that can help focus you as you go about your work:

LEVELINGS APPROACH FOR PLANNING

L	EVELS of students' language and literacy
E	XPECTATIONS and purpose
V	OCABULARY requirements
E	MBED context into lessons
L	EARN relevant background information
I	NPUT is comprehensible
N	ARROW and cut-away extra or unnecessary content
G	ENERATE opportunities for participation and independence
S	ELF-REFLECTION and assessment

LEVELS OF LANGUAGE AND LITERACY

Before you even begin to plan, ensure you know the levels of your BMLs' English language and literacy. This will help you to correctly plan your lesson while differentiating for their "just right" level of resources (books, texts, written materials, etc.).

EXPECTATIONS AND PURPOSE

Be clear on exactly what you aim to achieve with your lesson or activity. Decide what your primary objective is. For example, if you ask students to do a writing activity, is it to have them express an idea about an issue or topic? Is it to give them practice applying their phonemic awareness skills or handwriting skills? Whatever the primary purpose is will determine what you will assess as your learning outcome and what you can then "cut away".

If you have decided that the primary purpose of your writing assignment is to have your students express their ideas and opinions, then you can decide not to mark or assess their spelling errors for example. Similarly, if your students are required to locate facts about a country for their Social Studies project, then you can easily have BMLs research independently through their MT. This will help you know how to specifically differentiate your lessons either by process (how they will learn), product (what they will create) or content (information they will access) (Tomlinson, 2001).

VOCABULARY

Identify specific topic or subject-related vocabulary words that BMLs will need to learn in order to fully participate in the lesson. Have your BMLs create a *MT Word Wall*. If they already know the meanings of these words in their MT, this will greatly help them access the learning.

Vocabulary-learning should be targeted and planned. Opportunities for daily activities must be created within the timetable. Some deliberate learning along with explanations and rich discussions will help BMLs gain greater control over keywords through multiple exposures. This should continue as they advance through the unit of learning.

EMBED CONTEXT INTO LESSONS

All lessons should begin by embedding context and activating all students' prior knowledge. This will not only make the learning relevant and meaningful, it will help BMLs (and all learners) better comprehend and engage with what you are teaching. Keep in mind that BMLs at the FL stages will usually require more explicit context than students at the TL stages in order to build up their understanding about a topic; however, do not assume that more proficient BMLs no longer require context. They often still do because of cultural aspects they cannot always understand or relate to but also because their assignments are now much more text- or language-heavy than they were previously.

For instance, a lesson that aims to teach students about buildings or structures could encourage BMLs to select buildings which are based in the countries they come from. This could then create a natural link to their culture and prior knowledge base. Similarly, an essay about environmental concerns could first be approached by having students watch videos on the topic, especially if they do not have much experience with the topic or issue first-hand.

LEARN BACKGROUND INFORMATION

Most lessons require some background information on the topic being explored. Ensure your BMLs have enough background knowledge and understanding about what you will be teaching them, especially since many of the topics may not be something they directly know about. Extended "teacher talk" (explanations) or difficult readings are not the preferred methods for teaching BMLs since it is very passive and also difficult to build context from on its own. It can disengage BMLs who are still at earlier stages of English proficiency since verbal information is often beyond their level of comprehension.

Instead, make this an active process, with BMLs reading in their MT, researching, watching video clips, etc. Invite them to draw pictures or record short notes about what they have found. Never assume that your BMLs come to you with prerequisite knowledge. Imagine for a moment, a student who has been a refugee for most of his life. He comes with no prior access to schooling and cannot make prior connections to the class unit on "earth, moon and stars" because he knows nothing of space beyond what he has directly seen up in the night sky. This particular BML will need more concrete exposure to models, pictures or videos to help them build up the necessary background information before moving on.

INPUT IS COMPREHENSIBLE

Ensure that learning resources and materials are comprehensible to BMLs in such a way that they can access them independently or with minimal support. If BMLs are below the grade or year-level reading expectations, then you need to ensure that their learning materials are differentiated for them. In some cases, this can simply mean giving them a different text to work with. For example, if students are working on Shakespeare`s *Romeo and Juliet*, but your BMLs cannot access the text, you can easily get a simplified version (which is available in many levels, right down to books at Grade 3 or Year 4 level). Again, think about what the purpose of the study is. Is it to learn specifically about Shakespeare himself, or is it to learn about the universal theme of "love"? If it is to learn about Shakespeare, then you can focus on simplified text or videos that offer quality information. If it is to teach the universal theme, then you might even be able to do this by having the student read a famous story from their own culture that focuses on the same universal theme. They could even access it through their MT and later discuss it or write about it in English.

You must ensure all BMLs have equal access to the curriculum objectives but at the same time, students should be able to comprehend and access learning content. How you go about reaching those objectives should be open-ended and flexible.

Narrow Focus and Cut Away Content

Sometimes the learning activities you have planned for your NS are redundant or inappropriate for your BMLs. In fact, it may not even be worth the time and effort required for you to teach them in some cases.

When looking at the bigger picture of your lesson and the learning purpose, narrow down the highest-impact learning activities for your BMLs and focus only on those. "Cut away" any extra learning that you feel is unnecessary at this particular moment in time.

This might be because of the heavy amount of support (i.e. spoon-feeding) the BML would require to complete the activity or the extended length of time it would take them to complete the work, thereby making it ineffective for independent learning. For instance, if you are teaching your English classes about "characterization" and students have to analyze both main and supporting characters from *Romeo and Juliet* over a one-week time-frame, then you will likely need to differentiate this task for your BMLs. In this case, understanding that characterization is the purpose of the learning is essential and so BMLs then need to focus primarily on this aspect. In order to narrow this task, you could "cut away" the excess amount of work to allow BMLs at the FL stages to focus on only 1 or 2 characters in detail. Depending on their levels, decide what they could independently complete in one week. BMLs could also be provided with a list of character traits to support them with this task.

You should always try to keep your BMLs learning the same (or similar) content as much as possible. You may adapt it to make it more culturally-relevant or "pitched" to their instructional level but remember not to create too much extra work for yourself. Capitalize on the routines you already have and what you know already works. The trick is to hone in on one or two important aspects of the lesson or topic and make it more concentrated or condensed for your BMLs. For example, if the class is working on comparing 2 different revolutions in their history class but your BMLs do not have any prior knowledge of the topic, you could focus in on the concept of "revolution" and have them work with that. If you already use small groups or allow students to work with a partner, keep these routines up. Do not plan flowery, alternative lessons that will take you one or two evenings to prepare. Instead, think of how these students could learn what they need to in the simplest possible way. Maybe you could write 2 or 3 guiding questions for them on a page, give them a familiar graphic organizer that helps them to organize their research and then ask them to work together in *MT groupings* if possible. Then check back with them along the way by allowing them to clarify and sum-up what they have learned.

In another example, you could also focus on a prerequisite skill the BML student may not have mastered yet. For example, if you are teaching a lesson about "advanced punctuation" but the BMLs in your class have not completely mastered "basic punctuation," you could assign them a journal-writing task instead. If students are already used to working with their journals, they will have no problem getting started and knowing what to do. As they work on this writing task, they will have natural opportunities to practice their punctuation skills at their own targeted levels. You can work with them at key points to check back over their work and to monitor or clarify their success with applying punctuation. If they still need help, it is easy to give a concentrated "mini-lesson" around a specific skill.

In a science classroom, a teacher plans to have his students carry out an experiment. Afterwards, they must complete a structured lab report to detail their findings. Knowing that he needs to focus his BMLs who are at the FL stages on the steps of the experiment and the actual results, he cuts away the excess writing to better allow them to focus and express what they have learned (using labels, drawings or diagrams). He could also encourage BMLs to write a short summary about what the experiment revealed afterwards, using their developing English if there is enough time. This differentiation is very efficient for the teacher and enables BMLs to participate fully and independently in *purposeful* learning. It narrows the focus to the essential elements and allows BMLs to demonstrate what they know and have learned.

It is important to note that some schools do not allow "modification" of curriculum (e.g. changing the grade/year-level curriculum expectations entirely), only "adaptation" or "accommodations," unless specific paperwork has been completed with the appropriate signatures. Be sure to know your school's parameters with this. Encourage your staff to develop policies and written procedures to outline any stipulations related to curriculum differentiation and modification.

GENERATE OPPORTUNITIES FOR PARTICIPATION AND INDEPENDENCE

Within every lesson, you must make sure that your BMLs have opportunities to participate in meaningful, relevant ways. Ensure they are able to function independently and create plenty of opportunities to practice and build their oral, listening, reading or written English. Differentiate learning activities to match their instructional levels. Adapt your environment, schedules and routines to support this. Make sure that your learning activities require your students to do *most* of the work and *most* of the talking. When teachers consistently dominate the air-time, students are not given enough time to talk, problem-solve or demonstrate what they know. A good rule of thumb is to use the 70/30

Principle: the teacher can talk for only 30% of the class time while the other 70% is reserved for the students to discuss, interact or perform meaningful activities.

One of the most effective things you can do as a teacher of any subject is to use different groupings with your students. This can greatly maximize their participation. Train students up to learn how to manage within a group learning situation. Teach them how to take on specific roles so that they can operate collaboratively, yet independently. When you pull back and allow students to start to rely on each other and themselves for their learning, then you have more freedom to work flexibly with individuals and groups. You can move from student-to-student or group-to-group, observing, engaging and assessing your students. Keep in mind that new BMLs may find group work overwhelming and may not be comfortable participating at first. If this is the case, you can work directly with them, building their comfort level over time.

Remember, if a BML consistently needs an adult to help them complete the majority of the activity, then it is not at their "just right" or instructional level. It is either too challenging or simply not scaffolded enough. Be sure to check their reading levels or ask a colleague if you are unsure. Once you need to start spoon-feeding students, something has gone wrong. Learning will not be meaningful or purposeful if BMLs are not able to access it independently. It will quickly begin to demand more and more of your attention and time. Instead, take a step back and look again at your BMLs' levels and what they can do on their own. Reposition your activity to help them gain entry into the learning.

SELF-REFLECTION AND ASSESSMENT

BMLs must be guided to self-reflect and evaluate their own learning and strategy-use. They need specific opportunities for practice and should have clear targets to direct their learning. Direct feedback about their work as well as explicit modeling or instruction will allow them to see where they should put their focus.

Students who have opportunities to self-reflect on their thinking (metacognition) are better able to self-direct and improve their work. Traditional "marking" of student work does not always have impact with BMLs and is unproductive in many cases. It is much more effective for you to teach them how to actively think and self-monitor according to more specific goals or targets.

Sitting and conferencing with students, even for just a few minutes, can allow you to make greater impact in directing them to specific targets or "next steps." Creating regular opportunities to self-assess and reflect on their own learning will build greater mastery, helping them reach the next level. Tools like checklists, learning logs, rubrics and even guided questions can be helpful in this process.

Always consider the issue of "fair assessment" when working with BMLs. It is important to understand that tests and evaluations must reflect what they can do rather than simply highlighting weaknesses. Differentiating assessment may be required in order to get an accurate picture about what a BML knows or can do. This can involve "authentic" or "performance-based assessments" that enable you to directly observe your BML while they perform specific learning skills or tasks. This can also include your analysis of learning products (e.g. project work).

Depending on BMLs' English proficiency, they may not comprehend written tests or be able to fully express their knowledge in writing. BMLs, especially those in the FL stages, may have difficulties recalling keywords, even if they have seemed competent earlier.

Understanding your specific BMLs' needs and what they are capable of will help you apply the most appropriate forms of assessment. In some cases, only simple differentiation will be required, such as reading test items aloud or even allowing them to provide answers verbally. In any case, ensure your assessment fairly reflects BMLs' *actual learning* rather than being reduced to a measurement of their language proficiency.

PUTTING IT ALTOGETHER

In the 3 examples below, you will see how the learning within different subjects can be differentiated for BMLs.

SECONDARY – GRADE 10/YEAR 11 ENGLISH

LEARNING EXPECTATIONS:

1. Students will respond critically to texts.
2. Students will identify major themes within texts.
3. Students will use expository writing effectively, using supporting evidence, facts and relevant details.

LEARNING UNIT OVERVIEW

A 6-week learning unit was designed around the book, *The Hunger Games*, by Suzanne Collins. This unit will cover 4 weeks of reading focus and a 2-week writing focus. All students are required to read specific chapters before each class and then work with a partner to discuss relevant events, thoughts, feelings and themes using guided questions.

Students will record relevant notes during their discussions with each other. They will all come together as a class to share their "big ideas" while the teacher facilitates and directs their learning. The teacher draws students' attention to any other relevant points and records the information on a central chart which can be used for later reference. Each day, the teacher assigns short journal writing activities to students in order to help them better reflect on their learning and thoughts as they go about their readings and discussions. Students are asked to think deeply about the themes and make connections to the content. In some cases, these strategies are modeled by the teacher. Journals are a learning activity designed to build student's proficiency with writing and target skills. Each day, the teacher sits with one or two students to go through their journals and give them feedback about their work.

Once the novel is completed, students will then be required to write an expository essay of approximately 500 words, choosing between 3 topics: Describe how our society is a reflection of both a "dystopia" and "utopia"; Is struggle a requirement for triumph? or Discuss the major Universal Themes in the *Hunger Games* and how they contribute to the plot of the story. The first week will have students explore features of expository writing and will have them compare different examples. Students will plan their writing using a graphic organizer and will show this to their teacher before beginning their first drafts. During class time, the teacher sits with target students individually to conference with them and provides focused feedback and goals to work on. All students are given new targets or goals to work on within their writing. At the end of their assignment, students self-assess their work and take part in peer-assessment tasks according to a pre-defined rubric.

At the end of the unit, the teacher will gather the students during one period and allow them to read their favourite excerpts from their writing, either from their essays or their journals. For BMLs, the teacher might have them pre-record their excerpt on a video to share (where they can practice "getting it right" if they are not confident speaking in front of an audience) or they may also choose to read or discuss their work with another student one-on-one until they feel more confident.

TEACHER CONSIDERATIONS IN PLANNING: LEVELINGS APPROACH

<u>L</u>

The teacher knows the literacy levels of all students and uses this information to determine whether they can read the novel in English or in their MTs. They also know what specific targets individual students need to practice in order to reach the next level in their English literacy.

<u>E</u>

The expectations and purpose in this unit directly relate to the curriculum and help students think critically and deeply about universal themes in literature which are common to all individuals (e.g. suffering, good vs. evil, power, love, loss, etc.). Students are also expected to express their ideas in response to the text as well as advancing their literacy skills through expository writing.

<u>V</u>

The teacher will provide students with a vocabulary list for each chapter. Students will be provided with daily, deliberate vocabulary practice as well as opportunities to use and apply these words in discussions and writing. BMLs reading the novel in their MT will make bilingual dictionaries for learning vocabulary words in the MT and in English. Students will also be encouraged to use their Mini-Thesaurus and other word lists for character traits, etc.

<u>E</u>

Prior to starting the novel, the teacher will engage students in discussions and journal writing to connect them to personal experiences and knowledge of universal themes. Students will see how universal themes are common to all human beings.

<u>L</u>

The teacher will need to be sure students understand background knowledge and ideas related to "dystopia" and "utopia" as well as the specific genre, "dystopian fiction." Connections can be drawn to other books and movies but students who have no experience with these examples can be shown images related to these themes for better comprehension.

<u>I</u>

BMLs who cannot yet access the English version or who cannot read in their MT can watch the movie and then create a *Story Map* after each chapter to highlight main events and details. The teacher can support this in a small group. BMLs will be able to use this information to build their comprehension while still participating in large group discussions.

N

For BMLs at FL1 or FL2, the teacher will have students write the expository piece in their MT if possible. If this is not possible, the teacher can cut-away the larger expository writing task and focus more time and energy on developing the Story Map. These students will then identify and focus on one universal theme. They can either write a short paragraph about the theme to provide evidence, or draw pictures of scenes from the movie where that particular universal theme was demonstrated (along with words or labels). BMLs at FL3 can also work with the Story Map and should use it to help them write at least 2 paragraphs-one page about one universal theme. BMLs at FL4 and above will use graphic organizers and pre-writing strategies to help them complete their writing goal about one, two or three universal themes (depending on the individual student). The teacher will have narrowed the essay to best fit students while still providing a good level of challenge.

G

With this class format, there is flexibility and opportunity for BMLs to actively participate in small and large group tasks as well as to work with the teacher if required. They will find the information is accessible to them so they can work independently. They will use their story maps to support them in whole-group discussions of events.

S

Working with a rubric provides many opportunities for BMLs to self-reflect and evaluate key skills and behaviours. BMLs will also receive feedback from peers and the teacher throughout their learning activities. They should also be encouraged to apply their specific literacy goals/targets to their work throughout the unit.

MIDDLE SCHOOL – GRADE 6/YEAR 7 SCIENCE

LEARNING EXPECTATIONS:

1. Students will understand the properties of flight.
2. Students will construct a scientific investigation demonstrating knowledge of scientific processes and variables.
3. Students will collect, display and interpret data accurately.
4. Students will communicate findings, facts and information using appropriate formal language, speech volume and eye contact.

LEARNING UNIT OVERVIEW

In this 4-week unit, students will discover the principles of "flight." They will take part in a variety of hands-on experiments to help them visualize the concepts of "Bernoulli's Principle," "drag," and "lift," etc. Students will also learn important features and elements of a formal scientific investigation, including "independent" and "dependent variables;" along with use of the scientific method and the collection and interpretation of data.

The unit will start with students discussing and brainstorming what they know already about airplanes and flying machines. They will first work with partners to record their knowledge and later share in a large group. The teacher will focus students on the vocabulary for the unit and especially work with BMLs to create a MT Word Wall throughout the unit.

Students will be encouraged to create questions for inquiry and will be given time to explore those questions through research and note-taking. Students will return to the large group to create a class chart, documenting their information. The teacher will facilitate discussions and direct further learning opportunities.

The teacher will introduce students to concepts of flight and the essential principles. Students will watch videos, and then take part in a paper-airplane-making activity in order to observe and document these phenomena through their models.

Students will then be introduced to scientific concepts that relate to investigating (such as the scientific method, independent/dependent variables and then data collection). They will gain further practice working with these concepts and then will be asked to work in heterogeneous groups to design their own investigation. Students will create 4 different styles of paper airplanes and then hypothesize which will travel the largest distance. Students should base their hypotheses on their previously-learned knowledge. They will design their investigation to test their hypotheses over several trials with each paper airplane as they collect relevant data. Students will be required to write up a "lab report" later in order to document their results. Each group will present their findings to the class.

Teacher Considerations in Planning: LEVELINGS Approach

L

The teacher needs to know students' reading and writing levels in order to make sure they can match a range of differently-leveled books to students in the class. BMLs will be encouraged to access MT resources online.

E

This learning unit will emphasize the scientific process through experimentation, writing lab reports and presenting information. Students will be evaluated on their content, not grammar or spellings. An English subject expectation for presenting is embedded in this unit but BMLs who are not yet ready to speak in front of the whole class will be encouraged to present to a small group or adult only.

V

Students will learn and practice key vocabulary words for this unit: *airplane, flight, wings, tail, drag, Bernoulli's Principle, lift, hypothesis, investigation, variables, data, trials,* etc.

E

Students' real life experiences with flying machines (airplanes, hot air balloons, helicopters, etc.) will be explored. They will also be encouraged to discuss their previous knowledge and experiences with creating and flying paper airplanes. Connections will also be drawn to students' prior experiences designing experiments.

<u>L</u>

All students need a basic knowledge of "flight" as well as the purpose of scientific investigations. Videos and discussions will be used.

<u>I</u>

The teacher needs to ensure that books and reading materials are accessible for a range of literacy levels. Students can access videos in English or in their MTs to support their concept learning. Translation tools can be used as well as pairing BMLs in MT groupings when appropriate.

<u>N</u>

The teacher should narrow the focus of the unit to "how planes fly." BMLs should be able to explain this process with notes, diagrams or information they have discovered (either in English or their MT). The teacher will need to work with BMLs to discuss and clarify their research, in some cases providing them with a more "broken down" mini-lesson if they have not understood something. In some cases, the teacher may need to cut-away detailed information about "variables" if it cannot be easily understood or explained (in English or another language). If BMLs are new or are still at early levels of English, the teacher can decide that this would not be considered "essential learning" at that time; focusing instead on the other important components. In this unit, the teacher and students' focus should be on carrying out the experiment and being able to communicate the results (in different ways depending on what is appropriate for each BML).

<u>G</u>

The teacher will ensure that all BMLs have the opportunity to work independently, in pairs and in small groups throughout the unit. Since the unit also has a very hands-on component, students can easily observe and follow their peers. BMLs are encouraged to participate in the presentation based on what is appropriate for each of them.

<u>S</u>

At the end of each lesson, students will self-reflect on their learning with guiding questions posed by the teacher and with short yes/no questions to assess understanding of concepts. There will be a summative test at the end of the unit but BMLs, depending on their levels, can have an adapted test or assessment. For BMLs who cannot sit a formal test because they do not have literacy skills, the teacher can collect data about student learning through work samples, photos or anecdotal observations.

PRIMARY SCHOOL LEVEL - GRADE 3/ YEAR 4 SOCIAL STUDIES

LEARNING EXPECTATIONS:

1. Students will understand how the "past" impacts the "present" and "future."
2. Students will use both primary and secondary sources to research and locate information.
3. Students will recognize and describe key aspects of their community.

LEARNING UNIT OVERVIEW

Students will learn about their local area and community and draw contrast between its history and its present. Students will all be required to contribute to making a class movie that culminates their research and findings about their community. This can later be shared with parents and other community members. Students will be involved in a variety of activities that include: making maps of their communities (with key landmarks and features), researching the history of the community as well as contrasting the current state of buildings, homes, nature/wildlife, industry and educational institutions. Students also will come to understand how the community has changed over the past 50-100 years.

Students will have the opportunity to find, gather, collate and research information about the topic from family members, members of the community, online sources and from old newspapers and magazines. The teacher will also invite 2 senior citizens, who are longstanding members of the community, to come and share their first-hand memories and experiences with the students through photographs, newspapers, old artefacts and discussions. Before the visit, all students will be required to brainstorm good interview questions for the visitors and then the class will narrow down all of the questions to 10. Two students will record the interviews of the visitors on film.

Throughout the unit, the teacher will integrate their learning with English reading and writing tasks. Students will participate in a variety of writing activities that include: note-taking, journal writing (writing from the perspective of a child from the past, writing about their reflections on life in the past, etc.) as well as writing letters to community members to invite them to visit their classroom. Students will also create a "time capsule" as a class and fill it with important items to document their lives in this particular year. They will also include individual pieces of biographical writing to describe and share their personal lives and histories. Throughout the unit, video footage will be taken and a group of students will work with the teacher at the end to edit the videos and create a 10-minute movie about their unit. This will be shared with parents and the school community.

Assessments will be based on performance tasks in conjunction with specific rubrics.

Teacher Considerations in Planning: LEVELINGS Approach for Grade 3/Year 4 Social Studies

L

The teacher knows individual literacy levels and uses that information to support students as they carry out key tasks within the unit. BMLs will have numerous opportunities to apply their individual writing targets/goals.

E

The expectations will remain the same for BMLs. Although new students may not have much knowledge about their new community, this unit will provide them with opportunities to learn more about it.

V

The teacher will focus BMLs on specific content-related vocabulary words which can be worked on through deliberate activities and games along with: MT Word Walls and Bilingual Dictionaries. They will also be opportunities to use words in class discussions and writing. Key words should include: *community, past, present, future, artefacts, primary sources, secondary sources, interviews, research, time-capsule, maps, landmarks, etc.* An important element in this unit is discussion and sharing of experiences, ideas and findings. This will allow students to gain more practice using the target vocabulary words in-context.

<u>E</u>

Within this unit there are numerous opportunities for BMLs to connect with familiar contexts. The study of their community, landmarks and people will naturally scaffold their learning in practical ways. They may also think about other communities they have lived in previously.

<u>L</u>

All students will be familiar with the concept of "community." The teacher can support BMLs to make connections to their previous communities when learning more about their current one.

<u>I</u>

BMLs will be able to gain meaning from the learning through observations, direct interactions (e.g. with places, people, etc.) and practical activities. This will support their learning but the teacher should be sure to clarify any points of confusion. Books and articles may be above their level of comprehension depending on their language proficiency so they may need to work in a small group supported by the teacher to help them with the research component. Students can work in MT groupings to brainstorm interview questions and can also think of the questions in their MT first before translating them into English.

<u>N</u>

The teacher may need to cut away at the research task for BMLs at the early FL stages. Since local information may not be available in the students' MTs, they can get support from the teacher for this task. The teacher can provide students with pictures and short question prompts focusing on key elements. Questions such as: "How did the school building change in 50 years?" or "Where do people get their food in this community?" can prompt students to use pictures and think about what they already know (or have seen) in order to identify differences/similarities over time. This type of activity can allow students to participate meaningfully but with a much more narrowed focus on *specific elements* or concepts that the teacher decides are important take-aways. BMLs could also write short responses and even draw pictures. The teacher should clarify as needed. They might also decide to reduce the quantity of writing expected for some BMLs at the early FL stages. Some BMLs may also find it difficult to take on the perspective of a child from the past and write *as that child*. Instead, this task could be differentiated to have students write about their own experience as a child in the community in the *present* time.

<u>G</u>

In this unit, there are many opportunities for BMLs to apply their language and literacy skills. Since there are several hands-on activities, students will be able to fully take part with some differentiation. Activities can also be adjusted to allow independent work with writing tasks and interview questions.

<u>S</u>

Rubrics will be used to target key skills and behaviours. BMLs will get a chance to evaluate their own work as well as peer's work according to the rubric criteria. The teacher will also assess student work through observation and with the set rubrics.

DIG DEEP:

1. How can planning your units with the "big picture" in mind help you to differentiate for your BMLs?

2. Why do we need to know our BMLs' ability levels and language-levels in order to plan effectively? How can this impact the success of your specific lessons?

3. What are the essential elements you need to keep in-mind during your planning when working with BMLs?

BREAKOUT:

4. Reflect upon a previous lesson that you taught. What aspects do you identify that worked well and what could you have improved on? Were you able to maintain the challenge levels and independence levels for your BMLs?

5. Why does it make sense to use BMLs' mother-tongues to help bridge the language barrier?

6. Why does "narrowing and cutting away" content help the student? Explain how it helps the teacher to "work smarter."

EXPLORE:

Analyze one of your learning units or lessons. Use the LEVELINGS Approach to understand where you may need to fine-tune or focus the learning for your BMLs. What did you discover?

[8]

Supporting Literacy Development

IN THIS CHAPTER YOU WILL...

- Understand the importance of building quality literacy experiences into the school day
- Recognize why all BMLs need to engage in individual reading programs regardless of their grade or year levels
- Learn important considerations for developing literacy programs in schools
- Understand how subject teachers and English teachers can work together on shared literacy goals

GROUNDING QUESTION:

What good literacy practices or programs does your school already have in place?

Literacy is the gateway to academic success for all students. Proficient readers and writers hold the key to unlocking a world of benefits that continue to compound and move them forward, not only in isolated reading and writing skills, but also by enabling them to open the door to more challenging cognitive skills and academic experiences.

Consider this: students who lag in literacy do not get the full benefits that reading provides them. As good readers continue to progress, they make gains not only in reading, but in their ability to learn from what they are reading. This is critical.

Students who struggle in literacy can be restricted in their ability to further their subject and world knowledge as well as their vocabulary.

What we have already learned about BMLs is that they need to make roughly 1½ years progress in one academic year in order to simply catch up to their NS peers. This can be a difficult goal to reach especially since many BMLs are already 2 or more years below their grade or year-level expectations and do not always have access to support.

On the other hand, there are schools where BMLs do make good, ongoing progress in their academic learning and do meet their short and long-term goals. In many of these schools, you will find teachers who are trained to understand the needs of BMLs. You will also find very high-quality literacy programs and policies are in place.

From what we already know about vocabulary, we can understand that reading and writing are key vehicles for vocabulary development. Vocabulary in turn, influences other important aspects of literacy like reading fluency and comprehension. It also enables students to become more independent and competent readers and learners.

It is not only important that schools design high-quality literacy activities but that administrators and teachers are aware of how these activities add value to student achievement. The bottom line is that teachers need to be given the right training and flexibility to enable them to develop programs that better support BMLs' literacy development. Literacy should be a top priority within each school since it relates to every subject and almost every task or learning activity. It is easy to understand why students who are not successful in literacy do not feel successful in school.

We believe there are fundamental, whole-school strategies that schools can implement to enable good progress for BMLs' reading and writing development. These initiatives do not only relate to English teachers or those who teach literacy to BMLs, but they can and should include approaches for subject teachers as well.

While subject teachers do understand that English is integrated within their academic tasks and programs, some may not feel comfortable in knowing exactly where to put their focus or even how to align literacy goals efficiently with objectives or standards. While it is certainly true that subject teachers do not have much extra time to actively "teach" separate English skills to BMLs, they can definitely support and reinforce the strategies already being applied within BMLs' English classes.

This means that schools need to have clearly-defined goals and strategies that are communicated across the school and to all staff members so that each teacher can build these into their programs. This allows subject teachers to mirror key techniques already being applied with BMLs in the English class. This kind of approach can have significant positive effects on students but it can also provide subject teachers with a very clear focus for their teaching.

ESSENTIAL COMPONENTS OF QUALITY LITERACY PROGRAMS FOR BMLs

If you recall, in Chapter 5 we examined the components of "Vocabulary Programming" through the activities listed on our pyramid graphic. The base referred to "environmental experiences," the middle reflected "academic experiences" and the peak pointed to "deliberate vocabulary instruction." It may not come as a surprise to you that the same pyramid outlines quality literacy programming as much as it does for vocabulary. The reason is that language, literacy and vocabulary are as interconnected as a spider's web. Engaging in literacy-based activities also stimulates an individual's English language and vocabulary.

If we explore these components further, we can build an understanding about the essential elements that good schools as a whole, need to implement. While many of these may actually fall under the responsibility of the English teacher or Literacy specialist, we cannot understate the power of harnessing the whole school team in supporting student literacy across all subject areas.

PROVIDING A LITERACY-RICH ENVIRONMENT

Many of you will already know the value of a literacy-rich environment. This can include many different elements that support BMLs' language, literacy and subject-content. For example, it can include print-rich word walls, labels, charts, poems, vocabulary lists as well as collections of print and reading materials. These print materials are typically linked to themes or subjects students are learning about. Making sure these resources are organized in a way that allows BMLs to refer to them and use them is essential.

Having a literacy and print-rich environment not only allows BMLs greater access to vocabulary and reading materials, but it also provides a point of focus for teachers to direct their students' attention towards. We have always loved the Reggio Emelia approach to early childhood education and how they elevate the learning environment to the status of a child's "third teacher." They understand that a child's environment plays a pivotal role in communicating information and teaching them. A high-quality, literacy-rich environment should never be underestimated.

Since students spend a great deal of their time within the learning environment, it is critical to maximize space as much as possible. Think about how your school and classroom environment can contribute to your BMLs' learning:

- Does the environment support what the students are learning?
- Is there easy access and visibility to materials, charts or word walls?
- Are materials and resources changed regularly in order to add impact?
- Do BMLs actually make use of displays and word walls? If not, how can they better engage students?
- Are books and other reading materials available within the classroom and do they reinforce what is being taught? Are they available in a variety of levels?
- Do word walls contain useful words that BMLs need to know?
- How can BMLs' cultures and MTs be incorporated into the environment in useful ways?
- How many different ways can students engage with their print-and literacy-rich environment?

PHONICS AND EARLY LITERACY PROGRAMS

Every school must ensure they have strong early literacy programs available for all students. While we have already learned that BMLs can typically acquire foundational literacy skills like phonics and early reading fairly easily, it is important to embed these concepts into rich literacy and language experiences.

Rather than employing a pre-packaged program, all teachers working with young BMLs need to be aware that these students will learn best when learning is integrated with context-heavy or theme-based experiences. This is because young BMLs need to be able to make links to concepts easily. They do not usually possess the background knowledge that native speakers come to the classroom with. For instance, BMLs may struggle to make sense of decontextualized phonics patterns like "ch" because they may not have that sound in their own language and also because they may not yet know any English words that have "ch" in them. For many BMLs, learning the separate sounds can be a quick process; however, independently applying them can take longer. The BML needs time to build up the accompanying vocabulary and contexts to truly make sense of English sounds and patterns.

Older BMLs who come into the school with no previous knowledge of English literacy will require opportunities to learn about concepts like phonics and in some cases, even letter formations for beginning writing. If the BML already has established literacy in their own MT then this will be a great benefit to their English development. They will already have learned how to read in their language so they will likely understand the concept of how sounds come together to create whole words even if their orthography is very different to English. They will simply transfer this already-existing knowledge over to English and can often be "fast-tracked" through the basic letter sounds and phonics patterns. We have certainly seen BMLs with strong MT literacy learn the basic English phonics system in a matter of weeks with daily instruction. While it may take longer to master the pronunciation of some sounds, many of these BMLs can begin applying their knowledge for "learning to read" in English immediately.

BMLs with already-established literacy in their MT would benefit from explicit teaching about English, since it can initially be difficult for them to understand the annoying inconsistencies of English. If they are coming from a much more phonetic and consistent language background, they may be confused about why English does not work "logically" for spelling and decoding words. Some points for explicit teaching can include:

- English has many rules but it does not always "follow" the rules
- A number of words in English cannot be "sounded out" but must be recognized by sight (e.g. the "sight words")
- Two or three letters can come together to make one sound
- Some letters are "silent" and do not make any sound

INDIVIDUAL READING AND WRITING ASSESSMENTS FOR STUDENTS ACROSS THE SCHOOL

Knowing BMLs' literacy levels can help teachers understand how to "pitch" their lessons. This will benefit all teachers as they plan their lessons to enable BMLs to better access learning content. This kind of student information should be gathered by class teachers if the students are in elementary/primary or the designated English teachers if the student is in middle or secondary school. How teachers gather this information can vary from school-to-school.

Some teachers may prefer to use "running records" or "reading records" to assess BMLs' comfortable reading levels. This helps identify specific strategies that the student needs to reach the next level of challenge. This method is highly-preferable since it not only provides the teacher with the reading level of the student but also allows them to gain feedback about what they are doing well, including what their "next steps" should be.

Other types of assessments may be used by schools to determine BMLs' reading levels. Standardized tests or those which provide "Lexile Levels" can be easier to administer since they may rely less on a highly-skilled teacher; however, these tests do not always provide the "bigger picture" for BMLs, many of whom need to be taught more explicit "strategy-based teaching" to move to the next level.

Class teachers or English teachers should find the BMLs' comfortable reading level suitable for teaching (with some extra challenge) when students have around 90-95 % accuracy with good comprehension of text. However, when BML's are required to read independently (without support) their books should be slightly less challenging and allow them greater success with around 98% accuracy. When teachers work directly with BMLs for reading, they scaffold, allowing them to solve new challenges with decoding or vocabulary, for example. When BMLs are reading on their own, books need to be easy enough for them to gain meaning independently.

Schools need to ensure that the system they are using for reading is being followed-up within the class-room for daily practice. They should also have a monitoring system in place to evaluate BMLs' ongoing progress. Ideally, BMLs should be assessed by a designated individual every 4-6 weeks if they are more independent readers but more often if they are still developing their early literacy skills.

Similarly for writing, BMLs' work needs to be leveled according to an established system. "Exemplars" or writing samples can serve as models to cross-reference BMLs' work against. In this way, everyone can understand what level the student is working at independently. Again, this information should be noted for all teachers to access. Collecting a student writing sample to put into a portfolio or file every month can provide valuable insights about how they are progressing. Like reading, BMLs will need to be monitored and given tips and strategies for moving forward.

All teachers, including subject teachers, should be able to access this kind of student information very easily without having to search through individual student files. Posting this information on a shared drive or network can be ideal since it can be easily updated and accessed by all the BMLs' teachers when needed.

DAILY READING AND DAILY WRITING PRACTICE

This particular strategy is extremely impactful and ensures that students have the required time within the school day to dedicate to meaningful, individualized reading and writing. While we already know of the benefits of daily reading and writing especially in relation to vocabulary development, this is not always reflected in existing school programs.

Administrators and teachers must work together to build in at least 15-20 minutes of daily (silent) reading and writing for all students across the school. There are countless pieces of research to support the value of daily reading, not only for BMLs, but all students. For many BMLs, the school day is their only opportunity to gain access to reading and writing in English. As a result, reading and writing time should be given one of the highest priorities within the school. This will allow BMLs to read leveled books and work on the writing strategy goals provided from their last assessment. In this way, teachers can be sure that BMLs are getting access to daily literacy without leaving this responsibility to chance. It is simply not enough to hope that parents will follow-up with student reading or writing at home or that the BMLs themselves will be motivated enough to sit and read once they get home.

The value of authentic student writing must be recognized; not only as a means of building BMLs' language but also for enabling logical thinking processes, self-expression and self-reflection. In many cases, BMLs' educational programs are deprived of meaningful writing opportunities but filled with worksheets and "busy tasks." This is also pointed out by Dr. Jim Cummins in Danling Fu's book, *Writing Between Languages* (2009):

> *For most ELL students, writing represents the most challenging language skill to acquire to native-like levels because it demands use of vocabulary, grammatical structures, and rhetorical conventions that are very different from conversational language. Typically, students get relatively little opportunity in classrooms to engage with the creation of meaning through written language. As Danling Fu points out, much of the "writing" that ELL students carry out consists of little more than fill-in-the-blanks exercises or short responses to questions about academic content. One of the reasons for this poverty of writing experience is the perception by many teachers that ELL students must first learn English before they can write in English (p. xi).*

INDIVIDUALIZED READING PROGRAMS AND GUIDED READING

As already-mentioned, knowing the level of a BML's reading can provide a teacher with much-needed information from which to develop an individualized program. In some schools, teachers run "guided reading" programs with small groups of similar-ability students while others employ "individualized" reading programs. These are usually set up by the English or class teacher who aims to move the child forward in their reading.

From the reading assessment, teachers can then help BMLs to identify "next steps" in their reading and understand how they can begin to reach the next level of difficulty. Many schools use sets of leveled reading books to support students' developing reading and once students are trained up to know their levels, they can begin to self-select books independently if books are easily accessible. This is an important consideration. When books are readily available, students can exchange them on their own, thus requiring less "management" time by the teacher.

BMLs should always know what their "next steps" are and should be given opportunities to practice these within their leveled books. While many NS students can move on to "independent reader" status, this is not usually the case with BMLs. Monitoring of BMLs can and should be ongoing so that their progress is consistently being observed. BMLs needing more focused support or intervention can be easily identified with this approach.

In the middle years or upper years when many English teachers have long since stopped listening to or monitoring BMLs' reading, these students' literacy development may have stagnated in the meantime. They may have even completely disengaged from reading. This is not something that BMLs can afford to miss out on, especially considering the valuable benefits that continued reading provides.

Implementing daily reading and writing initiatives across the school will require additional training, scheduling and time to organize BMLs' information; however, it is extremely worthwhile with a high return-on-investment.

Setting up a 15-20 minute, daily silent reading practice within the schedule can allow a teacher the opportunity to sit with one student at-a-time. During this time, teachers can monitor student reading and provide them with one or two new strategies. They can also offer focused modeling and guided practice within this short period of time.

If the English teacher sits and conferences with a different student each day, then they could ideally get through their whole rotation of students around every 6 weeks. This is a great model that works well within an already established routine.

Systems will work best when staff are trained and confident and they are asked to work within already-working routines and practices within the school. This requires teachers and staff teams to work together to plan these kinds of initiatives. Working with daily routines also enables all students to become trained up in the expectations of the classroom and with little need for teacher direction. This is built-in value that adds to the success of the program.

READ-ALOUDS

Read alouds can be one of the most satisfying parts of a student's day, especially if it is an entertaining book or novel. This kind of shared reading experience allows the teacher to engage students in the topic of the text or book while they read and students listen. Read-alouds typically involve a storybook or class novel that is read over a longer period of time. It encourages students to enjoy a story, to further reinforce their vocabulary exposure, builds up their experience with elements of "plot" and reading comprehension strategies. Since read-alouds offer many benefits to students, they should be incorporated within the school day or week as much as possible. Finding time in the school day for read-alouds may be easier for classroom teachers since they tend to have several opportunities to read a chapter or two, whereas English subject teachers may have less chance to build the read-aloud into their programme. In this case, even if teachers can only find short pockets of time in their weekly schedule, it can still be valuable for students to listen to and follow the story.

Read-alouds can also prompt in-class discussions where students share their feelings, ideas and predictions about a book or text. Read-alouds can also include other types of shared reading like newspapers, articles or text that are based around a particular subject. They can be incorporated within all kinds of subject classes.

DISCUSSIONS ABOUT BOOKS AND LITERATURE HELP SUPPORT VOCABULARY AND READING COMPREHENSION

One way to support student learning around literature and books is through rich discussion. Discussion provides an ideal format to help BMLs draw greater meaning from a text or story. It allows students build further detail into their already-existing interpretations of events and characters. BMLs that have been able to comprehend big ideas but still struggle with finer details in text can benefit from discussion because it naturally scaffolds what they already know while extending their comprehension even more. It also gives them an opportunity to clarify information, make inferences and develop predictions about what might happen next.

Remember that having good quality discussions about a topic or book gives BMLs additional practice and exposure to vocabulary but also builds their engagement and interest. Incorporating controversial questions or provocative statements into dialogue can stimulate higher-levels of discussion and even debates around issues. This helps to bring learning into the real world for BMLs.

As we already know, BMLs' vocabulary knowledge directly impacts their reading comprehension. In our work, we see many students who are able to trick parents and teachers into thinking their reading skills are strong because they often seem to fluently "read" words from a difficult piece of text. In fact, while their "word decoding" skills may be strong, many of these students do not actually understand very much of what they have read. In most cases, this is simply because the vocabulary in the text is too difficult for them to comprehend.

In the article, "Reading Comprehension Requires Knowledge-of Words and the World," (2003), Professor E.D. Hirsch Jr. discusses the positive impact that can be made in reading and writing when students understand a topic deeply. When they know a particular topic intimately, they are more likely to learn (and understand) the related vocabulary and concepts. This has numerous benefits:

> *...texts and topics must be compelling enough that both the teacher and the children want to talk about what they read and deep enough that there is enough reason to revisit the topic. Such immersion in a topic not only improves reading and develops vocabulary, it also develops writing skill. One of the remarkable discoveries that I made over the many years that I taught composition was how much my students' writing improved when our class stuck to an interesting subject over an extended period. The organization of their papers got better. Their spelling improved. Their style improved. Their ideas improved. Now I understand why: When the mind becomes familiar with a subject, its limited resources can begin to turn to other aspects of the writing task, just as in reading. All aspects of a skill grow and develop as subject matter familiarity grows. So we kill several birds with one stone when we teach skills by teaching stuff (pg. 28).*

Meaning is at the heart of reading comprehension and so we can see that engaging students in deep learning contexts and through texts which support these concepts, not only builds their interest, but also provides them with repeated exposure to new vocabulary words. Then as students go about their reading and learning, new opportunities are created for them to learn and use these vocabulary words.

FOCUS ON "GENRE WRITING" OR TYPES OF WRITING

In most curricula in English-medium schools, there is a focus on exposing and teaching students the "genres" of writing so that they can understand there are different forms of writing for different purposes. Narrative writing, report writing and persuasive writing are all examples of writing genres that students are likely to explore throughout their education.

Each of these kinds of writing genres makes use of particular features that students should be made aware of. For example, report writing uses the "present tense" and includes relevant facts and details about a topic. Narrative writing uses a particular structure for the plot which follows sequences of "beginning," "middle" and "end".

Since most curricula expose students to the same genres of writing from year-to-year, it makes sense that students be taught these specific features and how to organize their work accordingly.

One way to do this is to introduce students to "graphic organizers" (sometimes called "writing frames") in order to help them lay out their ideas before they start writing.

English teachers and class teachers would be responsible for explicitly teaching BMLs these writing types as well as how to work with corresponding graphic organizers. Since many subject teachers also ask students to take part in different types of writing assignments, it makes sense for them to use the same graphic organizers that students are already used to using within their classes. Then there is no "down time" or additional learning time. This is a very high-impact strategy because it not only breaks down the assignment into manageable components for BMLs but it also supports them in working more independently.

Subject teachers also have their own formats for writing (e.g. lab reports for science, research reports for history, etc.) so they should provide BMLs with graphic organizers to reflect these particular formats.

Getting started, staff teams should collectively decide on the graphic organizers that will be used within and across the school and these should be actively taught within the English class. This would then allow BMLs to fine-tune their writing skills across subject areas. They will be better prepared and will know how to attack their writing assignments with greater independence and accuracy. This allows subject teachers to spend more time with BMLs on the content of their work rather than focusing on the writing itself.

Since BMLs benefit greatly from repetition and practice, this whole-school approach creates significant impact. It allows English teachers to focus on the initial teaching of writing genres and formats then allows BMLs to build greater proficiency through further reinforcement within their subject classes.

READING AND WRITING "CONFERENCING"

To build on students' reading and writing progress, teachers must provide them with direct feedback about their reading and writing. Again this can be done within the class framework for 15 minutes of reading and writing or even with other types of assignments.

The objective is for teachers to help BMLs reach the next level of difficulty by looking at the errors within their reading or writing samples. They think about what strategy the student needs to move forward. Ideally this strategy should be a "high-impact strategy"—one that would make a big difference in the BML's reading or writing. For instance, if the student frequently repeats words as they write, they could be taught to use a mini-thesaurus or adjective list to replace them. If they do not use paragraphs, they can be given a quick demonstration (using real books with paragraphs) on what the purpose of paragraphing is and how to do it. The idea is to model ideal strategies for students who then have an opportunity to "try it out" under the guidance of the teacher. During this session, the teacher should record the student's new strategy or strategies on an index card for them. Then BMLs take this card with them and apply the strategy whenever they are doing writing tasks—either in the English class or in their other subject classes. When the BML and teacher conference again, the teacher should check on that particular skill to see the progress they have made. At this time, they should either clarify the strategy if more instruction is needed or they should move onto a new goal.

Conferencing with BMLs is a much more effective way to give feedback than simply correcting their work or writing lengthy comments on it. It allows the teacher to demonstrate a strategy explicitly, showing them where the problem is and how to fix it. It also gives students the opportunity to ask questions and try out the new strategy with support. Then, there is a clear follow-up for the student to work with over the next few weeks.

With many opportunities for BMLs to practice their reading and writing during the school week, students should always be focused on applying the goals written on their individual index cards. This can be incorporated any time there is writing within the school day, either in the English class or in their subject classes. Subject teachers can support student goals by having them put their index cards onto their desks during writing assignments. Then they can understand what BMLs are working towards and can reinforce this.

Once students know and can follow the routine, this approach can work extremely well. If it is incorporated as a whole-school practice, it can have very powerful effects.

PARTICULAR ENGLISH CHALLENGES FOR BMLs

It is fairly common for BMLs to have significant gaps in their written skills as compared to their oral language or reading skills. As we know, this does not necessarily indicate a learning disability. This can be a result of normal development of second (additional) language acquisition. For example, if an individual is developing their CALP, they may be better at oral communication than written simply because they are not yet proficient in the more academic features of written expression. They will likely need further practice and targeted support.

Even if BMLs have gained good oral and written skills, they may still experience difficulty with formal language and writing that is required in secondary and sometimes even middle school. These can include "metaphoric competence" and "passive voice."

Metaphoric competence refers to having skill in the use of symbolic or figurative language. Metaphors, symbolism and idioms make up this component. BMLs often lack proficiency with these higher-level language skills because they are often a neglected aspect of language teaching (Sabet & Tavakoli, 2016). In most cases, BMLs attempt to translate figurative or metaphoric language word-for-word but are still not able to comprehend because there is an alternative or hidden meaning to the words or phrases. For example, to "kill two birds with one stone," does not mean that you will actually kill birds; it means that you will accomplish two things at once. Similarly, "I heard it through the grapevine," means that you have heard a rumor or gossip through your friends or family. You can see how easy it would be for a BML to get confused when coming across figurative language or metaphors. BMLs must have direct exposure and experience to these phrases or concepts in order for them to gain the subtleties of the English language.

Idioms can be taught early on with explicit instruction. BMLs at the later FL stages can be taught many idioms as long as they are explained well and provided with relevant examples and contextual cues like pictures, for instance. There are numerous lists of high-frequency idioms that students are likely to come across and these can easily be focused on through "Idiom Booklets" which allow BMLs time to write the idiom, provide an example and meaning as well as draw a picture to support recall.

Metaphors and symbolism are more difficult to grasp, especially because they require a higher-level of cognition or abstract thinking to comprehend the meaning within a unique context. For instance, "all the world's a stage..." requires the learner to draw a link or comparison between the world and stage in order to build up the meaning within the target context. Understanding metaphor is a very complex cognitive task that requires extensive instruction to build familiarity and proficiency. Roessingh & Elgie (2009) describe the "critical threshold" of metaphoric competence to occur around 15 years of age for NS. At this time, students are required to cope with more complex cognitive-based language features. More advanced metaphoric language is commonly used in secondary school but again, students will need explicit training and practice around these language devices.

An easy way to explain metaphor without any words is to show images of artwork that is ironic or controversial, such as the works of *Banksy*, the graffiti artist. Asking students to examine images and think about the message can help them understand that metaphors work the same way—they have to delve beyond the surface words or meaning to truly comprehend the underlying message. Essentially, they must "read between-the-lines."

Passive voice can often be another stumbling block for BMLs. In English grammar, sentences are categorized as either "active" or "passive:"

> *In an active sentence, the person or thing responsible for the action in the sentence comes first. In a passive sentence, the person or thing acted on comes first, and the actor is added at the end, introduced with the preposition "by." The passive form of the verb is signaled by a form of "to be"...In a passive sentence, we often omit the actor completely: The uncertainty principle was formulated in 1927 (Corson & Smollett, 2015).*

Even native English speakers may find the concept of "passive voice" confusing but it is important to draw attention to this concept so your BMLs can be clear on it as well. BMLs can begin to learn about passive voice around TL1 stage when they are more advanced in their English proficiency. NS typically begin actively learning about it around 11 or 12 years of age since it is used extensively within science (lab) reports and also within fiction writing. BMLs will require specific instruction and modeling with this, first to recognize the grammatical structures and then to apply them within their own work when required.

INTENSIVE LITERACY SUPPORT

While many schools have additional support programs for students struggling with literacy, this support may not always get the desired results. It may lack targeted focus or a clearly-stated goal or it may not be intensive enough to get results. Support sessions that are offered once or twice weekly may simply not be enough for BMLs who need to fill their gaps. This model is often justified internally so that teachers can spread themselves across a greater number of students.

While it does start out with the right intention, this kind of support usually becomes diluted. A much better approach would be to do a shorter-term intervention of daily sessions with the target student(s). This way they benefit more from day-to-day practice and feedback.

In many cases, one to two months of intensive, goal-oriented support is enough to help students make significant progress in target areas. Then once students have met their goal(s), the teacher can select new students for daily sessions. This approach gives the teacher a much clearer direction for his or her work and enables them to pick up where they left off the previous day. Students are likelier to make greater gains, especially when instruction is embedded with the following components: goal-setting, teacher modeling, direct feedback and guided practice. There should be plenty of opportunities for students to learn through real reading and writing rather than worksheet-style activities. This will allow students the opportunity to receive direct feedback about their strategy-use while reading and writing.

LITERACY IN THE MOTHER-TONGUE

For many of our *MT Literate* BMLs, maintaining literacy in their MT is equally as important as reading and writing in English. BMLs that are able to speak, read and write in their own language are able to reach a higher level of functioning with their language(s). They will be better able to express themselves as well as connect with their culture through print. For many BMLs, keeping up their literacy skills can also give them an edge in educational or employment opportunities later on.

In addition to teachers, both parents and BMLs themselves should understand the importance of maintaining the MT and continuing literacy. As already discussed, it is highly recommended that BMLs continue their MT development through MT classes if at all possible. These classes should support the development of language and literacy skills so that BMLs have opportunity to read and write in their MT as much as possible—supporting them to become more balanced bilinguals. Schools can collaborate with external organizations, cultural associations and even community members or volunteers to provide MT classes. Lessons can be organized after-school or on the weekends. In some schools, MT classes are organized within the school day when students would normally study a foreign language. There are several models that are implemented successfully but schools need to think about what will work best for their BMLs and their school.

The English-medium school can also support MT literacy by including MT reading and writing when appropriate. Having a good selection of MT books and resources in the school library and even within individual classrooms is a good idea. This sends an important message to BMLs because it communicates that their MT is a valuable resource worth maintaining. Building MT literacy initiatives into the school can also ensure that students, parents and teachers understand this important message.

BMLs Studying Additional Languages

Some schools require students to take 1-2 foreign language classes at-a-time in addition to English. These classes may even be mandated by governments, but schools should try to ensure that BMLs, especially BMLs in the Foundational Language stages do not have to focus their efforts on learning too many languages at one time if at all possible. While we are not saying that BMLs cannot learn an additional language(s), we simply encourage school staff to consider the value of that additional foreign language, especially for BMLs who may still find learning English overwhelming.

If the language is the language of the country and BMLs are likely to encounter that language in their day-to-day interactions, then it should be given importance. However, if it is simply part of the educational program for students to learn more languages then teachers will have to understand that this means students' energy and focus will be diluted. Since BMLs typically need more time to catch up in their English language and literacy, they can definitely benefit from additional time in English rather than a language that has little practical value for them. This does not mean that students should receive "ESL" type support or "English lessons" in place of foreign languages but they should have access to valuable and rich experiences in English or even their MT if possible.

This can translate to many different options for schools. One idea is to have BMLs explore an independent study where they focus on learning more about their class topics or themes. This would allow them further opportunity to apply their English skills purposefully through *more* reading, writing, speaking and listening.

Taking Literacy Seriously

Schools must take a careful look at their literacy policies and practices if they want to make a positive impact on BMLs' success. They must examine the bigger picture to understand how their literacy programs and policies contribute to student achievement. Upon thorough examination, schools may notice gaps in their literacy programs that need attention. They may find that old practices are not working or do not reflect their growing knowledge base about BMLs. This can stimulate school teams to find new ways of servicing students—either with their existing staff and timetables or outside-the-box in terms of new initiatives or scheduling.

In any case, there is always room for improvement and once it is understood just how valuable literacy is for BMLs, staff can work together to make positive changes that reflect this within their policies and programs.

Having all staff—class teachers/English teachers and subject teachers—work together on shared goals for literacy can create a more holistic or "wraparound" service for BMLs. This will ultimately optimize their quality of learning as well as add impact to their learning.

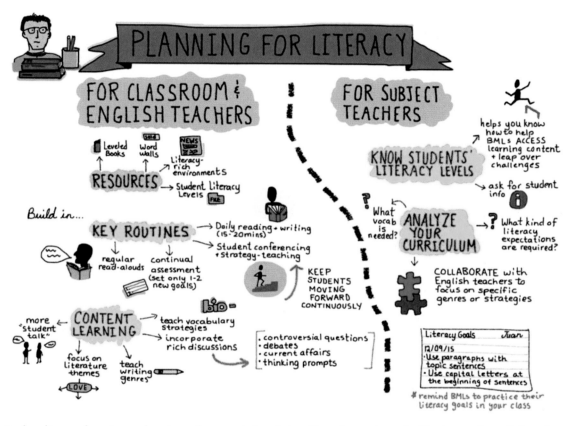

Student literacy-learning and goals can be extended to their subject classes through effective teacher collaborations

DIG DEEP:

1. Why is it critical for BMLs to have ongoing literacy programs?

2. Why is "conferencing" more impactful than "marking" BMLs' writing?

3. How does vocabulary support literacy development?

BREAKOUT:

4. How does your classroom environment support literacy development? How could you make it "literacy rich?"

5. How could a teacher create time in their schedule to conference with BMLs? What are the practical considerations for implementation?

6. How easy is it for you to listen to each of your BMLs reading on a regular basis? How could you schedule this into your classroom routines?

EXPLORE:

What kind of literacy programs does your school have in place? Are they effective? What could be done to create greater impact in literacy development for the BMLs within your school?

Appendix

1. SAMPLE PARENT INTERVIEW SHEET

2. LANGUAGE HELPERS:

    Arabic

    Dutch

    French

    German

    Hindi

    Japanese

    Korean

    Mandarin

    Polish

    Russian

    Spanish

    Urdu

SAMPLE PARENT INTERVIEW SHEET

Child's Full Name: Other Names:

Date of Birth: Date:

Address: Phone:

Mother's Name/Contacts:

Father's Name/Contacts:

Emergency Contact:

CHECK ALL THAT APPLY:

☐ MT LITERATE   ☐ PRACTICAL PROFICIENCY   ☐ ENGLISH DIALECT
☐ MT NOT LITERATE   ☐ BML WITH IDENTIFIED SPECIAL NEEDS
☐ YOUNG BML LEARNER   ☐ NO/DISRUPTED SCHOOLING

CHILD'S BACKGROUND INFORMATION:

Child's Country of Birth:

Nationality and Passport:

Custody Arrangement (if applicable):

Child's L1:   Child's L2:

Additional Languages:

MOTHER'S BACKGROUND INFORMATION:

Mother's Date of Birth:

Mother's Country of Birth:

Mother's Nationality and Passport:

Mother's L1:   Mother's L2:

Additional Languages:

FATHER'S BACKGROUND INFORMATION:

Father's Date of Birth:

Father's Country of Birth:

Father's Nationality and Passport:

Father's L1:   Father's L2:

Additional Languages:

SIBLINGS AND FAMILY MAKEUP (parent's marital status, etc.):

List siblings and ages:

EXPATRIATE/OVERSEAS FAMILY HISTORY (List all countries lived in and dates):

FAMILY LANGUAGE BACKGROUND:

Main/all languages spoken between parents (include % of time):

Main/all languages spoken between this child and mother (include % of time):

Main/all languages spoken between this child and father (include % of time):

Main/all languages spoken between this child and siblings (include % of time):

Main/all languages spoken between this child and their grandparents/extended family members (include % of time):

Does this child have refugee status? Are they an asylum-seeker? If so, please provide relevant background information and details, regarding refugee camps or any possible trauma the child may have experienced:

EDUCATIONAL BACKGROUND OF STUDENT:

List Previous Schools Attended:

Grade/Year:	School & Country:	Curriculum & Language Medium:	Previous Support:	Comments:

Additional Information:

DEVELOPMENTAL HISTORY:

Any complications with pregnancy and/or delivery?

Were the developmental milestones on-target for walking and talking?

Any health concerns? (e.g. allergies, surgeries, health conditions)?

Has the child had a hearing screening test? If so when?

Has the child had a vision screening test? If so when?

Has the child ever received specialized referrals or supports?

For motor skills?

For speech/language?

For social/emotional/behavioural?

For education?

Has your child been previously identified as a bilingual/multilingual learner or EAL/ELL/ESL learner? Have they received any additional support?

Has your child been previously identified as student with special educational needs? Have they received any diagnoses? If so, what? Have they received any intervention or support (provide details)?

TO BE COMPLETED AFTER PARENT INTERVIEW AND AFTER STUDENT OBSERVATION

(Include dates and attach any samples – to be put into student's main file)

ASSESSMENT:	DATE:	RESULTS:
Reading Assessment (Indicate Year/Grade Level Equivalent)		
Writing Assessment (Indicate Year/Grade Level Equivalent)		
If Applicable: Mother-tongue Writing Assessment (Indicate Approximate Year/Grade Equivalent)		
Mathematics Assessment (Indicate Year/Grade Level Equivalent)		
Stage on the *ELP Map*:		
Long-term Vocabulary Goal:		

Additional Comments:

Signature of Person Completing Form:

LANGUAGE HELPER: ARABIC

MAIN AREAS SPOKEN

- The Levant area: Syria, Lebanon, Jordan, Palestine
- The Arabian Gulf: Kuwait, Bahrain, Iraq, Oman, Qatar, United Arab Emirates, Kingdom of Saudi Arabia
- Africa: Egypt, Sudan, Algeria, Tunisia, Libya and Mauritania, Yemen, Somalia, Djibouti, Comoros

NUMBER OF SPEAKERS WORLDWIDE

There are over 390 million speakers as a first and additional language.

ABOUT THE LANGUAGE

- Arabic is a Semitic language that has many spoken variations, often referred to as "dialects" (based on different regions as listed above).
- Written Arabic is very different to spoken Arabic. In most languages, the written form of the language is a written representation of the oral language where the syntax, grammar and vocabulary are similar in both. However in Arabic, this is not the case. The written and spoken languages are very distinct (a reasonable comparison might be Modern English and Shakespearean English).
- There are 2 forms of written Arabic: Classical Arabic and Modern Standard Arabic. Classical Arabic is the written language derived from *The Holy Quran* (Holy Book) and has not changed or evolved over the centuries.
- Many Muslims can read Classical Arabic only from *The Holy Quran* and most authors/writers today do not write using Classical Arabic. The literary language used across the Arabic-speaking world is called: Modern Standard Arabic (MSA). MSA is not a specific spoken dialect but rather a formal language understood by all Arabic speakers. It is used for written texts and as well across news and radio broadcasts. Arabic speakers' colloquial spoken language is their regional dialects so when they learn to read and write, they must learn to write using syntax, grammatical features and vocabulary which are different from their own spoken dialects. As a

result, it can be a difficult process for some mother-tongue speakers to fully master the written form.

- Arabic can be described as a very descriptive or "flowery" language and there is a rich culture of poetry and stories written in Arabic.
- Arabic is also a Semitic language and therefore shares similarities with other Semitic languages, such as Aramaic and Hebrew. In terms of writing, several other languages use the Arabic script, such as Persian/Farsi, Urdu, Pashto and Kurdish.
- Arabic is a phonetic language with each letter shape representing a particular sound. The letter sounds (phonics) are consistent and reliable, unlike English, where one letter can make several different sounds.
- MSA has 28 letters of the alphabet – 22 consonants and 6 vowels.
- The English letter sounds p, v, x, ch and "hard g" are not typically used in Arabic (with the exception of some specific regional dialects).
- Directionality of print is read from right-to-left, opposite to English.
- Directionality of numerals is the same as in English, with numbers read from left-to-right.
- Arabic does not make use of capital letters as in English, but letters can have up to 4 different ways of being written, depending on their position within the word (beginning, middle, end or if it stands-alone).
- Arabic has categories of "long" and "short" vowels in words; "short" vowels are usually written in words for early teaching of reading; however, most are omitted later on (e.g. after the individual recognizes words by sight).
- The punctuation system in English has more rigid rules than Arabic.
- There are several forms of the 2nd person pronoun, "you" as compared to English.
- All nouns are either masculine or feminine with adjectives matching the masculine or feminine noun.
- There are fewer rules for making plurals than in English.
- The indefinite article ("a/an") does not exist in Arabic so often the word "one" is replaced instead when speaking English (e.g. "One dog came and bit me.").
- The definite article ("the" which translates to "al" in Arabic) exists and is used more often in comparison to English.
- There is no verb, "to be," (within the present tense) in the Arabic language (e.g. "I am a teacher" would be translated as "I teacher").
- Arabic uses a largely V-S-O word order but can also make use of S-V-O occasionally

- Some verb tenses which exist in English do not exist in Arabic (e.g. the present perfect tense, (have been/gone, has seen, etc.).
- There are no exact modal verbs (can, should, will, etc.) or auxiliary verbs that translate exactly to English

POSSIBLE CHALLENGES FOR ARABIC SPEAKERS LEARNING ENGLISH

- Arabic speakers can find the vowel sounds particularly challenging as English concepts of "short" and "long" vowels are very different to theirs.
- They may have problems pronouncing some of the letter sounds in English (e.g. "p" is often replaced by a "b" as in "Bebsi" for "Pepsi").
- They may have problems in differentiating what they perceive as similar sounding short vowels, "i/e/u."
- Arabic speakers may find English spellings tricky, especially when trying to identify and apply the short vowel sounds.
- Correct letter formations and directionality of print in English can be a challenge until established.
- Arabic speakers may have challenges with the irregular word stress patterns in English.
- The correct use of "who" and "which" may be a challenge for Arabic speakers since there is no distinction of human and non-human nouns in Arabic.
- Arabic speakers can over-use the definite article "the."
- Arab speakers can find English word order (S-V-O) challenging.
- They may find the concept of "capital letters" difficult to get used to.
- The punctuation system in English is more rigid than in Arabic. Arabic speakers tend to use more commas and often what we consider "run on sentences" would be acceptable in the Arabic language.
- In Arabic, use of repeated synonyms can be appropriate while in comparison it may seem redundant in English.
- The usage and rules for the "passive voice" in Arabic are easier than in English so this can be a challenge for some Arabic speakers.

ABOUT ARAB CULTURE

Religion is often deeply linked to many cultural aspects in the Arab world. The majority religion in the Arab world is Islam. The degree to which people follow the religion can vary from individual-to-individual with some people following the religious principles strictly while other Muslims do not practice the religion at all. There are also large communities of Christians in the Middle East so one should not to assume that all Arabs or Arabic-speakers are practicing Muslims. There are also smaller Jewish communities.

Family is extremely important to most Arabs and they often maintain close ties with their extended family members.

Their value of "time" can be different in comparison to the West in that they tend to focus on what is important in the "now" rather than strictly adhering to appointments. Arabs like to "keep face" which means they do not like to be put in situations where they might make a mistake or be publicly embarrassed (e.g. admitting blame, etc.). In many Arab cultures, individuals do not like to say "no" to someone directly since they feel uncomfortable (e.g. in terms of accepting invitations, etc.).

Arabs are very hospitable people who will go to great lengths to extend invitations or gifts to others. This can be uncomfortable for Westerners who are not used to this but they should feel free to accept the gift or invitation, otherwise it could cause offense.

Some Islamic children are separated from the opposite sex in schools around middle-school and are encouraged to socialize with the same-sex. Some Islamic women and men do not always shake hands when greeting the opposite sex. It may be more appropriate if you are greeting the opposite sex to not extend your hand out to them at all and instead just smile and say hello, only extending your hand if they do first.

Some Islamic women (although not all) may choose to cover their hair with a hijab (scarf) or the full face and hair with a "niqab". This is a personal preference.

In regards to names, a general convention is for the individual to have a given name first, the second name is the father's first name and then the third name is the family name. If there are additional names in-between, this is usually the grandfather's name. For example, "Saleh Mahmoud Hamad Al-Saud" would indicate that "Mahmoud" is Saleh's father's name and "Hamad" would be the grandfather's name. "Al" means "the" and "Hamza" would indicate the family Saleh comes from. Similarly, "Ibn" or "Bin" means "son of" and can sometimes be found within Arabic names.

SCHOOLING

Education in the Arab world varies from country-to-country. Although many Arab countries have compulsory and public schooling, the quality and age of starting varies. There is a strong culture of private schooling in many countries within the Arabic-speaking world.

Students are generally expected to learn how to "do" rather than how to think critically outside of textbooks or prescribed activities. Often, family or close friend obligations take precedence over study commitments. Students value completion of coursework diplomas and certificates. Students are used to competing with each other in class, often comparing themselves to each other. They value academic subjects that are related to career goals and many have high educational aspirations.

Language Helper: Dutch

MAIN AREAS SPOKEN

Dutch is primarily spoken in The Netherlands, Belgium (referred to as the "Flemish" language) and Suriname (South America). It is also spoken in Aruba and the Dutch Caribbean and is a very close relative to "Africaans," which is one of the languages spoken in South Africa.

NUMBER OF SPEAKERS WORLDWIDE

There are over 23 million Dutch speakers as a first language.

LANGUAGE ORIGIN

Dutch stems from the Indo – European family and West Germanic branch of languages. It shares many similarities to the English language.

ABOUT THE LANGUAGE

- Dutch shares many similar words with English (cognates) but they are pronounced differently. This can often make it easier for Dutch speakers to recognize and understand English words.
- Dutch is a more "direct" language than English, with fewer tendencies to show "politeness" as compared to the English language.
- Dutch shares a similar word order, grammar and vocabulary to German.
- The alphabet is the same in both English and Dutch; however, the pronunciation of letter sounds is not the same (especially vowels and other more "guttural" sounds). There are a number of consonant and vowel combinations.
- Dutch phonics is highly-reliable so words are usually pronounced as they are spelled.
- There are no silent letters in Dutch.
- The stress and intonation patterns in Dutch and English are relatively similar.
- Dutch has 3 genders: masculine, feminine and neuter.

- Dutch follows S-V-O as in English as well as S-O-V.
- There is no verb "to do" in Dutch.
- Like English, Dutch has regular and irregular verbs.
- Dutch has many of the same tenses but they are not used in the same way as compared to English.
- Dutch uses fewer capital letters. It does not use capital letters for days of the week, months of the year, people or titles.

POSSIBLE CHALLENGES FOR DUTCH SPEAKERS LEARNING ENGLISH

- Dutch speakers may be challenged in "sounding polite" in English since it is acceptable for them to answer with a simple "yes/no" in their language.
- They may find it difficult to master the "th" sound (may replace with the "d" sound instead).
- Dutch is a much more phonetic language so it can be a challenge for Dutch speakers to master English spellings.
- Dutch vowels and letters look similar but are pronounced different. Vowels do not have a "long" or "short" sound, just one sound.
- They will likely find it difficult to know the differences between similar words in English like, "to/too" or "they're/their/there" etc. since there are no homophones in Dutch.
- Rules for double consonants (e.g. bell) may be difficult.
- The use of English tenses can be a challenge for a Dutch speaker.
- Putting together more complex sentence structure may be a challenge.

ABOUT DUTCH CULTURE

Dutch people are practical and disciplined. They place great emphasis on the family unit. They tend to be private people in regards to their personal affairs and may find it uncomfortable to be asked personal questions directly. Dutch will usually use first names with known acquaintances but often address new people with "Mr." or "Ms." etc.

Dutch culture emphasizes egalitarian beliefs and this is carried forward in their governmental policies and practices. Everyone in society is valued and given respect and opportunity to share their opinions. This is true even in the workplace and school environments.

Appearances and social conventions are important in Dutch culture. People value being neat and organized and people are hard-working and detail-oriented. Being on-time is important as are maintaining schedules and appointments.

Dutch are straight-forward and may sometimes seem "blunt" in regards to their preference for directness. They might seem to "get to the point" quickly without flowery conversation or small talk. They honour their word and tend to be fair and focused on facts and information.

SCHOOLING

In The Netherlands, students start compulsory schooling at the age of 5, and carry on until at least the age of 16. Secondary schooling can finish at the age of 17 or 18.

Education in The Netherlands is child-centered and provides students autonomy and opportunities to be creative and solve problems.

Language Helper – French

MAIN AREAS SPOKEN

French is spoken in France, Monaco, Belgium, Canada as well as some areas in the Middle East, Caribbean and Africa. It is one of the most popular languages to learn as an additional-language around the world.

NUMBER OF SPEAKERS WORLDWIDE

There are over 130 million speakers as a first and second language.

LANGUAGE ORIGIN

French is a Romance language derived from Latin, similar to other Romance languages like: Spanish, Italian, Portuguese, Catalan and Romanian.

ABOUT THE LANGUAGE

- French shares many similar words with English (cognates).
- There are many "false friends" which can look like similar letters and words but are not pronounced or used the same as in English.
- French uses the same 21 letters and 5 vowels although they are pronounced differently to English. French also has additional sounds which are made by symbols (accents/ diacritics) which are placed over/under specific letters. Letters are written in both upper and lower case, similar to English.
- French does not have the "th" sound.
- There are 2 pronouns for "you": a polite form ("vous") and an informal form ("tu").
- All nouns and objects are either masculine (le livre) or feminine (la table) and the corresponding adjective changes its spelling to match the noun (e.g. le livre noir, la table noire)
- There is no corresponding word for "it" in French.

- Most plurals end with an "s" (e.g. voiture becomes voitures); however this "s" is silent.
- Definite and indefinite articles are used in French.
- Word stress patterns in French are more consistent than in English which tends to be more irregular.
- French and English share the same basic sentence structure of S-V-O but they do differ in more complex grammar structures.
- The adjective can come before or after the noun but typically comes after.
- French has similar tenses to English.
- In French, the present tense and the present continuous tense are the same (e.g. je me brosse mes dentes = I brush/I am brushing my teeth).
- French uses "reflexive verbs" where the action is being done to oneself.
- The letter "h" is a silent letter in French.
- Capitalization is used less often in French. Although many rules are the same, the 1st person pronoun ("I/"je") is not capitalized. Days of the week, months of the year, nationality, street names, etc. are also not capitalized.

POSSIBLE CHALLENGES FOR FRENCH SPEAKERS LEARNING ENGLISH

- French speakers may become confused with the number of "false friends" when they begin learning English (e.g. pronunciation of the vowels). They may find English spellings challenging since they have the same letter formations as English yet they sound differently.
- They may have a tendency not to pronounce the "th," sound, the "h" or the "s" (at the end of a word).
- They may find the pronunciation and stress patterns in words challenging.
- They may not apply capitalization rules easily.
- They may confuse their use of tenses such as the present and present continuous tenses (e.g. "I am going to school every day.").
- They may put the adjective (describing words) after the noun rather than before it.
- They may find telling time in English challenging.
- They may not be easily able to formulate questions since they do not have the verb, "to do" (e.g. "Do you...?").

ABOUT FRENCH CULTURE

The French have a very strong culture rich in traditions and arts. They take great pride in their country and place great value on their traditions and customs.

While the French are predominantly Catholics, France separates the "State" from "Church" or religion. This is reflected in the legal system.

SCHOOLING

In France, students enter primary school at the age of 6 and education is compulsory until the age of 16. After, students can carry on in secondary education for university or vocational training.

The French education system values high academics rather than the creative and discovery process. The teacher's role is still traditionally held as the font of knowledge. There is a strong emphasis placed on exams all through the schooling system. Students who do not pass the exams or do not achieve the expected results repeat the academic year again.

Writing in correct French is very important to French teachers. French students are expected to be well-versed in various forms of writing in order to pass the "Baccalaureat" (end of high school exam).

Language Helper – German

MAIN AREAS SPOKEN

German is spoken in Germany, Austria, Switzerland, and Lichtenstein; some parts of Northern Italy as well as Luxembourg and Belgium. German is also widely-learned as an additional language.

NUMBER OF SPEAKERS WORLDWIDE

There are over 95 million speakers as a first language and 10- 15 million speakers as an additional language.

LANGUAGE ORIGIN

German is a West Germanic language and has many similarities to: Afrikaans, Dutch and English.

ABOUT THE LANGUAGE

- The German language shares many similarities to English and so has many cognates which make it easy for Germans to recognize these words in English. There are also many "false friends" which may look like German words but are completely different in meaning.
- German has a very similar stress pattern to the English language.
- They do not have the "th" sound.
- The German script is very similar to English.
- German has 30 letters of the alphabet. 26 (21 letters and 5 vowels) are similar to English; however, there are 4 additional letters: ä, ö, ü, and the ß (the double s).
- Although the vowels look similar to English, they are not pronounced in the same way.
- German and English have many differences with tenses and their uses. There is no present/past continuous and no future tense in German.
- All nouns in German are gender-based: feminine, masculine and neutral.
- The indefinite article in German has 3 forms: masculine, feminine and neuter.

- The definite article has 2 forms.
- The word order is most often "S-V-O" but can also make use of "S-O-V."
- German has many modal verbs but there is no verb "to do" in German.
- Use of capitalization is quite similar to English; however, all nouns are capitalized, even within sentences.

POSSIBLE CHALLENGES FOR GERMAN SPEAKERS LEARNING ENGLISH

- German speakers may find grasping mastery of the English vowels sounds and their uses a challenge since their phonics system is more consistent as compared to English.
- They may become confused by the "th", "v," "w" and "f" sounds of English.
- German speakers may find the use of English tenses quite challenging at times.
- They may struggle with English rules for capitalization.
- They may not be easily able to formulate questions that have "do" in them.

ABOUT GERMAN CULTURE

German society values structure, good productivity, thriftiness and punctuality. They are a people who like order and feel comfortable when time is respected. As a result, they like calendars, appointments and schedules to be respected.

At first, Germans might seem to be "cold" to people outside their culture since they can take time to get to know others before opening up. Germans have a strong sense of community and family values. In German culture, perfectionism and expertise are respected highly and German people would rarely like to admit fault or an error, even jokingly.

SCHOOLING

Students attend free and compulsory schooling from the ages of 6 up to the age of 17 or 18. After Grade 4, students are streamed into one of 3 schools which prepare them for university or vocational studies.

The Germans value education and offer free education to their citizens. Post-secondary education is also free, not only to citizens but non-citizens as well.

Language Helper – Hindi

MAIN AREAS SPOKEN

Hindi is one of the official languages of India and is widely spoken in northern and central India along with Nepal, Pakistan and Bangladesh. It is also spoken in Mauritius, South Africa and Fiji as well as numerous other countries where large numbers of Indians have settled.

NUMBER OF SPEAKERS WORLDWIDE

There are over 425 million speakers of Hindi as a first-language and over 120 million additional-language speakers across the world.

LANGUAGE ORIGIN

Hindi belongs to the Indo-Aryan (Indo-European) language family and is also derived from the ancient language of Sanskrit.

ABOUT THE LANGUAGE

- The Hindi language shares many loanwords (cognates) from Arabic, Persian and Turkish languages due to a long history of invasions. It is very similar to the Urdu language although they do have different scripts (Urdu uses the Arabic script).
- Although Hindi is an official language in India, there are some Indians who do not speak the language, for either political reasons or because they speak English or another regional, Indian language. There are two main dialects of Hindi found in the Eastern and Western regions of India as well as other dialects within smaller areas.
- Hindi is structured differently to English since it follows a S-O-V pattern (e.g. "She apple eats").
- In Hindi, each noun is masculine or feminine and this is shown by adding an ending on the word.

- There are no articles ("a" or "the") in Hindi nor are there specific words for "he" or "she."
- The Hindi language has many more personal pronouns than in English since there are different ways to address specific individuals depending on the level of respect or relationship.
- The Hindu script appears very similar to the ancient script of Sanskrit with a line that connects the letters at the top. The writing direction is from left-to-right as in English.
- There are 33 consonants and 11 vowels and the language is extremely phonetic with each letter representing a different sound. There are no capital letters but there are similar forms of punctuation.
- Hindi does not use as wide a variety of adjectives in comparison to English. Adjectives can be repeated twice to indicate their intensity (e.g. "little, little cat" for "tiny cat" in English).
- Prepositions come after the noun in Hindi (e.g. "on the table" is translated to "table on") and are called "postpositions."
- In Hindi there is no auxiliary verb for "to do," so instead of using "do..?" or "does..?" for asking questions, intonation is used to indicate meaning.
- Hindi uses similar verb tenses to English but they do not easily correspond to those used in English.

POSSIBLE CHALLENGES FOR HINDI SPEAKERS LEARNING ENGLISH

- Hindi speakers may struggle with pronunciation and being understood because of the different types of intonation patterns they are used to in Hindi.
- They may find English letter formations challenging until established.
- They may make errors with the English S-V-O.
- English spellings may be difficult because they are not as predictable as in Hindi; Consonant clusters (e.g. "fl-" or "str-") are not common in Hindi so students may struggle to decode and pronounce them.
- They may not apply capitalization rules easily.
- There are very different intonation patterns in English compared to Hindi so students may not easily be understood.
- They may find it challenging to use the definite article and may insert the word "one" in place of "a" or "the."

- They may speak in the "present continuous tense" in place of the "simple tense" (e.g. "I am speaking to my mother everyday.").
- They may not easily formulate questions in English because they do not have "to do."

ABOUT INDIAN CULTURE

Indian culture is extremely diverse since there are a variety of distinct cultures and languages within the country. Since there are so many different languages, it is common for Indians to use English or Hindi to communicate with one another as a common language since they may not speak the same mother-tongues.

Although Hindi is one of the official languages of India, many South Indians (from the State of Kerala) do not typically speak Hindi. English is commonly spoken by many and their English dialect is heavily influenced by Hindi vocabulary; individuals may use words which are not recognized in Western English (e.g. "do the needful," meaning, "follow-up," or "same, same" to mean "the same thing"). Most educated Indians will speak English quite well and take pride in speaking English, often preferring to use it over their own mother-tongues. This can create a challenge in convincing parents of the value of speaking their own language in addition to English since many believe that English is "better" than their own MT.

Indians have very strong familial ties, with extended families often living together.

General Indian culture is very hierarchical. Individuals like to know their status in relationship to others and responsibility is taken by bosses and others at "the top."

Typically, Indians do not like to say, "no." This can make them very uncomfortable since they do not like to disappoint others.

SCHOOLING

The education system in India is teacher-centered and the teacher is revered and considered to hold the knowledge. Learning is primarily by rote and there is not much opportunity for students to think critically or learn outside of the school workbook. There is a great deal of emphasis placed on education and going on to higher education following secondary school.

Language Helper – Japanese

AREAS SPOKEN

Japanese is spoken throughout Japan as well as other parts of the world where large numbers of Japanese immigrants have settled.

NUMBER OF SPEAKERS WORLDWIDE

There are over 110 million speakers of Japanese as a first language and 10 million speakers as an additional language.

LANGUAGE ORIGINS

Japanese does not stem from any other linguistic family or group as far as researchers know. Many Japanese characters from the Japanese Kanji script originate from Mandarin Chinese.

ABOUT THE LANGUAGE

- Japanese is very different to English but there are still many cognates which are shared between the languages.
- There are 3 Japanese scripts: Katakana which is used for foreign words that have been adopted by Japanese; Kanji is the Japanese writing system which is based on Mandarin symbols and Hiragana is the basic Japanese system. Children raised in Japan would learn all 3 of these systems for literacy.
- Japanese learn both pictorial and phonemic systems.
- The vowel sounds in English are not represented in Japanese.
- The "l," " r," " o," " v," sounds do not exist in Japanese and there are very few consonant clusters which make one sound (e.g. str-).
- Intonation and stress patterns in Japanese are very different to English and are very regular in comparison.

- In Japanese, an individual's hierarchy and position in society is very important, so pronouns and sentence structures can change to convey this cultural aspect. For example, there can be 5 different forms of the pronoun "I" depending on whom the speaker is talking to. The pronouns for "he" and "she" are also more complex in Japanese.
- Japanese nouns are all neutral, the same as in English.
- There are no capital letters in Japanese script and the full stop or period is a small circle rather than a "dot" used in English.
- Japanese does not use plurals, so the noun simply stays the same (e.g. they may specify number or amount instead).
- Indefinite and definite articles do not exist in Japanese.
- There are significant differences between English and Japanese sentence structures. Japanese is typically an S-O-V language but there is more flexibility in how they arrange their sentences without the meaning changing.

POSSIBLE CHALLENGES FOR JAPANESE SPEAKERS LEARNING ENGLISH

- Mastering the English vowel sounds and letter sounds which are not present in their language can be challenging for Japanese speakers. This would also be true for their pronunciations.
- Mastering writing letter formations can be difficult although the directionality is the same as English.
- Japanese speakers may have problems hearing the differences in letter sounds, especially vowels.
- There are no capital letters in Japanese so the rules of capitals and their uses can be a challenge to Japanese speakers.
- Understanding the spelling rules of plurals in English can be a challenge since this does not exist in Japanese.
- English verb tenses and the conjugations of verbs can be difficult for Japanese.
- Irregular tenses can be a problem since there are very few of these in Japanese.
- Speaking and writing in English using the correct S-V-O word order can be difficult.
- They may not easily be able to formulate questions in English because they do not have "to do" (e.g. "Do you have any money?").

ABOUT JAPANESE CULTURE

Japanese culture is very rich with longstanding traditions and ways of operating. Japanese people highly value hard work and put the needs of the group ahead of the needs of the individual.

There are many rules of behaviour that Japanese adhere to, mainly affecting their outward appearance and presentation to others. Respect, honour and hierarchy are important aspects of Japanese culture. Japanese bow to indicate hello/goodbye, thank-you or sorry. Japanese may also use less eye contact than Westerners are used to and can find direct eye contact slightly aggressive. Japanese do not like to say "no" to others since it is deemed impolite.

Japanese can be sensitive to hygiene and cleanliness. They react strongly to body odour and strong scents. Blowing one's nose in public is frowned upon.

SCHOOLING

Japanese children enter school at 6 years of age. School is compulsory for 9 years (elementary and middle school) but 98% of children go on to complete secondary school.

Teachers and education in general are very highly regarded in Japanese society. Japanese students would never talk back or question a teacher. Japanese students believe that it is their responsibility to make sure they understand the course work or curriculum and they would reply positively if asked by a teacher if they understand, even if they do not. Japanese would rather not understand something or pretend to understand rather than have the teacher and classmates know they do not understand. They always avoid "losing face".

Some Japanese students do not like to leave mistakes on a page. They would prefer to erase the whole line rather than just simply add a word.

Japanese students prefer not to give their opinions individually. They might be embarrassed by being singled out. In Japan, there is not the same emphasis placed on individualism as there is in the West. Japanese children generally do not like to be singled out from their classmates even for doing good work. "Saving face" is very important.

Language Helper - Korean

MAIN AREAS SPOKEN

Korean is spoken in the Korean Peninsula in northeast Asia (North and South Korea) as well as some areas in provinces of China that border North Korea.

NUMBER OF SPEAKERS WORLDWIDE

There are around 50 million native speakers in the Republic of Korea (South Korea) as well as another roughly 24 million in the Democratic People's Republic of Korea (North Korea). In addition there are nearly 3 million speakers living in provinces bordering the Chinese/Korean border. Large numbers of Korean speakers migrated and now live in Japan, Russia, the U.S.A. as well as Thailand and Singapore.

LANGUAGE ORIGIN

The Korean language is distinctive and may have extinct relatives. There are some similarities found between Korean and Japanese. There are several "dialects" but only 2 main dialects: the "Seoul dialect" in South Korea and the "Pyongyang dialect" in North Korea.

ABOUT THE LANGUAGE

- The Korean writing system originally used 3 main scripts. These systems were similar to those developed in Japan. The Koreans also borrowed a large number of Chinese words, and also invented about 150 new characters.
- There are distinct differences in regards to the writing, pronunciation and grammar between South Korea and North Korea.
- South Korea tends to make use of English pronunciations of words whereas North Korea uses traditional pronunciations.
- The modern written system is called, "Hangul."

- There are 24 letters of the alphabet: 14 consonants and 10 vowels.
- There are double vowel combinations similar to English.
- The Korean alphabet is highly phonetic and consistent.
- There are no upper or lower case letters in Korean. There are no capital letters at the beginning of sentences or for proper names.
- Some English sounds are not present in Korean (e.g. "th," "v").
- The directionality of writing is from top-to-bottom, left-to-right.
- There are spaces between words as in English.
- Korean typically uses the "subject-object-verb" order (S-O-V) with the verb coming at the end of the sentence.
- The subject of a sentence is often left out and simply inferred from the context.
- The adjective comes before the noun, similar to English.
- Korean nouns are gender neutral which is similar to English.
- There are no indefinite (the) or definite (a) articles.
- There are no auxiliary verbs in Korean (e.g. shall, can, do, etc.)
- There is no use of "he" or "she" in Korean. It is very common to use the gender neutral 3rd person equivalent to "it".
- Typically, the family names are said or written before the given name
- Nouns are not pluralized in Korean— the meaning, either singular or plural, is indicated from the context or a number. Repeated consonants emphasize the intensity of the noun.
- There is a very extensive system used to express the differences in social status between speakers and the level of familiarity between the speaker and the listener. This is done by adding "honorific" suffix endings on to the end of the noun to indicate the level of honor attached to it. There are 7 speech levels in Korean and each level has its own unique set of verb endings which are used to indicate the level of formality of a situation although only a few are used on a day-to-day basis.
- In the Korean language, people seldom refer to each other by their proper name and more commonly by their position in the family relative to the speaker. Each family member has a specific title depending on their position within the family structure and there are many specific titles used to classify all family members.

- There are 2 types of number systems in Korean: the first is the native Korean system used for numbering items 1-99 and age; the second is the Sino-Korean system based on Chinese numbers which is used for dates, money, addresses, phone numbers and all numbers more than 100. Numbers from 1-99 are constructed logically, for instance 13 is "ten three" 47 is "four ten seven."
- There is an absence of "stress" in the spoken language.
- Verbs are not conjugated in agreement with the subjects of a sentence.
- Punctuation is fairly similar to English.

POSSIBLE CHALLENGES FOR KOREAN SPEAKERS LEARNING ENGLISH

- Korean speakers can find the vowel sounds particularly challenging as they do not have the equivalent sounds.
- They may find English spelling challenging because of its inconsistent nature.
- Pronunciations of specific letter sounds they do not have in their language will be difficult.
- Korean speakers may find mastering "stress" patterns in words challenging since their language does not have variation in stress.
- There are no upper or lowercase letters in Korean script so mastering this concept can be a particular challenge.
- Learning articles (the, a) can be difficult.
- Mastering the word order can be a problem.
- Learning auxiliary verbs may be difficult.
- The correct use of verbs and in particular the "passive voice" in English can be challenging for native Korean speakers.
- The use of pronouns in English is challenging.
- Koreans may have a problem using "my" and prefer to use "we" instead.
- Mastering the names of the numbers in English can be tricky since it does not follow the more logical system that Koreans are used to.

ABOUT KOREAN CULTURE

Koreans have a strong, hierarchical culture. The higher status person always initiates and leads the conversation. In a classroom setting the teacher would be the one to initiate the conversation as teachers are highly regarded in Korea. Children would never call an adult by their name so a teacher would be called "Teacher". A Korean student in a Western or international classroom may need time to adjust to calling his/her teacher by their name. It is customary for younger people to bow their heads slightly when greeting older people but the elder should not do it back. Direct eye contact can be considered rude, especially if it is to a superior or elder; lowering the eye gaze is considered respectful.

Korean time-keeping is not the same as in the West. It is often acceptable to be late and Korean students would not think of apologizing for being late.

SCHOOLING

Education is a central value in South Korea. Children typically start kindergarten at around 4 years old and complete high school in the 12th grade at around 17 or 18 years of age. There are numerous private schools in addition to the public schools. Schooling is free and compulsory for students in primary and middle school (up to grade 9). Students attend school 220 days per year and spend around 13 hours of study per day including after-school work. The majority of Koreans attend post-secondary studies. Many families have a desire for their children to learn English.

Teachers and educators are very highly regarded in Korean society. Korean students would never talk back to a teacher or question a teacher. Korean students believe that it is their responsibility to make sure they understand the course work or curriculum. They would always reply positively if asked by a teacher if they understand even when they do not. They would rather not understand something and pretend to than have the teacher and classmates know they do not understand and "lose face".

Koreans are used to a school system where students work and study very hard and are expected to pass exams with near/full marks or A's. Most of the learning style is "rote-memorization" rather than risk-taking and discovery-style learning. Students expect to have plenty of homework and to study long hours.

In Korea, the family name comes before the given/first name. So for instance, with the name Park Sun-Yi, Park is the family name and Sun-Yi the first name.

The Koreans are quite physical with each other especially between classmates. Classmates often touch arms during pair work and seeing girls walking hand in hand is quite common. Boys tend to play fairly rough.

In Korea, there is not the same emphasis placed on individualism as there is in the West. Korean children do not like to be singled out from their classmates even for doing good work. "Saving face" is very important.

In Korea, primary children go to school at 8am and finish at 3pm. The secondary students go to school at 6am and finish at 6pm. Korean society is highly competitive. This can lead to increased stress on students, encouraging cheating in schools to get ahead. Cheating is seen as "cheeky" at worst.

A high percentage of Korean high school students attend Academies after school. This is a private school where they relearn and review the subjects taught in the regular school so they can attain higher grades on tests. It is common for them to study at the Academy until midnight.

Language Helper – Mandarin (Chinese)

MAIN AREAS SPOKEN

Mandarin is the official language of Mainland China. It is also spoken in Taiwan, Singapore, and around Southeast Asia as well as several countries and regions where Chinese immigrants have settled.

NUMBER OF SPEAKERS WORLDWIDE

Over 1.35 billion people around the world speak Mandarin. There are estimated to be over 850 million speakers as a first language and 500 million as an additional language.

LANGUAGE ORIGINS

Mandarin stems from the branch of Sino-Tibetan Chinese. Since it is a pictorial language, the same written character can be pronounced differently in various dialects throughout China but carry the same meaning. There are 2 main scripts traditional (with more strokes) and simplified versions (less strokes). Mainland China uses the simplified written language. The traditional version is seen more outside mainland China and within historic writing.

ABOUT THE LANGUAGE

- Mandarin is a language which uses very few words to get the meaning across. It is "compacted" or "concentrated" with meaning.
- Mandarin is a very different language to English and it is rare to find any cognates.
- Modern Mandarin is written from left-to-right and top-to-bottom.
- There is no alphabet in Mandarin. It is a pictorial language. Words derive meaning from pictures rather than separate letters combined to make up a word.
- There are 2 pronouns for "you" - a formal and informal/casual.
- There are no verb conjugations to make tenses. Mandarin speakers use the pronoun then the infinitive of the verb (e.g. "I to go", "you to go", "they to go"). Time words are used to help con-

vey the meanings of tenses directly (e.g. "Yesterday I to go" = "I went yesterday").

- All nouns are neutral as in English.
- In Mandarin "he" and "she" are pronounced the same way although they are written slightly differently.
- There are no plurals (e.g. 1 book, 10 book)
- There are no definite or indefinite articles
- Stress patterns are regular in Mandarin, unlike English.
- Pinyin is a system that was developed for transcribing Mandarin into phonetics (sounds) and this is widely taught in schools.
- There are never any words in Mandarin which start with a vowel sound.
- Mandarin is a tonal language. This means that the same word can be pronounced 4 different ways and have 4 distinct meanings, depending on the tone of voice used.
- The auxiliary verb "to do" does not exist in Mandarin.
- Mandarin sentence structure is similar to English (S-V-O) where the adjective comes before the noun.
- The numbering system if Mandarin is very different to English. It is a much simpler concept than in English (e.g. "12" in Mandarin is "ten two"; "24" is "two, ten four"; "42" is "four ten two," etc. This makes mental maths and number manipulation much easier for Mandarin speakers.
- Days of the week and months of the year are also much simpler in Mandarin: months of the year would be the number character first and then the character for month (e.g. one month = January, nine month = September). Similarly, days of the week would be written as the number character first and then the character for the day after (e.g. "Three day" is Wednesday; "six day" is Saturday).
- Telling the time is very similar to English.
- There are no capital letters in Mandarin; however, the use of other punctuation marks such as full stops (periods), question marks, and exclamation marks are similar to English.

POSSIBLE CHALLENGES FOR MANDARIN SPEAKERS LEARNING ENGLISH

- Mandarin speakers may have a tendency not to speak with "elaborate" or descriptive sentences since their language is concentrated and they can use fewer words to get the meaning across.
- Mandarin speakers may struggle to remember the days of the week, months of the year and names of numbers in English.

- Mandarin script is pictorial and so individuals may struggle to formulate the letters in English correctly.
- They may likely be familiar with basic phonics but not with the more complex phonics rules (e.g. with diphthongs, silent "e", etc.).
- Mandarin speakers may struggle with formulating the correct tenses when speaking or writing in English. They do not conjugate verbs so they may mix or confuse tenses when speaking or writing. This concept is not an easy one for them to grasp and remember.
- They may struggle when using "he" and "she" as they are pronounced the same in Mandarin.
- They may not be easily able to formulate questions in English.
- They may not apply capitalization rules correctly.
- They may find expressing their ideas in correct sentence structure difficult when translating from Mandarin to English.
- They may struggle to decode and pronounce various letter sounds, blends and clusters.
- There are very different intonation patterns in Mandarin to English so students' pronunciation may not always be easily understood.
- They may find it a challenge to use the definite and indefinite articles in English and may insert the word "one" instead of "a" or "the".

ABOUT CHINESE CULTURE

China is one of the oldest civilizations in the world. It is a very diverse country and as a result, there are many dialects, religions, cultural traditions, values, style and even foods, which all differ regionally.

There are many dialects of Chinese language which each has its own variations, similarities and differences to the main language. However, the written language is the same. This means that people from 2 different speaking dialects in China may pronounce a word differently but they would write it the same. This is possible because Chinese is a pictorial rather than phonological (based on sounds) language. The official language in China is Mandarin and schools teach in Mandarin.

In Chinese society, being part of a collective group or family is more highly valued than the individual. Family ties, community and societal acceptance are very highly regarded. The collective and social benefits outweigh the individual. For many decades, Chinese couples were only be allowed to have one child per family. This law has since been changed.

SCHOOLING

In China, schooling starts at the age of 6 or 7 and students must complete a minimum of 9 years of mandatory education. Students then go onto senior high school or vocational school until around 17 years of age.

China has significant regional differences and the conditions in schools can vary greatly. As the population in China is very large, there is a very high level of competition for entrance into good schools, colleges and universities. As a result, students often feel pressured to perform well in tests and exams in the rigid education system. Chinese students attend classes five or six days a week from early morning (about 7am) to early evening (4pm or later). In addition, it is very common for students to also attend "cram school", in the evening and on weekends.

Teachers are highly regarded in Chinese society. Students do not question or answer back to a teacher. Students treat teachers with complete respect. Lessons are very rote-based and students are required to memorize information. There is little emphasis on creativity or thinking "outside-the-box."

LANGUAGE HELPER – ABOUT POLISH

MAIN AREAS SPOKEN

In addition to being spoken in Poland, large numbers of Polish speakers can be found around the world, especially in Canada, Australia, USA, UK and Brazil. It is also a second language in some parts of Russia, Ukraine and Lithuania.

NUMBER OF SPEAKERS WORLDWIDE

There are around 40 million speakers worldwide.

LANGUAGE ORIGIN

Polish comes from the branch of Western Slavic languages within the family of Indo-European languages. It shares many similarities with Czech, Slovak and Serbian.

ABOUT THE LANGUAGE

- The Polish language has a fairly predictable stress pattern, unlike English.
- Polish speakers do not use as much intonation in their speech as English.
- Polish follows fairly consistent spelling rules.
- Polish uses many letter sounds which are not present in any other languages.
- Polish does have lower and upper case letters (capital letters) but does not use them for the days of the week and months of the year. It does use them at the beginning of sentences and for names of people.
- Polish is considered a very formal language. Other people are not referred to by their first names unless they are known very well. Instead, they use equivalents for "Mr," "Mrs" or "Miss".
- All nouns in Polish are masculine, feminine or neuter.
- Adjectives agree with nouns in terms of gender and within the sentence and adjectives generally come before the noun (like in English).

- There are no indefinite (the) or definite (a) articles in Polish.
- Word order in English and Polish is generally similar, Subject –Verb – Object (S-V-O); however, in Polish it is possible to move words around in the sentence, and to drop the subject, object or even sometimes verb, if they are obvious from context and still make sense.
- Polish does not have the equivalent of auxiliary or "helping verbs" such as "to be", "to have", "to do," etc.
- There are fewer vowels in Polish as compared to English and there are no similarities between their sounds.
- There are several cognates shared between Polish and English but there are also many "false friends" which look like similar words but have very different meanings.
- Punctuation rules are similar to English.

POSSIBLE CHALLENGES FOR POLISH SPEAKERS LEARNING ENGLISH

- The irregular stress patterns in English can be a challenge for native Polish speakers learning English and they can feel uncomfortable using them; their speech may sound flat or monotonous to English speakers.
- Mastering the English sounds can be challenging since many letters may look similar but have different pronunciations, especially vowels.
- There are no definite or indefinite articles in Polish so mastering their use can be a challenge for Polish speakers learning English.
- They may have problems with subject-verb agreement due to the rules of tenses; there are more tenses in English than Polish.
- They can mix word order within their sentences.

ABOUT POLISH CULTURE

Poles are typically traditional and family-oriented. Most are Catholics and their religion is deeply connected to their culture and customs. They are generally proud of their culture and country.

Poles tend to be more formal and will use titles when greeting each other until getting to know someone personally. They tend to be direct in their communication style and value relationships. Proper etiquette and good behaviour are stressed within the Polish culture.

SCHOOLING

The Polish education system values what the student can do with their knowledge and how they can apply information practically.

Free, compulsory schooling begins at 6 years of age and continues up to the age of 18. Students typically study in the Polish language but do learn additional foreign languages. Parents can also choose to educate their children in private schools. Students in upper secondary school can attend vocational or technical programs.

Language Helper – Russian

MAIN AREAS SPOKEN

Russian is the official language of Russia and many other countries such as: Belarus, Kazakhstan, Tajikistan, Moldova, as well as Abkhazia and South Ossetia. It is widely spoken in many satellite countries which geographically touch Russia's borders: Romania, Finland, Ukraine, Republic of Crimea, Odessa, Lithuania and Latvia, Estonia. In Israel, a large number of people speak and understand Russian.

NUMBER OF SPEAKERS WORLDWIDE

There are approximately 144 million native speakers of Russian in the world. There are another 40 million people who speak Russian as a second language.

LANGUAGE ORIGIN

Russian is part of the Slavonic branch of the Indo-European languages and shares many similarities between Ukrainian and Belarussian along with other Slavonic languages.

ABOUT THE LANGUAGE

- The Russian alphabet is written in a very different script to English called Cyrillic. Some letters look similar to English ones; however many are false friends.
- The alphabet consists of 33 letters. There are 21 consonants and 10 vowels.
- Russian has a highly-predictable spelling system.
- Russian does not have the "v," "w," sounds.
- Directionality of print in Russian is similar to English.
- In Russian, there are two 2nd person pronouns– a polite and informal form
- All nouns in Russian are masculine, feminine or neuter.
- The ending of verbs change to indicate masculine, feminine or neuter, matching the pronoun.

- Making plurals in Russian is more complex than English. In Russian all nouns change their forms and have different endings depending on what role the noun plays in the sentence (i.e. the subject or object etc.)
- There are no articles in Russian.
- Russian has three tenses: past, present and future.
- Russian and English word order and syntax are very different. Russian word order is very flexible. Subject, object and verb can move around within the sentence and not change the meaning. Russian sentences can be arranged in almost any order without causing any misunderstanding.
- In Russian, adjectives agree with the noun in gender (masculine, feminine or neuter), number (singular or plural) and case.
- There are no words in Russian which sound the same but have different spellings and meanings (e.g. "homophones").
- There are very few auxiliary verbs in Russian (e.g. will, do, have, should, could, etc.).

POSSIBLE CHALLENGES FOR RUSSIAN SPEAKERS LEARNING ENGLISH

- Mastering the long and short vowel sounds, dipthongs (2 vowels making one sound) and digraphs (consonant clusters: sch- etc.) can be a particular challenge for Russian speakers.
- Pronunciations of specific letter sounds as well as differentiation of short vowels can be a challenge.
- The sounds, "v" and "w" are difficult as well as the "-ng" at the end of words (i.e. long).
- Russian speakers can sound brusque because of the intonation in their language as compared to English; this can be very challenging for them to master.
- Mastering definite and indefinite articles in English can be difficult.
- Mastering English syntax and word order (Subject-Verb-Object) is challenging.
- Russian speakers often have problems with homophones since they do not have these in their language.
- Knowing how to ask questions can be challenging.
- Discriminating between the present tense and the present continuous tense can be difficult.

- Mastering the rules of conjugating the verbs in English can be a challenge for Russian speakers of English since it is much simpler in Russian.
- Mastering the use of the verb "to be" in the present tense can be difficult.

ABOUT RUSSIAN CULTURE

There are many different cultural/linguistic groups in Russia since it is a very diverse country. Family is very important to Russians. It is common for generations to live together: grandparents, parents and children. Russians appreciate honesty and being upfront when things are not going as planned.

Russians like to show their emotions and physical contact in public is very common. It is natural for them to greet family members and friends with kisses on the cheek. Traditionally men used to give each other 3 kisses on the cheek as well but this custom has now moved to a handshake greeting.

Historically, Russia has been a Czarist and then Communist state. Older generations may have a more pessimistic outlook on life based on the old Communist way of life. The younger generations today are much more exposed to Western influences.

The good of the group is valued more than individualism in Russian society. Russians tend to help their friends and family rather than compete. They are very patriotic.

Russians are not accustomed to saying "Please", "Thank you" and "Excuse me," frequently so they can seem rude or brusque. However, they are very warm and open once they build trust and rapport.

The main religions in Russia are Christian (Greek Orthodox) and Islam. Russians have a strong history of art and culture and place emphasis on creative skills.

SCHOOLING

Schooling is compulsory for students from the ages of 6-15. Students complete 2 more years of secondary education if they wish to pursue post-secondary studies.

The education system offers individuals from different mother-tongues the opportunity to be educated bilingually. The education system is very strong and taken seriously in Russia. Students are very studious and critical thinking is encouraged.

Language Helper – Spanish

MAIN AREAS SPOKEN

Spanish is one of the most widely-spoken languages in the world. It is spoken as a first language within Spain, in most parts of Latin America as well as the Caribbean region. It is also common to find Spanish speakers in the USA and in The Philippines. It is widely studied as a foreign language around the world. There are a variety of spoken dialects based on different regions. In Spain, there are also other languages spoken, such as Basque, Catalan and Galician.

NUMBER OF SPEAKERS WORLDWIDE

There are around 427 million speakers worldwide

LANGUAGE ORIGIN

Spanish is a Romance language and is part of the Indo-European language family.

ABOUT THE LANGUAGE

- There are 27 letter of the alphabet, 26 are identical to those in English with the exception of an additional letter ñ ("ch" and "ll" used to be considered letters of the alphabet but are not any longer).
- Writing is similar to English in that it follows left-to-right directionality.
- Although the letters look similar to English, many are not pronounced the same way.
- Spanish nouns and adjectives are either masculine or feminine.
- Spanish uses definite (el/los, la/las) and indefinite articles (un/una, unos/unas) which correspond to the singular or plural forms of nouns.
- Spanish typically uses a Subject-Verb-Object (S-V-O) structure like English but can be more flexible in terms of where the words are placed. Subject pronouns can also be omitted from the sentence with the meaning being inferred from context.

- Spanish uses a highly-reliable spelling system.
- There are only 3 double consonants used in Spanish (cc, ll, rr); this is very different to English which uses many double consonants.
- Spanish pronunciation uses a regular stress pattern as compared to English which is very irregular. In English, some words have the first syllable stressed (YESterday) and at other times the second syllable is stressed (toMOrrow) with no predictable pattern or rule.
- There is no auxiliary verb, "to do" in Spanish.
- In Spanish the adjective comes after the noun and the ending of the adjective changes to correspond with the gender of the noun it is matching.
- Punctuation is fairly similar to English with the exception of question marks and exclamation marks. Questions begin with an inverted question mark and finish with a regular question mark. This is the same for exclamation marks. Some Spanish does not use speech marks (quotation marks) for direct speech but instead uses a dash –
- Capitalization is not used with days of the week or months of the year.
- In Spanish, there is no auxiliary verb "to do."
- In Spanish, nouns have a singular and plural form, similar to English.
- Spanish does not make much use of ordinal numbers (i.e. fifth, twelfth, etc.).
- There are numerous cognates between Spanish and English but there are also many "false friends" which look like a particular word but have a different meaning.
- In most Spanish-speaking countries, numbers make use of a comma where a decimal would be used and a decimal (period or full-stop) where a comma would be used to separate groups of numbers.

POSSIBLE CHALLENGES FOR SPANISH SPEAKERS LEARNING ENGLISH

- Difficulties pronouncing "voiced" consonants which come at the end of a word.
- May have problems with differentiating and using English vowel sounds.
- Spanish speakers have less intonation as compared to English so this can be a point of difficulty.
- Since Spanish words are decoded letter-by-letter, speakers tend to apply this to English decoding which does not always work because of silent letters and rules about pronouncing double vowels.

- Spanish speakers can tend to write with one consonant instead of using double consonants (i.e. "prety" for "pretty").
- Challenges differentiating between "do," "does" and "did."
- Spanish speakers may apply the "masculine/feminine" rule to nouns in English by referring to a noun as "him/her."
- They may apply the plural form to words inappropriately like "lightnings" for "lightning."
- Spanish speakers can tend to add an "e" sound at the beginning of words which start with an "s" consonant cluster, such as "eschool."

ABOUT SPANISH CULTURE

Spanish people value personal relationships and the family. They have a rich history and culture of the arts. They are fairly traditional and most are Catholic.

Spanish people are quite sociable and enjoy social interactions. They can become quite animated as they speak and may interrupt one-another as they talk. They tend to use hand gestures while speaking.

In general, Spanish people like to look good in others' eyes and so they like to "save face." They do not like to show or indicate they do not understand something.

please note that this cultural information is for Spain only, not South American cultures

SCHOOLING

In Spain, compulsory schooling is available for students from the ages of 6-16 years and is free up to the age of 18. Education in South America is varied in terms of availability and quality compared from one country to another.

Language Helper - Urdu

MAIN AREAS SPOKEN

Urdu is the primary language of the country of Pakistan and parts of India. It is one of the official languages of India and co-official language in many regions of India and Afghanistan. It is also spoken in many other parts of the world where large Urdu speaking communities have settled, Botswana, Fiji, Guyana, India, Malawi, Mauritius, Nepal, Oman, Qatar, Saudi Arabia, South Africa, Thailand, UAE, UK and Zambia.

NUMBER OF SPEAKERS WORLDWIDE

There are over 159 million native and second language speakers of Urdu worldwide.

LANGUAGE ORIGIN

Urdu belongs to the Indo-Aryan branch of the Indo-European language family.

ABOUT THE LANGUAGE

- Urdu is very similar to the Hindi language in basic grammar and vocabulary.
- The stress pattern in Urdu is very different to English. Its use is not as important as in English in changing the meaning of a sentence.
- Urdu uses the Arabic script for writing and the writing direction is right-to-left.
- There are 57 letters of the alphabet in Urdu.
- In Urdu each letter has 4 distinct written forms depending on its position in a word: initial, middle, final or isolated.
- There is no distinction between upper and lower case letters.
- Urdu script only shows the consonant and long vowels. It does not indicate the short vowels (similar to Arabic).
- Urdu has many words to describe family members-indicating whether the family member is from the maternal or paternal side of the family and what their position is in relation to the speaker.

- In Urdu there are 3 forms of the 2nd pronoun "you" to express different levels of respect (formal, informal and extremely formal).
- Plurals are made by changing some letters inside the singular noun.
- All nouns in Urdu have a masculine or feminine gender.
- There is no definite article in Urdu and speakers use the word "one" when speaking English where the indefinite article should be.
- Urdu uses S-O-V (subject-object-verb) word order. The verb usually falls at the end of the sentence.
- Urdu does not have prepositions but has postpositions instead.
- The adjective comes before the noun similar to English; however, it has to correspond to the gender of the noun (i.e. masculine or feminine).
- Urdu speakers use adjectives much less frequently than English speakers. When an adjective is repeated twice it emphasizes the intensity (e.g. "little, little" to mean extremely little).
- There is no verb "to have" in Urdu.
- There is no auxiliary verb "to do" so asking questions in English using "Do...?" or "does...?" can be challenging for Urdu speakers. Questions are usually indicated by a rising tone at the end of the sentence.
- Urdu and English share similar tenses, however, it is acceptable in Urdu to mix tenses within a sentence.

POSSIBLE CHALLENGES FOR URDU SPEAKERS LEARNING ENGLISH

- Learning to master some consonants and vowel sounds in English can be a particular challenge as similar sounds do not exist in Urdu.
- If the student is already literate and able to write in Urdu, they may become confused with the writing direction in English.
- Differentiating short and long vowels in English can be a challenge for Urdu speakers learning English.
- They may have problems learning and understanding the concepts of upper and lower case letters since this does not exist in Urdu.
- Mastering the correct intonation and stress patterns in English can be challenging.
- English word order can be challenging
- Mastering prepositions in English may be difficult.

- Understanding the full role of verb tenses in English can be a challenge for Urdu speakers.
- Mastering the use of articles may be difficult.
- Using the verb "to have" and "to do" appropriately can be challenging to master.
- Proper use of English adjectives can be a challenge for Urdu speakers.
- Mastering the structure for asking questions can be challenging for Urdu speakers learning English. They may raise the tone of their voice at the end of a sentence to express a question.

ABOUT PAKISTANI CULTURE

Although there are Indians who also widely speak Urdu, Urdu is the official language of Pakistan. Pakistanis often adheres to Islamic traditions of family values, and modesty (in regards to dress and manners) when dealing with others. The family unit is most highly respected as are elders within the family. Since there are many layers of hierarchy in Urdu language and society, it is often polite to ask someone how they want to be addressed.

There are many underdeveloped areas in Pakistan and in several communities girls are not given the same access or opportunities as males. In contrast, there are also very wealthy families in Pakistan and these individuals may be highly educated and have access to the best schools and education. They are often very proficient in English as well as Urdu.

In Pakistan, there can be a mix of direct and indirect communication between people depending on their status and ages. In general, one speaks more indirectly when speaking to elders, and more directly when speaking to friends and family. For Pakistanis, it is acceptable in conversation to talk over on another and interrupt without it being considered rude.

It is very rude to say "no" when directly asked to do someone a favour. It is considered better to respond more indirectly with a "maybe" or "Inshallah" (God-willing) and then the asker can infer that the answer is likely a "no."

Indirect eye contact is quite normal especially as a sign of respect from the younger generation to the older and between men and women (since that can often be misconstrued). In some conservative families, interactions between boys and girls are not encouraged or permitted after the age of puberty.

SCHOOLING

Government schooling in Pakistan is free and compulsory from the ages of 5-16 years. The schooling system is loosely modeled on the English education system.

Pakistan has a poorly-funded public education system. Although education is free, the standards are not always high. There are many private schools that parents can send their children to and post-secondary education is very desirable. Pakistanis who can afford to send their children to higher-education have strong aspirations for their children's career paths.

Glossary

Additive Bilingual: where the learning of an additional language (L2) does not take away from, or replace the development of the first language (L1).

Assimilation: the process of enculturating a person or specific cultural group into the "dominant culture" and language of another cultural group.

Balanced Bilingual: this refers to an individual having fairly similar proficiency in both languages. Individuals can become balanced bilinguals when they actively use and apply both of their languages regularly.

BICS or "Basic Interpersonal Communication Skills:" this can be thought of as "social language" or "conversational language." BICS can take anywhere between 6 months to 2 years for a new English speaker to master. BICS requires the learner to have knowledge and use of high-frequency vocabulary words. The term "BICS" was coined by Dr. Jim Cummins.

BML/BMLs: Bilingual and multilingual learner(s)

CALP or "Cognitive Academic Language Proficiency": can also be thought of as the "academic language" required for a learner to be successful in the educational environment. CALP requires the learner to have knowledge and use of more advanced, academic vocabulary and usually takes between 5-7 years to master. "CALP" was coined by Dr. Jim Cummins.

Code-Switching: the practice of alternating between 2 languages (or 2 dialects of the same language) during conversation. It usually occurs unconsciously between individuals who speak the same languages.

Dynamic Assessment or "DA:" refers to a test-intervention-retest situation where a teacher works with a student on specific, targeted skills in order to make direct, quick impact in one area; or to gain further information about a student's ability to learn. It also allows a student to demonstrate how they learn in a more controlled situation.

Expatriate or "Expat": a person who chooses to live and/or work abroad, away from their own country.

Foundational Language (FL): encompasses 4 stages on the *English Language Progression Map* and reflects the base of vocabulary needed for acquiring the language we use for everyday communication and developing early literacy skills. Foundational Language is comprised (largely) of high-frequency words.

Interlanguage: occurs when a new speaker attempts to speak in the new language but is not yet fully proficient. They often apply language or grammar patterns which do not originate from any of their languages. It seems to be an "in-between" language that fades away as they gain greater proficiency with their new language.

L1 (L2, L3, etc.): This refers to an individual's "Language 1," meaning the first language they have acquired or learned; L2 is the second language they have acquired and L3 would be the third, etc.

Language Interference: a term to describe what happens when people apply knowledge from one of their languages to another. This knowledge may be phonological, grammatical, lexical, or orthographical (spellings). Usually, the speaker or writer tries to apply linguistic rules in the same way as they work in their first language. This also shows evidence of language transfer.

Mother-Tongue or "MT": The mother-tongue is commonly referred to as one's first language. According to Tove Skutnabb-Kangas, it can also refer to: the first language one learned, the language one identifies with the most, the language one is identified with as a native speaker by others, the language one knows best or the language one uses most.

Native Speaker or "NS:" this refers to "Native Speaker" or "Native Speakers," typically referring to English native speakers within the context of this book.

Sequential Bilingual: when an individual learns their first language (L1) and then learns another after the age of 3. This can occur when individuals are immersed in a new culture or language or are later educated within a bilingual education setting.

Simultaneous Bilingual: those who learn their two languages at the same time. This usually occurs when individuals are spoken to in one language by one parent and a different language by the other parent. Both languages grow simultaneously.

Subtractive Bilingual: when the learning of another language (L2) takes away from the development of the first language (L1) and then begins to replace it. This can occur when individuals begin to assimilate into a "dominant culture" without continuing to grow or develop their L1.

Thinking Language or "TL:" encompasses 2 stages on the *English Language Progression Map* and refers to the language students acquire in order to perform a wide-variety of higher-level and abstract thinking tasks. In these stages, students are building more advanced academic vocabulary which allows them to comprehend and communicate complex thoughts and concepts with greater ease.

Translanguaging: this is a term first used by the academic Cen Williams and refers to "the ability of multilingual speakers to shuttle between languages, treating the diverse languages that form their repertoire as an integrated system". In other words, speakers of more than one language mix, use and apply all their languages in unique ways in order to fully express themselves and be understood.

References

Aguirre, A. (2003). Racial and ethnic diversity in America. Santa Barbara, CA: ABC-CLIO.

American Speech-Language-Hearing Association. The advantages of being bilingual. Retrieved January 22, 2015 from: http://bit.ly/111Gwzw

"Annual Report on Ontario's Publicly Funded Schools 2012." People for Education.

Artiles, A. J., & Zamora-Durán, G. (Eds.). (1997). Reducing disproportionate representation of culturally diverse students in special and gifted education. Reston, VA: Council for Exceptional Children.

Bay, M., Bryan, T. & O'Connor, R. (1994). Teachers assisting teachers: A prereferral model for urban educators. Teacher Education and Special Education, 17(1), 10-21.

Beck, I.G. & McKeown, M.G. (2006). Different ways for different goals but keep your eye on the higher verbal goals. In R.K. Wagner, A.E. Muse & K. Tannenbaum (Eds.), Vocabulary Acquisition: Implications for reading comprehension (pp. 182-204). New York, United States: Guilford Press.

Beck, I.G., McKewon, M.G. & Kucan, L. (2013). Bringing words to life, second edition: Robust vocabulary instruction. New York: Guildford Press.

Biemiller, A. (2001). Teaching vocabulary: Early, direct and sequential. American Educator. Posted to: http://bit.ly/2nVAA8h

Biemiller, A. & Slonim, N. (2001). Estimating root word vocabulary growth in normative and advantaged populations: Evidence for a common sequence of vocabulary acquisition. Journal of Educational Psychology, 93(3), 498-520. http://dx.doi.org/10.1037/0022-0663.93.3.498

Biemiller, A. (2011, Winter). *Vocabulary: What words should we teach?* http://bit.ly/2bHyPXN

Biemiller, A. (2012). Words for English language learners. TESL Canada Journal, 29(6), 198-203.

Blankstein, K.R., Toner, B.B., & Flett., G.L. (1990). Cognitive components of test anxiety: A comparison of assessment and scoring methods. Journal of Social Behaviour and Personality, 5, 187-202.

Bloom, P., & Keil, F. (2001). Thinking through language. Mind and Language, 16(4), 351-367.

British Columbia Ministry of Education (1999). English language learners: A guide for classroom teachers. British Columbia.

British Columbia Ministry of Education. (2009/2015). Students from refugee backgrounds: A guide for teachers and schools. Retrieved April 2014 from: http://bit.ly/2oYnTJ7

Butzkamm, W., & Caldwell, J. (2009). The bilingual reform. Tu¨bingen: Narr.

Cassady, J. C., & Johnson, R. E. (2002). Cognitive test anxiety and academic performance. Contemporary Educational Psychology, 27, 270–295.

Chall, J.S., & Jacobs, V.A. (1983). Writing and reading in the elementary grades: Developmental trends among low-SES children. Language Arts, vol. 60,(5), 617-626.

Chall, J. S. & Jacobs, V. A. (2003). The classic study on poor children's fourth-grade slump. American Educator, 27,(1), 14-15, 44.

Chomsky, N. (1957). Syntactic structures. The Hague: Mouton.

Clark, E. (2003). First language acquisition. Cambridge: Cambridge University Press.

Clyne, M. (2003). Dynamics of language contact: English and immigrant languages. UK: Cambridge University Press.

Coleman, J. (2010). A case study of the responses of two mainstream primary teachers in a non-metropolitan area to the refugee English language learners in their classes. Retrieved from Australian Catholic University Database: http://bit.ly/2nCg2Qv

Collier, V. (1989). How long? A synthesis of research on academic achievement in a second language. TESOL Quarterly, 23, 509-531.

Collier, V., & Thomas, W. (1989): How quickly can immigrants become proficient in school English? Journal of Educational Issues of Minority Students, 5, 26-38.

Collier, V.P. (1995). Acquiring a second language for school. Directions in Language and Education, 1(4). Washington, DC: National Clearinghouse for English Language Acquisition.

Corson, T. & Smollett, R. (2015, January 18). Passive voice: When to use it and when to avoid it? Posted to: http://bit.ly/2013QMx

Coxhead, A. (2000). A new academic word list. TESOL Quarterly, 34(2), 213. http://dx.doi.org/10.2307/3587951

Coxhead, A. (2002). The academic word list: A corpus-based word list for academic purposes. In B. Kettemann & G. Marko (Eds.). Teaching and learning by doing corpus analysis (pp. 73-89). Amsterdam: Rodopi.

Cummins, J. (1979). Cognitive/academic language proficiency, linguistic interdependence, the optimum age question and some other matters. Working Papers on Bilingualism, No. 19, 121-129.

Cummins, J. (1981a). The role of primary language development in promoting educational success for language minority students. In California State Department of Education (Ed.), Schooling and Language Minority Students: A Theoretical Framework. Los Angeles: Evaluation, Dissemination and Assessment Center California State University.

Cummins, J. (1984). Bilingualism and special education: Issues in assessment and pedagogy. Clevedon, England: Multilingual Matters.

Cummins, J. (1984). Heritage languages in Canada. [Ottawa]: Dept. of the Secretary of State of Canada, Multiculturalism.

Cummins, J. (1986). Empowering minority students: A framework for intervention. Harvard Educational Review, 56, 18-36.

Cummins, J. (2000). Language, power and pedagogy: Bilingual children in the crossfire. Clevedon: Multilingual Matters.

Cummins, J. (2001). Bilingual children's mother tongues: Why is it important for education? Sprogforum, 7(19), 15-20.

Cummins, J., Baker, C., & Hornberger, N. (2001). An introductory reader to the writings of Jim Cummins. Clevedon [u.a.]: Multilingual Matters.

Cummins, J. (2007). Promoting literacy in multilingual contexts. (Ontario Ministry of Education: Literacy and Numeracy Secretariat, What Works: Research Into Practice (Research Monograph #5).

Cummins, J. & Hornberger, N. (2008). Bilingual education. New York: Springer.

Cummins, J. & Persad, R. (2014). Teaching through a multilingual lens: The evolution of EAL policy and practice in Canada. Education Matters, 2 (1), 3-40.

Department for Education and Skills, Qualifications and Curriculum Authority (2012). Marking progress: Training materials for assessing English as an additional language. United Kingdom.

Figueroa, R. A. (1990). Best practices in the assessment of bilingual children. In A. Thomas & J. Grimes (Eds.), Best Practices in School Psychology ll (pp. 93-106). Washington, DC: National Association of School Psychologists.

Figueroa, R. A. (2000). The role of limited English proficiency in special education identification and intervention. Washington, DC: National Research Council.

Figueroa, R. A., & Hernandez, S. (2000). Our nation on the fault line: Hispanic American education. Testing Hispanic students in the United States: Technical and policy issues. Washington, DC: President's Advisory Commission on Educational Excellence for Hispanic Americans.

Finegan, E., & Besnier, N. (1989). Language. San Diego: Harcourt Brace Jovanovich.

Flynn, S., Foley, C. & Vinnitskya, I. (2004). The cumulative-enhancement model for language acquisition: Comparing adults' and children's patterns of development in first, second and third language acquisition of relative clauses. International Journal of Multilingualism, Vol 1 (1), 3-16.

Fu, D. (2009). Writing between languages: How English language learners make the transition to fluency, grades 4-12. Portsmouth: Heinemann.

Grosjean, F. (2000, March 26). Myths about bilingualism. Posted to: http://bit.ly/2buXLBY

Grosjean, F. (2010, October 12). Myths about bilingualism. Posted to: http://bit.ly/2nVxNvV

Grosjean, F. (2013, January 19). Retaining an Accent: Why some people retain an accent in a second language. Posted to: http://bit.ly/2oB9zdc

Grosjean, F. (2014, November 30). Chasing down those 65%: What is the percentage of bilinguals in the world today? Posted to: http://bit.ly/2oAUesR

Gyorffi, M.L. (2015). Language policy: (Fact Sheets on the European Union). Retrieved from: http://bit.ly/2oGqQP6

Harper, C. & de Jong, E. (2004). Misconceptions about Teaching English Language Learners. Journal of Adolescent and Adult Literacy, 48,(2), 152- 162.

Haynes, J. (2007). Getting Started with English Language Learners. Alexandria, Va.: Association for Supervision and Curriculum Development.

Hembree, R. (1988). Correlates, causes, effects and treatment of test anxiety. Review of Educational Research, 58(1), 47-77.

Hill, J.D. & Flynn, K.M. (2006). Classroom instruction that works with English language learners. Alexandria, VA: ASCD.

Hirsch, Jr., E.D. (2003). Reading comprehension requires knowledge—of words and the world: Scientific insights into the fourth-grade slump and the nation's stagnant comprehension scores. American Educator, 27(1), 10, 12-13, 16-22, 28-29.

Horwitz, E.K., Horwitz, M.C. & Cope, J. (1986). Foreign language classroom anxiety. Modern Language Journal, 70, 125-132.

Hudspath-Niemi, H. & Conroy, M. (2013). Implementing response-to-intervention to address the needs of English-language learners. New York: Routledge.

Humphreys, M.S., & Revelle, W. (1984). Personality, motivation, and performance: A theory of the relationship between individual differences and information processing. Psychological Review, 91, 153-184.

Jordà, M. (2005). Pragmatic production of third language learners of English: A focus on request acts modifiers. International Journal of Multilingualism, 2(2), 84-104. http://dx.doi.org/10.1080/14790710508668378

Klingner, J., & Artiles, A. J. (Eds.). (2006). English language learners struggling to learn to read: Emergent scholarship on linguistic differences and learning disabilities. Journal of Learning Disabilities, 39, 99-156; 386-398.

Konnikova, M. (2015, January 22). Is Bilingualism really an advantage? Posted to: http://bit.ly/1JhvtU5

Krashen, S. (1982). Principles and practice in second language acquisition. London: Pergamon Press.

Krashen, S., Scarcella, R., & Long, M. (1982). Child-adult differences in second language acquisition. Rowley, MA: Newbury House Publishers.

Krashen, S.D. & Terrell, T.D. (1983). The natural approach: Language acquisition in the classroom. London: Prentice Hall Europe.

Krashen, S. (1985). The input hypothesis. Harlow: Longman.

Krashen, S. (1987). Principles and practice in second language acquisition. New York [u.a.]: Prentice-Hall Internat.

Krashen, S. (1988). Second language acquisition and second language learning. New York [u.a.]: Prentice Hall.

MacIntyre, P.D. & Gardner, R.C. (1991). Methods and results in the study of anxiety and language learning: A review of the literature. Language Learning, 41, 85-117.

MacIntyre, P.D & Gardener, R.C. (1991a). Methods and results in the study of foreign language anxiety: A review of the literature. Language Learning, 41(1), 283-305.

MacIntyre, P.D. & Gardner, R.C. (1991b). Language anxiety: its relation to other anxieties and to processing in native and second languages. Language Learning, 41, 513-554.

MacIntyre, P.D. & Gardner, R.C. (1994). The subtle effects of language anxiety on cognitive processing in the second language. Language Learning, 44(2), 283-305.

Mackay, R. (1993). Embarrassment and hygiene in the classroom. ELT Journal, 47(1), 32-39.

Marzano, R.J., Pickering, D.J., & Pollock, J.E. (2001). Classroom instruction that works: Research-based strategies for increasing student achievement. Alexandria, VA: ASCD.

McKeon, D. (2005). Talking points on English language learners. National Education Association Research. Retrieved on September 28, 2014: http://www.nea.org/home/13598.htm

Minister for Education, Government of South Australia (2007). Count me in! A resource to support ESL students with refugee experience in schools.

Montanaro, S. (2001). Language acquisition. NAMTA Journal, 26(2), 1–7.

Nation, P. & Waring, R. (1997). Vocabulary size, text coverage and word lists. In Schmitt, N. and M. McCarthy (Eds.): Vocabulary: Description, Acquisition and Pedagogy (pp. 6-19). Cambridge: Cambridge University Press.

Nation, I. (2001). Learning vocabulary in another language. Cambridge: Cambridge University Press.

Nation, I.S.P. & Meara, P. (2010). Vocabulary. In N. Schmitt (ed.) An Introduction to Applied Linguistics. Edward Arnold. Second edition. pp. 34-52.

Nation, P. (2012 October). Vocabulary size and young native speakers of English. Paper presented at the CLESOL Conference. Palmerston North, New Zealand.

Nation, I.S.P. (2013). What should every EFL teacher know? Seoul: Compass Publishing.

Nation, I.S.P. (2013). What should every ESL teacher know? Seoul: Compass Publishing.

Nation, P. (2014). How much input do you need to learn the most frequent words. Reading in a Foreign Language, 26 (2), 1-16.

Nation, P. (2014). What do you need to know to learn a foreign language? New Zealand: Victoria University of Wellington.

Nation, P. (2015). Principles guiding vocabulary learning through extensive reading. Reading in a Foreign Language, 27 (1), 136-145.

National Education Association (Policy Brief). Professional development for general education teachers and teachers of English language learners. Retrieved Oct 2, 2014 from: http://www.nea.org/assets/docs/PB32_ELL11.pdf

National Association for Language Development in the Curriculum. [Statistical data summarized by bar graph: EAL pupils 1997-2013]. Number and percentage of pupils learning English as an additional language from 1997-2013. Retrieved November 22, 2014 from: http://www.naldic.org.uk/research-and-information/eal-statistics/eal-pupils.

National Association for Language Development in the Curriculum. EAL essential part of new teachers' standards. Retrieved November 22, 2014 from: http://bit.ly/1yAlbch

New York State Department of Education, Office of Bilingual Education and World Languages (2015). Definitions, CR Part 154.2.

New South Wales Government Education and Communities (2013). Language diversity in NSW government schools in 2013. (CESE Bulletin, Issue 5). NSW: Office of Education. Retrieved from: http://www.cese.nsw.gov.au/images/stories/PDF/2013-LBOTE-Bulletin_v4.pdf

NSW Department of Education and Communities (2014). English as an additional language or dialect: Advice for schools. Darlinghurst, NSW.

Ontario Ministry of Education (2008). Supporting English language learners: A practical guide for teachers. Queen's Printer for Ontario.

Ortiz, A. A., & Graves, A. (2001). English language learners with literacy-related disabilities. International Dyslexia Association Commemorative Booklet (pp. 31-35). Baltimore: International Dyslexia Association.

Pappamihiel, N.E. (2002). English as a second language students and English language anxiety: Issues in the mainstream classroom. Proquest Education Journal, 36(3), 327-355.

Premier, J. A., & Miller, J. (2010). Preparing pre-service teachers for multicultural classrooms. Australian Journal of Teacher Education, 35(2). http://dx.doi.org/10.14221/ajte.2010v35n2.3

Puchta, H. & Williams, M. (2011) Teaching Young Learners to Think. Innsbruck and Cambridge: Helbling Languages and Cambridge University Press.

Queensland Government (2013). English as an additional language or dialect. http://bit.ly/2o7OHJN

Ridge, N., Farah, S. & Sami, S. (2013). Patterns and perceptions in male secondary school dropouts in the United Arab Emirates. (Working Paper No. 3). Retrieved November 22, 2014 from: http://bit.ly/2nVDF8z

Rist, R. C. (1977). On understanding the processes of schooling: The contributions of labeling theory. Exploring Education 2nd Ed. Allyn & Bacon, 2001: 149-157.

Roessingh, H. & Kover, P. (2003). Variability of ESL learners' acquisition of cognitive academic language proficiency: What can we learn from achievement measures? TESL Canada Journal, 21(1), 1.

Roessingh, H. (2005). BICS-CALP: An introduction for some, a review for others. TESL Canada Journal, 23(2), 91.

Roessingh, H. (2008). Variability in ESL outcomes: The influence of age on arrival and length of residence on achievement in high school. TESL Canada Journal, 26(1), 87. http://dx.doi.org/10.18806/tesl.v26i1.392

Roessingh, H. & Elgie, S. (2009). Early language and literacy development among young English language learners: Preliminary insights from a longitudinal study. TESL Canada Journal, 26(2), 24-45.

Roessingh, H. & Douglas, S. (2012). Educational outcomes of English language learners at university. Canadian Journal of Higher Education, 42 (1), 80-97.

Roessingh, H. (2013). A look at grade 2 writing: Successes and challenges in early literacy development. Learning Landscapes, 7(1), 269-281. Retrieved from: http://bit.ly/2o7Uxe5

Roseberry-McKibbin, C. & Brice, A. (2005). What's 'normal,' what's not: acquiring English as a second language. Retrieved September 2014, from http://www.ldonline.org/article/5126/

Sabet, M.K. & Tavakoli, M. (2016). Metaphorical competence: A neglected component of communicative competence. International Journal of Education & Literacy Studies, 4(1), 32-39.

Safont-Jordà, M. (2011). Early requestive development in consecutive third language learning. International Journal of Multilingualism, 8(3), 256-276. http://bit.ly/2oBdPcG

Sanchez-Boyce, M. (2000). The use of interpreters in special education assessments. Unpublished doctoral dissertation. University of California at Davis.

Schmitt, N. & Schmitt, D. (2012). A reassessment of frequency and vocabulary size in L2 vocabulary teaching. Language Teaching, 47(04), 484-503. http://bit.ly/2nInFWi

Shaffer, D. R., Wood, E., & Willoughby, T. (2002). Developmental psychology: Childhood and adolescence (First Canadian Edition). Scarborough, ON: Nelson/Thomson Canada Ltd.

Shephard, T.L., Linn, D. & Brown, R.D. (2005). The disproportionate representation of English language learners for special education services along the border. Journal of Social and Ecological Boundaries, 1(1), 104-116.

Shreve, J. (2005). Educators are poorly prepared for ELL instruction. Retrieved Oct 30, 2014 from: http://www.edutopia.org/no-train-no-gain

Skutnabb-Kangas, T. (1984). Bilingualism or not-the education of minorities. Clevedon, Avon: Multilingual Matters, p.378.

Skutnabb-Kangas, T. (2008). Human rights and language policy in education. In Volume 1. Language Policy and Political Issues in Education, eds. Stephen May and Nancy H. Hornberger. Encyclopedia of Language and Education, 2nd edition. New York: Springer, 107-119.

Swan, M. & Smith, B. (2001). Learner English: A teacher's guide to interference and other problems. Second Edition. Cambridge, UK: Cambridge University Press.

Tereshchenko, A. (2014). New migration new challenges: Eastern European migrant pupils in European schools. King's College Department of Education & Professional Studies: London. Retrieved December 21, 2014 from: http://bit.ly/2nVLyul

Thomas, W.P., and V.P. Collier. (1997). School effectiveness for language minority students. Washington, D.C.: National Clearinghouse for Bilingual Education.

Thomas, W. P., Collier, V. P., & Center for Research on Education, Diversity & Excellence (2002). A national study of school effectiveness for language minority students' long-term academic achievement. Washington, DC: Center for Research on Education, Diversity & Excellence.

Tomlinson, C. (1999). Mapping a route toward differentiated instruction. Educational Leadership, 57 (1), 12-16.

Tomlinson, C. (2001). How to differentiate instruction in mixed-ability classrooms. Alexandria, Va.: Association for Supervision and Curriculum Development.

Torlakson, T. (2012). Overview of the California English language development standards and proficiency level descriptors. California, USA.

Valdés, G., & Figueroa, R. A. (1994). Bilingualism and testing: A special case of bias. Norwood, NJ: Ablex.

Victoria State Government Education and Training. [Summary statistics for Victoria schools, March 2014]. Retrieved from: http://bit.ly/2o7Jn9g

Weaver, G. R.(1986). Understanding and coping with cross-cultural adjustment stress. In R.M. Paige (Ed). Cross-cultural Orientation. New Conceptualizations and Applications. Lanham MD: University Press of America.

Webb, S. & Nation, I.S.P. (2013). Teaching vocabulary. In The Encyclopedia of Applied Linguistics, ed. Chapelle, C.A. Oxford, UK: Wiley-Blackwell.

Wilkinson, C. Y., & Ortiz, A. A. (1986). Characteristics of limited English proficient and English proficient learning disabled Hispanic students at initial assessment and at reevaluation. Austin: University of Texas, Department of Special Education, Handicapped Minority Research Institute on Language Proficiency. (ERIC Document Reproduction Service No. ED 283 314).

Williams, S. & Hammarberg, B. (1998). Language switches in L3 production: Implications for a polyglot speaking model. Applied Linguistics, 19(3), 295-333.

Wilson, D.M. (2011, March-April). Dual language programs on the rise: Enrichment model puts content learning front and center for ELL students. Harvard Education Letter, 27(2). Retrieved from: http://bit.ly/2oB4BNt

Young, D.J. (1990). An investigation of students' perspectives on anxiety and speaking. Foreign Language Annals, 23, 539-553.

Zamora, P., testimony, Briefing before the U.S. Commission on civil rights, minorities in special education, Washington, DC, Dec. 3, 2007, transcript, p. 110 (hereafter cited as Zamora Testimony, Briefing Transcript).

Made in the USA
Monee, IL
06 October 2020